The
SAN PEDRO RIVER

The SAN PEDRO RIVER

A Discovery Guide

ROSEANN BEGGY HANSON

THE UNIVERSITY OF ARIZONA PRESS

TUCSON

The University of Arizona Press
© 2001 Roseann Beggy Hanson
First Printing
All rights reserved

∞ This book is printed on acid-free, archival-quality paper.
Manufactured in the United States of America

Library of Congress Cataloging-in-Publication Data

Hanson, Roseann Beggy.
  The San Pedro River : a discovery guide / Roseann Beggy Hanson.
     p.   cm.
Includes bibliographical references (p.   ) and index.
  ISBN 0–8165–1910–2 (paper : acid-free paper)
  1. San Pedro River (Mexico and Ariz.)—Guidebooks.   2. San Pedro River
Valley (Mexico and Ariz.)—Guidebooks.   I. Title.
  F817.S25 H36 2001
  917.917—dc21

                                                    2001000227

British Library Cataloguing-in-Publication Data
A catalogue record for this book is available from the British Library.

This book is dedicated to Jonathan, always my best supporter, field companion, and friend, and to all the people of the world who care about and fight for the last of our wild places everywhere. Never think one person can't do something about exploitation and injustice.

CONTENTS

ACKNOWLEDGMENTS

This project began as a joint publishing endeavor between me and Friends of the San Pedro River (FSPR). Circumstances in my life necessitated bringing in the University of Arizona Press to keep it going, and I am very glad I did.

Dot Rhodes, the primary engine running FSPR, really got the ball rolling and kept it rolling. This project would not have happened without her support and hard work. Steve Cox, now former director of the University of Arizona Press, did not hesitate to pick up the ball; I much appreciate his confidence in my work. Christine Szuter, the book's editor and now director of the press, embraced the book and helped move it along.

Without the expertise and dedication of the Bureau of Land Management's San Pedro field office staff, I would have floundered. I can't thank them enough for their help, especially for review of the manuscript: Dave Krueper, Jack Whetstone, Dorothy Morgan, Jane Pike Childress, and Howard Kahlow.

Numerous people read drafts of the book, and to them I am extremely indebted. This always sounds like a canned statement, but writers cannot have enough readers. Many thanks to Janice Emily Bowers, Linda Morley, Dot Rhodes, Helen Snyder, Sally Spofford, and Julie Stromberg, as well as the staff at the BLM.

Additionally, I would like to thank the following people—

For patience, manuscript reading, invaluable comments, patience, support to keep writing, patience, and love: Jonathan Hanson.

For tips, hints, ideas, interviews, information, and help: Hank Brodkin, Raymond M. Turner, Harley Shaw, Sue Morse, Kim Fox, Rose Clinton Smith, Sandy Flowers, Sheri Williamson, Ronnie Sidner, Steve Huckett, Katie Salwei, and Gary Nabhan.

For field trip companionship and great story material: Jack Dykinga, Dennis Caldwell, Chris Wolner, Harley Shaw, Sue Morse, and Sandy Lanham.

For prose repair and encouragement, members of my former writing group: Peter Friederici and Christine Paige. And for absolutely the best line-editing a writer could desire, Virginia Croft—it is her craft that created the final polish.

Last, but nowhere near least, I want to thank three people who contributed greatly to the Discovery Guide sections. Tucson artist Terri Gay created the maps; as always, she did a perfect job in record time. Dave Krueper of the BLM offered his unpublished guide to birdwatching in the RNCA as an invaluable resource. And Katie Salwei edited and annotated the horseback sections.

A NOTE ON Mexico. A very astute reader of the final manuscript pointed out to me that much of what I have to say about our neighbor to the south is negative: the drug smuggling, the depletion of natural resources, the pollution. This was purely by accident, for I love Mexico and spend much of my work and personal time traveling there. I did not have time or room in the manuscript to insert more stories about the fine conservation work being done in Mexico by biologists and citizen activists. I apologize to them for not doing a better job representing their work. I did intentionally avoid as much political discussion as I could, for this is not a book about the politics of nature; it is a celebration of nature and culture. My fervent hope is that this book will introduce people to the many facets of the San Pedro River and that these new friends of the river will then seek out ways to help ensure its future as a free-flowing river, both in the United States and in Mexico.

The
SAN PEDRO RIVER

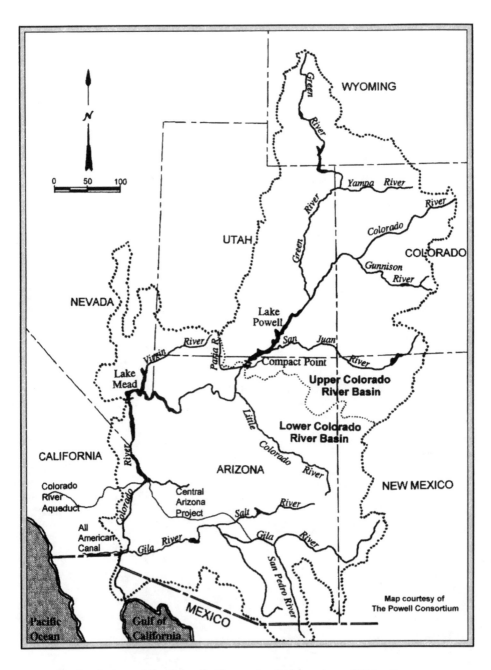

The San Pedro and the Colorado River watershed (courtesy of Water Resource
Research Center, University of Arizona)

INTRODUCTION

Stories Make a River

In the hills called the Sierra de los Ajos, the earth squeezes forth a tiny trickle of water that is the seed of the San Pedro River.

The Sierra de los Ajos and its neighboring Sierra de la Mariquita spill northwest off the foothills of the great Sierra Madre Occidental, two of dozens of *sierritas,* or "little mountains," that fan out from the foothills like toes sinking into the grassy plains of northeastern Sonora, Mexico.

Fed by other rivulets from the hills of Cananea, the San Pedro grows fatter with each passing mile. Like its sister river the Santa Cruz, 50 miles to the west, the San Pedro flows north into Arizona.

Near Cananea, a Mexican copper mining town, the young river begins to get its legs under it, murmuring quietly as it winds past great oily slag heaps and noisy railroad tracks. The face of the water shines dark, reflecting sooty clouds belched forth from mine smelters.

Once past the town of José María Morelos, about 20 miles from the U.S. border, the San Pedro begins to shake off its early urban-industrial surroundings. Soon the river sees not railroad tracks on its banks but groves of big Frémont cottonwood trees. Here, fed by more streams from the sierritas of northern Sonora, the San Pedro begins to run like a river.

Because the San Pedro has not been significantly dammed—one cannot say completely undammed because along its length are numerous small agricultural diversion structures—or channelized with concrete

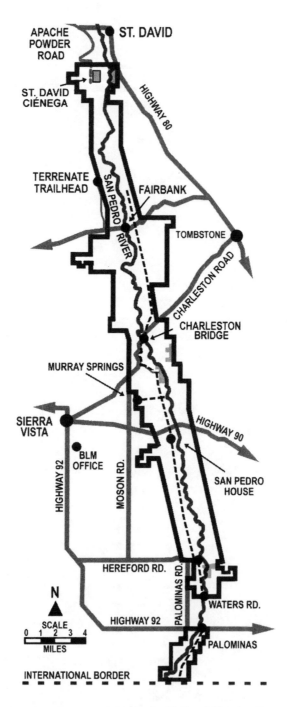

The Bureau of Land Management's San Pedro National Riparian Conservation Area

banks, it retains its natural form, the form once common to all south-western rivers before they were altered by industrialization and urbanization, as the Salt and Gila Rivers were. The San Pedro runs not straight, wide, and deep, but twisting and turning in elegant oxbows, slow and shallow, as it offers its water to the lush grasslands, *ciénegas,* and groves of trees that in turn stabilize its banks and shade its pools from the thirsty sun.

Along its last miles in Mexico, the San Pedro, a foot deep and perhaps 20 feet wide in the early spring, more or less in other seasons, sustains the cattle of several ranches and waters many agricultural fields. Its banks bear the hoofprints of these unnatural but grateful users. The understory on the banks also has provided sustenance to the bovines; it is eaten down to stubs or trampled into bare ground. Where the ground is not bare, it is covered by Bermuda grass introduced to the area in the great heaps of greenish brown fertilizer that dot the river's banks and seep deep-green and sharp-smelling rivulets into the water.

Under a canopy of shimmering light and greenness, the San Pedro River slides quietly under a rusty barbed wire fence into the United States, accompanied only by the songs of vermilion flycatchers and yellow warblers, the piercing calls of killdeer and flickers, and the swift shadows of sharp-shinned and gray hawks. There are no cattle on the banks here, only dense groves of young cottonwoods and willows, and there are few people except illegal entrants and the hardiest of bird-watchers and hikers to admire this last unfettered—undammed and unchannelized—of the Southwest's rivers as it enters its 40 miles of sanctuary, the Bureau of Land Management's San Pedro Riparian National Conservation Area, on its way 100 miles north to join the Gila River and ultimately to add its waters to the Gulf of California.

I AM STRUCK by the immenseness of the desert stretching before me: standing on the edge of a high escarpment on the western edge of the San Pedro River valley, I can see for more than 100 miles this clear summer day, a dark desert plain sloping east across the valley to the Dragoon and Tombstone Mountains, south to the Huachuca Mountains and the foothills of the Mexican Sierra Madre, north to the Rincon and Galiuro

Mountains, and if I turn to look behind me, west to the Mustang and Whetstone Mountains. And I am struck by both the fragility and power of the green ribbon far below me in the center of the valley, the San Pedro River, a bright green tropical snake in a charcoal brown desert.

Water is the source of the power. Water gives life to the groves of cottonwoods and willows, the *bosques* of mesquite trees, the sacaton grasslands, the shrubs and small plants—plants that feed huge numbers of insects (these forests are among the most biologically productive in the United States). The plants and insects feed more bird and mammal species than anywhere else in Arizona and most of the United States; and the water, plants, birds, and mammals have supported humans for perhaps as long as they have been in North America. Along this green ribbon people have hunted and farmed and raised families for more than 13,000 years, from the prehistoric Clovis Culture who hunted mammoths and bison to the agricultural Hohokam and Sobaipuris, from the military and missionary Spaniards to modern-day industrial Americans.

Yet if I squint slightly as I look down a thousand sloping feet to the river's snaking form, I can blur out the buildings and roads and see only a river flowing impossibly through a vast desert as it has for thousands and thousands of years. For millennia there have been people living in this valley, crowding close to the banks of the life-giving river like children clutching their mother's protective skirts, but their mark here is temporary in terms of the earth's clock, what we call geologic time. Nothing is constant, especially not the river. Although we humans can't perceive it in our short lifetimes, the river has changed character many times—lined by trees at one time, then lush with grasslands and marshes for another period, now lined with trees again. And it has writhed, and will continue to writhe, very much like a snake back and forth across the valley for many miles east or west, cutting down, down, down into its bed and then building up and up again. Where I stand was once the bank of the river before it cut down to its present level. The tendrils of its watershed have eaten away mountains too huge for us to comprehend, and it continues to nibble away at the Huachucas, the Whetstones, the Dragoons, the Tombstones, even the great Sierras in Mexico.

The power is immense—that power to change the land and to give life. And yet it is fragile. Today's human society is thirstier than it has ever been, and there are more of us than ever before. Perhaps we are finally more powerful than the force of this river, because now we have the power to kill this endangered naturally flowing southwestern waterway by sucking away the source of its life—its water.

The San Pedro Riparian National Conservation Area was established by Congress in 1988 to protect not only the plant, animal, and human resources of the San Pedro River but also the very source of that rich natural history, its water. The San Pedro is truly a "last great place," as named by the Nature Conservancy, where we can see our past—the stories of our ancestors—where we can read the story of all life in the Southwest, and our future as well, in the health of the trees and water. The conservation area is like a safety deposit box where we protect those stories as we piece together the big picture.

Up on the bluff above the river, I can see the big green snake as it rolls through the San Pedro Valley. Even with the hot, dry wind buffeting me where I stand, I can easily imagine the moist oasis down by the river, the millions of insects and thousands of birds gobbling them up, the sound of water flowing and birds singing and insects buzzing. That's the microcosm. The big picture is a little harder to conjure but no less important: the trickle of the river's birth in the foothills of the Sierra Madre, its life along the 50 or so miles I can see here by the town of Sierra Vista to where it fades into the blue haze 50 miles to the north, where it joins the Gila River, which flows past Phoenix and Gila Bend to the Colorado River, past Yuma and down to the Gulf of California, where the water gives life to the sea, to the fish and the fishermen, and ultimately is the source of much of the rain that feeds the Sierra Madre and that little trickle that is the seed of the San Pedro River.

THIS BOOK IS a celebration of the San Pedro River, a depository of some of its stories both human and animal, of plants and soil and water, as well as a guide to those stories. The seven chapters represent seven sections of the river, from the Mexican border to the confluence at the Gila River. Each chapter is a collection of natural and cultural history tales of the area, relating the author's personal experiences along the river and in the valley. And each chapter concludes with an "Exploration Guide" with maps and information on access, hiking, birdwatching, biking, horseback riding, and exploring historic sites.

The first six chapters describe the upper San Pedro, from the border to the St. David–Benson area, including the Bureau of Land Management's San Pedro Riparian National Conservation Area; chapter 7 describes the river from St. David–Benson to the confluence with the Gila River and provides a look at the future of the San Pedro, including threats to its condition and conservation efforts. The appendices provide lists of common plants, birds, mammals, and reptiles and amphibians; a directory of conservation and recreation resources; visitor information and regulations; a guide to other resources on the San Pedro; and a list of other southern Arizona riparian areas.

Use this book as a guide to exploring the river and for learning its many stories, as well as a way of getting to know the language of rivers. A river is not a simple linear thing flowing from point to point. It is the sum of many parts, a watershed of stories. The San Pedro River is not just a waterway; it is the microscopic water organisms and the beaver dams, the spadefoot toads and the green kingfishers, the Gulf of California and the limestone caves, the floods and the gray hawks, the ancient hunters and the black bears, the cottonwoods and the Spanish conquistadors, the mesquite trees and the songbirds, the mines and the birdwatchers.

In 1988 poet William Least Heat Moon wrote of the San Pedro River: "I am a Missourian living far from the San Pedro River, but I believe this emerald strand, still strung precariously with the iridescence of hummingbird bellies and scintillance of clear waters and the glow of cactus blossoms, is something that does not belong to me although I belong to it: its beauty, its history, and most of all its significance."

Know, enjoy, connect, protect.

CHAPTER I

BORDER TO PALOMINAS

*The Endless Water Cycle • Riparian Richness
• Summer's Mud-Loving Songsters • Thirteen Millennia of
Human Presence*

THUNDER FALLS OFF the shoulders of the Huachuca Mountains and boils east across the San Pedro River valley. The muddy San Pedro laps at the toe of my boot while the other boot swings on the sagging and rusting barbed wire fence that casually marks the international boundary with Mexico. When the thunder passes, the fence trembles, a message from the gods that I am not in an ideal location for experiencing a summer storm in southern Arizona.

At certain times when I am out in the field, an inner voice that I am sure belongs to my father reminds me to watch for rattlesnakes, to drink plenty of water, and to seek shelter when a thunderstorm approaches. My four siblings and I spent a lot of time running around the Arizona desert, and this litany of warnings was repeated so often it now lives permanently in my mind. Which isn't to say I often listen to it. I usually forget to watch for snakes until one buzzes a foot from my boot, and when the late-summer thunderstorm season arrives, I am drawn to the valleys to watch the storms cover the mountains with sheets of black rain and fill the dry riverbeds with ribbons of roiling chocolate water.

Which is why I am standing along the San Pedro this afternoon in late July 1997 while the Huachucas, also called Thunder Mountain by old-timers, cook up a storm that wets anew the hot, sandy bed of the San Pedro. Not a drop of rain fell between May and July, a typical summer dry season for this valley where the Sonoran and Chihuahuan Deserts meet, and as in nearly every other year, most of the surface flow retreated to the Cimmerian depths between bedrock and sand. But with the arrival of the summer monsoon season a few weeks ago, the river was again coaxed to the land of light and now flows under the tall gallery of cottonwoods and willows. Serious meteorologists do not like the way we Southwesterners use the word *monsoon* to describe our rainstorms, since it is more properly the name of a season of rain or a seasonal wind, depending on which scientist is objecting, but the word has stuck as a generic descriptor of summer storms, and I like its dramatic appeal.

When the thunderstorm finally breaks and rain chases the thunder down the mountain, it heads not to where I am at the border but northeast across the city of Sierra Vista and the army base at Fort Huachuca. Between a break in the trees downriver, I can see fingers of lightning probing a path in front of the storm's dark skirt of drenching rain. More thunder rolls across the valley. When rain clouds such as these liberate their cargo over an area on the earth's ground surface, the water follows the contours of the land. Flowing water always seeks the lowest elevation—usually the ocean, the basin of which is lower than the neighboring continent's upper landform (there are inland "sinks," such as the Willcox Playa in southeastern Arizona, that do not have outlets and collect water in vast shallow lakes that evaporate quickly). The courses the water takes to an ocean or sink form patterns: rainfall or snowmelt flows across the land surface to form small streams, small streams join together to form small rivers, small rivers join to form large rivers, all eventually flowing into one primary river that flows to the ocean. This network, representing a water catchment area, is known as a watershed. The watershed of the Colorado River, for example, stretches for thousands of square miles across the western United States, with its beginnings, or headwaters, on the western slopes of the Rocky Mountains. Each of the hundreds of rivers that flow into the Colorado River has its own watershed, defined by the surrounding landscape—the mountains and valleys that were themselves partially created by the erosional forces of the flowing water.

The San Pedro River is part of the Colorado River watershed. (See Introduction for map.) The river begins in the foothills of Mexico's Sierra Madre Occidental at about 6,000 feet above sea level and flows north 93 miles into Arizona; along its hundred-mile route from the border to its confluence with the Gila River, the San Pedro drops gradually from about

4,000 to about 2,000 feet. In addition to the Sierra Madre, its 4,487-square-mile watershed includes the Huachuca, Pinaleno, Catalina, and Rincon Mountains, all of which are massive enough to hold snowpack, an important source of the spring flows that determine part of the San Pedro's ecological character. Both large and small ranges collect rainfall—averaging 10 to 20 inches annually, but as little as 4.8 and as much as 25 inches—and their valleys channel it into the San Pedro; the smaller ranges include the Whetstone, Tombstone, Mule, Dragoon, Little Rincon, Galiuro, and Winchester Mountains. Two main tributaries of the San Pedro are the Babocomari River in the upper watershed, near Sierra Vista, and Aravaipa Creek, in the lower watershed near San Manuel.

After the water of the San Pedro merges with the Gila River, it heads west to join the Colorado River near Yuma, then turns south to complete its journey to the Gulf of California, or Sea of Cortés. But to say the water completes a journey is in fact a misstatement. The water only reaches its beginning on a journey that is an endless cycle: the hydrologic cycle, or more simply, the water cycle.

In the Middle Ages people thought that ocean water flowed from the earth's surface in subterranean rivers into the center of the earth, where it was heated to boiling. The steam of the boiling salt water rose toward the surface, into caverns, where it condensed and collected as fresh water. The fresh water, it was believed, then bubbled to the surface as springs, which formed rivers, lakes, and eventually fed the oceans, cycling back into the subterranean rivers to complete the circle.

Over three hundred years ago Frenchman Pierre Perrault published a landmark monograph on the origin of the water in the River Seine. After years of study, Perrault correctly deduced that annual precipitation over the Seine basin added up to enough water to keep the river flowing without benefit of subsurface steam caverns. With that publication in 1674, he became one of the first modern hydrologists.

Although Perrault proved that precipitation was the key to most surface water flows, there was still the question of where the rain or snow came from. Those medieval theories about vast underground stills cycling water from the ocean were in essence, if not in detail, on the right track. The earth's water does circulate in a vast cycle, but instead of filtering down to the core to boil up, it evaporates out of the oceans and fresh water basins and transpires from the leaves of plants into the atmosphere, where it forms into clouds, which, under the right conditions, condense and rain or freeze and release snow. In summer some of southern Arizona's thunderstorms are born in the atmospheric moisture over the Gulf of California.

Once water falls to the earth, it can take many paths on its journey through the water cycle. It may fall as rain, run off into a river, and journey back to the sea in a matter of weeks, or it may fall as snow over a polar icecap, where it will remain locked up for millions of years, a vast reserve of fresh water for future replenishment. Some water percolates down into the earth's skin, into underground aquifers where it sits or slowly seeps as springs into surface water features such as rivers or lakes. And some water is captured by the roots of plants, used to create energy, and transpired as vapor back into the atmosphere.

Humans use enormous amounts of water, adding many extra side trips to the water cycle. Water is temporarily taken out of one part of the water cycle, used, and returned to another part of the cycle to continue its journey. Wells pump water out of aquifers to irrigate agricultural fields; as they grow, the plants transpire some of the water into the atmosphere, while the rest runs off into streams and rivers, evaporates, or percolates back down to the aquifer. Water from wells or from huge reservoirs—which might be dammed rivers—is pumped into urban areas for household and industrial use. The waste water is flushed back into other surface or subsurface rivers or reservoirs, to flow out to the sea, evaporate directly to the atmosphere, or percolate back into aquifers. The 50,000 people of Sierra Vista, Fort Huachuca, and other San Pedro Valley communities draw their water from an aquifer beneath the San Pedro River basin.

All parts of the water cycle are connected. A disruption of one part causes the cycle to falter or fail. In the western United States, we are beginning to feel the effects of too many people using more water than is available locally. Sometimes in Los Angeles, water is rationed. In Colorado, Utah, Nevada, Arizona, and California, we have impounded the mighty Colorado River at so many sites—43, in fact—with dams for electricity, diversions for agriculture, and canals for sluicing water to rapidly growing cities such as Phoenix and Tucson that, except in years when floods reach enormous levels, it no longer runs all the way to the Gulf of California. We do not know how this lack of a once-huge freshwater inflow will affect the ecology of that sea, the weather patterns generated by the sea, and the people who depend on the bounty of the sea and the rain it sends north.

ACROSS THE RIVER from where I stand, deep inside a dense willow thicket, comes a rhythmic, almost wooden knocking that begins with slow cadence but builds in tempo and volume to a resounding "kuk-kuk-kuk-Kawalp-Kawalp-Kawalp!" In my rush to see the rising water of the river, I left my binoculars with my pack and mountain bike leaning against a cottonwood on the first river terrace, so I can't scan for the noisemaker, but I know it to be a yellow-billed cuckoo (*Coccyzus americanus*), a beautiful foot-long bird with a snowy belly and throat, brown back and head, and long black-and-white striped tail. Yellow-billed cuckoos are summer migrants to southern Arizona, where they seek out river corridors with tall trees and dense riverside thickets, their favorite nesting sites and hunting grounds for caterpillars and other insects. They usually arrive and establish breeding territories just prior to the summer rains, coming from as far away as Argentina; "rain crow" is a nickname for this beautiful but secretive bird that you are more likely to hear than see.

This greater roadrunner ran across the road in front of my bike as I pedaled south on the riverside two-track north of the border.

Although not similar in appearance, the yellow-billed cuckoo is related to the ground-dwelling greater roadrunner (*Geococcyx californianus*), an iconic desert bird. Both are related to the European common cuckoo, after which the famous cuckoo clock was named. The roadrunner is a permanent resident of the brushy understory along the river and up into the desertscrub. A large bird with a long tail and tall crest, which it raises and lowers frequently, especially when alarmed, the roadrunner earns its name by running at speeds of 15 miles per hour or more after its prey of lizards and snakes. A consummate omnivore, the roadrunner also eats insects, rodents, birds, and fruits and seeds. Despite its broad wings, it flies only infrequently and for short distances.

The San Pedro River is famous for its bird life. Biologists have determined that more than 100 species breed each spring and summer in the Bureau of Land Management's 40 river miles in the upper watershed. Another 250 species of migrant and overwintering birds annually use the river's corridor for feeding and shelter. In all, nearly 390 species—more than half of all birds known to occur regularly in the United States—have been recorded along this stretch of the San Pedro. The American Bird Conservancy named the San Pedro River its first Globally Important Bird Area in the United States, and the Nature Conservancy includes the San Pedro River in its list of Last Great Places in the Northern Hemisphere because the San Pedro's basin not only attracts a wealth of birds but is home to more species of mammals, reptiles, and amphibians than anywhere else in the country. It is a biological treasure trove.

It is obvious to the casual observer that the tall, dense vegetation, the cool shade, and the water are attractive to wildlife, but we have to look more closely at these components to understand why so many organisms depend on this habitat type. It is the structure of the plant communities and their complex relationships with the soil, weather, water flow, and wildlife that combine to make this habitat so biologically rich.

The swath of water-dependent vegetation growing along the San Pedro is known as riparian habitat, or a riparian area. In the arid Southwest, these ribbons of green have never comprised a large portion of the landscape: less than 5 percent of the original riparian areas of the Southwest remain intact, the remainder degraded by land clearing, groundwater pumping, and overuse.

The best way to understand the nature and rarity of riparian areas is to drive across the continent along a southern route from east to west. Somewhere around the middle of Texas, the rich green landscape and its abundant water begin to recede. The land sliding past your car windows begins to fade from dark green to intermittent green and prairie brown, from tall trees to occasional short shrubs to vast stretches of dark brown low desert dotted with a few tendrils of brighter green shrubbery. A hundred miles can roll by without your passing by a flowing body of water. The first big one is the Pecos River, which paints a shockingly green stripe down the Chihuahuan Desert in west Texas and eastern New Mexico.

After that it's another hundred miles of brown desert to the Rio Grande. Southern Arizona's San Pedro is the next big green ribbon for 250 miles.

The path of the San Pedro, like that of other rivers in the arid Southwest, creates an abrupt and absolute change in vegetation and local climate. If you get out of your car, you can walk through short, brownish thorn scrub, dust swirling around your feet and heat rising up your legs, and in just one stride enter the cool shade of 50-foot cottonwood trees, moist earth sinking under your feet. You can wade across the knee-deep water, cool and delicious feeling, emerge on the far bank under more cottonwoods and willows, walk another hundred feet, and in one stride reenter the short, brownish thornscrub, dust swirling around your feet. The cool, damp oasis with its multilayered canopy of trees and dense thickets harbors many microhabitats—habitats within a larger habitat—providing shelter and food for a great many organisms in a compact space. Consequently, riparian areas provide food and shelter for animals to a degree far greater than one would think, given how little surface area they take up. More than 80 percent of Arizona's vertebrate species—mammals, reptiles, amphibians, birds, and fish—are riparian habitat "obligates" (they live only in or need access to riparian habitats), while another 15 percent depend on riparian habitat for at least one life function. Of Arizona's federally listed threatened or endangered species, 60 percent are riparian obligates.

There are different types of riparian habitats in the Southwest. Along the San Pedro today the primary riparian habitats—the habitats that define the river as we know it—are the Frémont cottonwood–Goodding willow forest and the mesquite *bosque* (Spanish for "woodland"). Another southwestern riparian habitat is the *ciénega,* a natural, usually spring-fed marshland. There is a ciénega at St. David, and one hundred years ago ciénegas were the defining riparian habitat type along the San Pedro River, strung out like green pearls alternating with lush grasslands. The dry wash, or arroyo, is also considered a riparian habitat type. Its denser, more robust forms of desert trees and shrubs depend on periodic water flows rather than perennial, or year-round, flows. There are many arroyos leading to the San Pedro from the surrounding hills, providing important protected corridors in which wildlife can build homes and nests as well as move across the valley.

Cottonwood-willow forests, such as those that line the San Pedro

River, are among the most biologically productive forest type in the United States, host to more insects and more breeding bird species than any other forest. From 60 to 70 percent of western neotropical migratory birds—birds that spend the winter in southern tropical regions of North, Central, and South America and the spring-summer breeding season in temperate and sub-Arctic North America—are obligate users of cottonwood-willow forests.

Unfortunately, according to the Nature Conservancy, Frémont cottonwood–Goodding willow forests are also the most endangered forest type in the United States. Only 10,000 to 11,000 acres of this forest type remain, and most are severely degraded. A healthfully regenerating cottonwood-willow forest needs surface flows that periodically reach flood level, thus allowing seedlings to sprout in the wet soil of the banks. Without careful flood management, dammed river corridors cannot support sustainable cottonwood-willow forests. The Bureau of Land Management's San Pedro Riparian National Conservation Area protects 40 miles of this riparian habitat, probably the longest undammed or unchannelized, naturally sustaining cottonwood-willow forest canopy remaining in the state.

THE SUN HAS dropped behind the cloud-capped Huachucas when I climb on my mountain bike and head back north on the rutted old ranch road that parallels the river on the second river terrace, at the edge of the flat, grass- and weed-choked floodplain a quarter mile from the river. Several other ancient floodplains rise off to the east, now covered in Chihuahuan desertscrub. Recent rain has turned the road's deep, powder-fine river alluvium into tire-swallowing muck that makes for slow going as I pedal along, scanning the nearest cottonwoods for flashes of rare gray hawks. These small tropical raptors dive through the trees, snatching lizards and birds from the branches; I wonder if they would go for a late-afternoon snack of spadefoot toads, a dozen of which I have seen in and around the road's muddy puddles.

With the growing dark, a few of these small, dirt-colored amphibians have begun to bleat their nasal sheeplike calls. Except for the salamanders, amphibians are great songsters during the spring-summer mating season, with mostly males producing impressive choruses of bleats, trills, whistles, and hoots. Virtually all amphibians—frogs, toads, and salamanders—must reproduce in water because their eggs have no shells and would quickly dry out if exposed to air. A newly hatched amphibian is usually in a larval stage, like the tadpole of frogs and toads. It breathes through gills and gradually develops limbs and lungs that enable it to emerge onto dry land, but its skin remains moist and permeable to air. In fact, amphibians breathe through their skin as well as their lungs and so most must remain near or in water in order to survive.

Spadefoots, named for the little digging appendages on their hind feet, are among the most interesting of the San Pedro's amphibians. Of four possible spadefoot species in the Southwest, Couch's (*Scaphiopus couchii*) and southern (*S. multiplicatus*) spadefoot toads make the desert areas around the San Pedro their home. Adapted to the boom and bust of the short summer rainy season, these little toads remain buried alive for eleven months of the year, emerging only when the first rains arrive in summer. Mark Dimmitt at the Arizona–Sonora Desert Museum has completed studies that suggest it is the noise of thunder coupled with newly moistened soil that triggers their emergence (which is why they don't emerge at other times of year when it rains).

I found this young Couch's spadefoot toad splashing in a muddy puddle; his belly was very white and soft, and he squirmed a lot, trying to get away.

During their short terrestrial forays, the toads must hurry to mate and consume enough food to last them the next year underground. Spadefoots eat enormous quantities of insects; a researcher observed a Couch's eating 55 percent of its body weight—the equivalent of a year's supply of food—in termites in one sitting. Spadefoot toads develop from eggs to tadpoles to adults in a breathtakingly short amount of time (those waterholes dry up fast), usually around eleven days but as few as seven. At the end of the season, the adults and young adults use their spades to bury themselves in the mud, where their skin dries out to form a moisture-retaining leathery shell.

Other toads along the San Pedro include Southwestern Woodhouse's (*Bufo woodhouseii australis*), red-spotted (*B. punctatus*), Great Plains (*B. cognatus*), and Sonoran Desert (*B. alvarius*), formerly known as the Colorado River toad. The only known frog, and by far the most abundant amphibian, currently living along the San Pedro is the introduced bullfrog (*Rana catesbeiana*), a voracious predator that eats whatever it can get its large mouth around. Leopard frogs (*R. chiricahuensis* and others) were once more common in the Southwest, but habitat alterations, introduced species of fish, crayfish, and bullfrogs, and a fatal skin parasite have sent many leopard frog species spiraling toward endangered status. Introduced catfish and bass, both present in the San Pedro system, eat up frog tadpoles; crayfish alter pond ecology by eating just about everything, from plants to tadpoles. Long ago the repeated flash flooding and drying out of most southwestern streams provided a harsh enough habitat that most introduced species could not survive. But damming and other controls, as well as the development of permanent water features, such as stock ponds, allow non-natives to thrive and outcompete the natives. Along the San Pedro, where numerous permanent ponds allow non-natives to dominate, toads exist in smaller numbers than expected, but native frogs have disappeared.

I don't see any gray hawks by the time I reach a windmill about 2 miles south of Highway 92. Fallen into disrepair by the 1980s, the old windmill and cattle tank have been repaired by volunteers from Friends of the San Pedro River. Today the storm-freshened breeze spins the creaky fins so they blur into a roseate of galvanized steel. The shaft thumps faithfully up and down, sending a steady trickle of clear water into the shrub-lined cement catchment where wildlife, rather than cattle, now drink, especially during the hot, dry months of May and June. Tracks in the soft dirt tell tales of visiting coyotes, rabbits, quail, javelina, and mule deer. There are hundreds of old ranch and farm structures in the Riparian National Conservation Area—stock tanks, pumps, diversion dams, irrigation ditches—most of which are steadily being removed by the BLM or reclaimed by nature.

Human industry along the San Pedro is not new. People have been ranching, mining, farming, hunting, and raising families along the river for at least 13,000 years. Along most of the east side of the river from Palominas to the border lie hundreds of acres of old agricultural fields, probably cleared and cultivated beginning in the 1930s and continuing into the 1970s, now choked with amaranth, tumbleweed, burroweed, and Johnson grass where sacaton grassland once dominated. The road on which I'm riding could easily be part of the trail on which Spaniards Fray Marcos de Niza or Francisco Vásquez de Coronado, in 1539 and 1540 respectively, pushed north on their quests for fame and gold, or the route used by Father Eusebio Kino in 1692 to bring cattle and spiritual salvation to the Sobaipuri Indians. All along the river are old agricultural fields and irrigation dikes used by the Mogollon, Hohokam, and Salado cultures from around A.D. 1 to 1350. And just north of Highway 92, between Palominas and Hereford, is the Lehner archaeological site, perhaps the most important remains of the Clovis hunter culture yet found in the New World, a camp where animals such as mammoths, tapirs, and camels were butchered around 11,000 B.C.

After surviving twelve-and-a-half millennia of human use—including some astoundingly intensive wood cutting, water siphoning, and overgrazing in the late 1800s—the river by the early 1980s was finally facing imminent death as a free-flowing, healthy watercourse. The sleepy town of Sierra Vista and its neighboring army base, Fort Huachuca, awakened and began to thrive in the economic and military boom times. People flooded the northeastern slopes of the Huachuca Mountains and the San Pedro Valley. Too many wells began sucking water from the aquifer, threatening the natural surface flow of the river as the water table was lowered and the river's base flow followed suit. Still more people came, lured by jobs and the climate and the beautiful natural environment. The final straw came when a Phoenix land developer acquired 43,000 acres along the San Pedro and readied plans for massive development, sounding the death knell for the river, whose banks and adjacent floodplain had already been hammered into sometimes-defoliated barrenness by decades of overgrazing, gravel quarrying, and farming. Community activists rallied, and the BLM entered the picture.

The Bureau of Land Management's involvement with the San Pedro River actually is loosely tied in history to both the American and Mexican Revolutions. Shortly after winning independence from Great Britain, the Congress of the Confederation in 1780 called upon the new states to relinquish all claims to the western half of North America. Congress thus began its administration of 1.8 billion acres of land west of the original colonies for the benefit of all Americans. For the next two hundred years, during which time more U.S. property was acquired from Mexico and Spain, two-thirds of the land was carved up into new states or sold off to private corporations and individuals. The rest was eventually set up as national forests, wildlife refuges, and national parks and monuments.

After winning its independence from Spain in 1821, Mexico took control of the land in the San Pedro River valley. Shortly thereafter, settlers began filing petitions for ownership of ranches along the river. Between 1832 and 1833 two large land grants, each about 20,000 acres, were awarded: the San Juan de las Boquillas y Nogales went to Captain Ignacio Elias Gonzalez and Nepomucino Feliz, and the San Rafael del Valle to Gonzalez's cousin Rafael Elias González, who later became governor of Sonora. By 1840, because of intense Apache raids, the ranchers abandoned their land and cattle; the authors of several books and articles have estimated that 60,000 to 100,000 wild cattle roamed the area for the next twenty years, but evidence to support such large numbers is largely circumstantial.

The United States and Mexico went to war in 1846 and ended hostilities in 1848 with a treaty establishing the Gila River as the boundary between the two countries. After years of problems with the river border, a new border was drawn much farther south, and in 1854 much of the San Pedro River became part of Arizona Territory with the ratification of the Gadsden Purchase. In 1880 George Hill Howard bought the San Juan de las Boquillas y Nogales land grant; by 1899 Howard had sold the grant to George Hearst, father of William Randolph, who then sold the land to the Boquillas Land and Cattle Company in 1901. In 1905 William Cornell Greene acquired the San Rafael del Valle grant. Both continued as ranches and farms under various corporate ownerships.

In 1946 Congress created the Bureau of Land Management to supervise 270 million acres of public land, much of it leased for grazing and mining. During the 1960s and '70s the public lobbied for and won fundamental changes in public land management, and under the Federal Land Policy and Management Act of 1976, agencies such as the BLM began to manage not just for resource extraction but for recreation and conservation. Around this time interest developed in establishing a federally owned wildlife preserve along the San Pedro River. A January 13, 1978, front-page article in the *Tucson Citizen* reported that "an 80- to 100-mile stretch of the San Pedro River from a point south of Tombstone almost to Winkelman has been targeted as a 'unique wildlife area' by the U.S. Fish and Wildlife Service and is being considered for purchase under President Carter's National Land Heritage Program."

Meanwhile, Tenneco West, then owner of the two land grants, sold them to White Tanks Associates, the Phoenix land developer who made plans to create a massive housing development. The Arizona office of the BLM set to work on a land deal that, when signed and delivered in 1986, involved 1.7 million acres that were exchanged, transferred, or changed from one land agency to another, including the San Pedro land: White Tanks Associates swapped their 43,000 acres of San Pedro land for 40,947 acres of public land west of Phoenix. Other swaps and exchanges in the enormous deal settled decades of land debt that the federal government owed to the state of Arizona, including loss of land for the Central Arizona Project and the Navajo-Hopi Relocation Act of 1980.

On November 18, 1988, Congress passed the Arizona-Idaho Conservation Act, which created the San Pedro Riparian National Conservation Area along the boundaries of the two land grants, from Hereford north nearly to St. David. An additional 13,300 acres adjacent to the grant lands were also part of the exchange or purchased from willing private owners, bringing the total RNCA acreage to 56,300 acres. The conservation area begins at the Mexican border and, except for 2 miles between Palominas and Hereford, stretches for 34 linear miles, or approximately 40 river miles, to the St. David ciénega; the RNCA averages 2 to 3 miles wide, with one 5-mile-wide section just south of Fairbank. (See Introduction for map.)

According to the act, the San Pedro RNCA was established "to conserve, protect, and enhance the riparian area and the aquatic, wildlife, archaeological, paleontological, scientific, cultural, educational, and recreational resources of the public lands surrounding the San Pedro River" but public use would be managed such that it would "further the primary purposes for which the conservation area is established." The act gave the BLM broad authority to close or restrict public access in order to protect the resources, and it also established strict guidelines that the BLM must follow, including establishment of a management plan and advisory committee within a year of the act and regular reports made to Congress on the progress of the plan.

For an agency that has been called, sometimes with good reason, the Bureau of Livestock and Mining, the BLM made some controversial decisions upon acquiring the land. All mining, including gravel quarrying, was permanently prohibited, and all motor vehicles were prohibited along the watercourse and restricted to just a few miles of existing roads in the floodplain—much to the chagrin of southern Arizona's very vocal and powerful dune buggy and all-terrain-vehicle aficionados. But cattle were removed only for a 15-year-period. In 2003 grazing in the conservation area will be resurrected as a potential option, to be put before a public hearing. The ultimate decision will be made in Washington, where political winds blow capriciously.

Down around Palominas, where there are still a number of large cattle and farming operations, people are not too divided on whether grazing should be allowed in the conservation area. Third-generation ranchers such as Sandy Smith Flowers believe that grazing reduces fire-causing grasses in the riparian area, making for a healthier riparian area and a safer habitat for the nearby homes. A few months before my bicycle trip, in May, I drove down to Palominas, just a few miles from the Mexican border, to talk with Sandy's mother, Rose Clinton Smith, who was born there nearly a century ago. I wanted to hear about the "old" San Pedro, but I also learned about a different way of viewing the river, from people who live it.

Rose is a small, delicately featured woman who moves with the weight of her ninety-four years. But her bright eyes are sharp, and her mind is still filled with memories of life in the upper San Pedro Valley. Her father, John Clinton, immigrated to the United States from Ireland, served in the Spanish-American War, came to Bisbee at the turn of the century seeking mining work, and ended up applying for a homestead along the San Pedro River in 1905. Speaking softly and often gazing out the window as she reminisced, Rose said, "To anyone from Ireland, free land was unbelievable. Well, he was in a hurry to get a little piece! The first time, my father filed for 160 acres; that was what was allowed in those times."

Rose was born in Bisbee a year before her parents moved onto the ranch.

"My father had some cattle, did a little farming. They just depended on the summer rains; the whole year of rain was a lot more than it is now.

This was in the beginning of the first ten years of this century. . . . It was all open [range] back then, when my parents came here. They were one of the first settlers.

"The river isn't any different now than it was then. It's got the same amount of water—it never did have much water in it, except in the summertime or wintertime when it was raining quite a bit. There were some awful floods came down that river. Those weren't regular rainy season rains; I don't know what you'd call them. There were some big, heavy floods in the river then. Those were times we were definitely on the wrong side of the river [from Bisbee]."

Rose told me her parents lost a baby because of a flood; they couldn't get across the river to get a doctor to take care of the baby, and she died.

"A lot of times whirlpools from the floods would leave nice swimming pools that were pretty deep, and nice to swim in. There weren't any fish in the river; lots of minnows, though. There weren't any beavers around here. I think I remember cowboys who worked the river for a long time around here talking about them at one time. There must have been more water in the river then than there has been in my lifetime."

Rose became a schoolteacher in Cochise County, where she taught for forty years, including a long stint at the one-room Palominas School. She married Ted Smith in 1943.

"After we married, we moved onto the ranch. My brothers were all gone to school in different places. Ted farmed the ranch for a while; he raised sorghum hay. Ted built the house we're living in now. The old homestead house part is toward the back. We had a happy marriage."

Rose's voice trailed off until I couldn't hear it anymore, and she seemed lost in her memories, gazing out the window of the living room that her husband had added to the original homestead. Out in the garden Sandy's husband, Wes, and two of her sons were getting ready for a camping trip. In the scrubby mesquite surrounding the house, cattle lay in the meager shade, chewing their cud. One or two lowed in the distance, out east toward the river. Cicadas buzzed loudly.

As Sandy walked me to my truck, I asked her about the future of the Clinton Ranch in the face of the rapid development chopping up the valley around them. "Wes and I are going to keep it going as long as we can," she said fiercely. "It's what my family's always done."

As I PEDAL out to the highway, it is almost completely dark, and I can hear the hollow sound of a car passing over the bridge that spans the San Pedro's muddy storm water. I recall a series of pictures I saw about six years ago in a slide show presented to the Tucson Audubon Society by San Pedro biological technician Jack Whetstone. Taken from one of the bridges—either this one or the Hereford bridge, I can't recall exactly which—the first picture dates from when Tenneco owned the land and shows a wide, shallow, sunny expanse of river with a few small shrubs on the two widely separated, eroded banks. The river bottom is pocked with thousands of small, hoof-sized holes, and the water, a dark uric yellow-green color, trickles sluggishly between the holes. Looking at the camera are about thirty cattle standing in the river. The second picture, taken just a few years after the RNCA was established, shows a darkly shaded, narrow, deep watercourse flanked by tall young cottonwoods and willows and a thick, dense understory of shrubs. It was hard to believe it was the same place.

I am not against cattle grazing. But I am against land abuse. When large corporations control grazing land, short-term profit or tax breaks, rather than long-term health of the land and a family's legacy, are the only motivating factors for management of that land. There are thousands of acres of well-managed cattle grazing land in the West, much of it still in the hands of families like the Smiths. When a place as biological and culturally rich as the San Pedro is abused by big business, the whole cattle industry looks bad. We can't just instantly remove cattle grazing entirely from American public lands—we wouldn't, after all, be removing it entirely, only displacing it to areas that will also be affected, such as the tropical forests of Mexico and Central America—but we can remove cattle from riparian areas.

I load my bike on my truck and head west to the Huachuca Mountains, where I will camp under the pines in Carr Canyon. There are bright sulfur flashes in the bellies of black clouds hanging over the mountain, and my hopes rise for a nighttime storm. I love to lie awake and imagine the drops rolling off my tent, across the pine-needle carpet, down the gullies and washes to the San Pedro River, running muddy and healthy far below.

EXPLORATION GUIDE

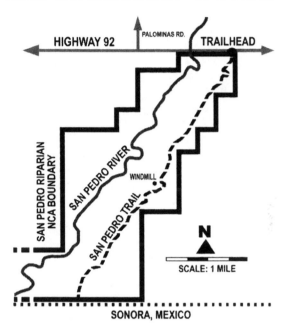

Border to Palominas San Pedro Trail and River Access Map

HIGHLIGHTS

The back road along this stretch of the river provides a unique access experience for four-wheel-drive vehicles and for mountain bikes. Birders who keep U.S. and Mexico lists enjoy the bonus of birding in two countries from one road. Palominas has a good country store and café for post-recreation refreshments, and Bisbee is just 10 minutes to the east.

MILEAGE

20 miles to the Palominas access point from the intersection of Highways 90 and 92.

DIRECTIONS

To get to the Palominas access point from the intersection of Highways 90 and 92, head south on Highway 92, which parallels the Huachuca

Mountains, then curves east at about 13 miles. Palominas is 5 miles east of the turn-off to Coronado National Memorial (Highway 61). Continue east from the bridge a half mile; the turn-off is on the right (south) here. The rough dirt road heads south 4.2 miles to the border. Four-wheel-drive is a necessity most of the year; there is a large incised gully about a mile from the highway, and only short-wheel-base four-wheel-drive vehicles with aggressive tires should attempt the steep ramp leading up the south side. No vehicles are recommended during times of rain. Park by the highway if you are mountain biking, hiking, horseback riding, or do not have a four-wheel-drive.

ACCESS

This is one of the few back roads open to motor traffic in the RNCA; it is the first section of the San Pedro Trail system.* All vehicles are restricted to the existing main back road. At the border the road turns west at some old corrals, then crosses the river (the border fence is not marked—the ranch at the corrals, on the other side of the fence, is in Sonora). Because most of the land on the west side of the river is private, it is best to turn around and return via the same road rather than cross the river. Also, when the river is flowing, quicksand is common in the riverbed.

A small measure of extra caution is advised in this area because of its proximity to the border; drug smugglers use the roads here, as does the Border Patrol. It is advisable to avoid overnights in this section. Do not be tempted to explore on the other side of the border fence; if you are questioned by Mexican officials and they find you without proper visas, you might find yourself in hot water.

To connect to the Palominas-Hereford section of the San Pedro Trail, take Highway 92 west to Palominas Road, then north to Waters Road. Take Waters Road east to the trailhead.

About the San Pedro Trail: This through-trail is a work in progress for the BLM and is mostly completed. Running from the border through the RNCA nearly to St. David, it comprises linked old two-track roads. Directions for following the San Pedro Trail are included in each chapter's "Access" section.

HIKING AND BACKPACKING

There are a few casual and short side trails that wander from the back road to the river, but for hiking the river, access is best along the riverbed itself. This can be wet during spring and fall (it's not recommended to hike the riverbed during summer rains because of flash floods), so wear hiking sandals, river shoes, old running shoes, or waterproof hiking boots and gaiters. The going can be rough through the occasional thickets of seep willow and rabbitbrush, but the scenic rewards are high as you explore the shady green world of the river corridor.

If hiking in the riverbed, start at the border and go with the flow north; if you try to hike south, you will run up against old flood debris that points north like the pikes at castle fortifications. A loop trip can be done from Highway 92 if you hike south on the road or through the floodplain (be prepared for low but dense weeds and stickers), then head back downriver about 2 miles (head east back to the road here to avoid problems on private property; legally you can walk the river as long as you stay in the current channel, below the high water mark).

BIRDING

The back road runs along the second river terrace, at the eastern edge of the half-mile-wide floodplain; to the east of the road, the hills rise into Chihuahuan desertscrub. Much of the floodplain is old agricultural fields; in summer keep your eye out for rare white-tailed kites and the more common Swainson's hawks, Chihuahuan ravens, western kingbirds, and Cassin's and Botteri's sparrows, which prefer grassland-mesquite habitat. About a mile north of the border, there is a backwater along the river where Cooper's hawks and nesting black-bellied whistling ducks have been seen. Around the river, expect to see northern beardless-tyrannulets, vermilion and brown-crested flycatchers, crissal thrashers, and other riparian specialties; look for gray hawks, especially during migration.

MOUNTAIN BIKING

This is a great ride, especially in late spring. In fall goatheads are a problem, so take plenty of tube-patching materials or spare tubes. Bike riders must stay on established trails. There is one really steep section near the beginning where the road crosses the first deep arroyo and climbs up the other side. There are numerous side roads that head down to the river.

HORSEBACK RIDING

Following the same route as mountain bikers is a good ride if you leave your trailer at the road head (the big wash prevents any trailers from being hauled back to the border). In summer it's best to start close to dawn to get the 4 miles of unshaded eastern exposure road under the saddle before it gets too hot. Except during very wet years, there is likely to be little water in the river in May and June, before the summer rains. There is permanent water at the windmill about halfway between the border and the highway. Riding in the riverbed is not recommended because of quicksand. If camping overnight (see information below), avoid grazing horses in a concentrated area, and do not picket horses together.

HANDICAPPED ACCESS

There is no access for low-mobility or wheelchair-bound visitors in this part of the RNCA, except for passengers in or drivers of four-wheel-drive vehicles.

CAMPING

There is no car camping allowed in the RNCA. With a permit from BLM, you can backpack and camp overnight anywhere in the RNCA except in research natural areas (RNA); there are no RNAs along this stretch. See the comments above, under "Access," concerning drug smuggling in this area. There are two campgrounds—Townsite and Ramsey Vista—in the Huachuca Mountains, at the end of Carr Canyon Road (a narrow, unpaved 9-mile mountain road; vehicles over 20 feet and trailers longer than 12 feet are not allowed). There are toilets, and water is usually, but not always, available at Townsite. For help finding RV parks, contact the Sierra Vista Chamber of Commerce at 800-946-4777.

ACCOMMODATIONS

Ramsey Canyon Nature Conservancy Preserve (bed-and-breakfast accommodations; 520-378-2785); Beatty's Miller Canyon Bed and Breakfast (520-378-2728); Casa de San Pedro Bed and Breakfast in Hereford (520-366-1300); and the San Pedro River Inn in Hereford (520-366-5532). There are many motels and hotels in Sierra Vista; contact the Chamber of Commerce (see above).

OTHER ATTRACTIONS NEARBY

Coronado National Memorial (520-366-5515) at the southern end of the Huachuca Mountains offers excellent information on the early Spanish exploration of the San Pedro River valley, including the namesake 1540 expedition of Francisco Vásquez de Coronado. Montezuma Pass, at 6,575 feet, offers views of the valley and into Sonora, as well as trail access to the Huachuca Mountains.

The Palominas Trading Post and Country Diner, at Palominas Road and Highway 92, is worth a stop after a hard hike or ride or morning birding excursion. It has a good old-fashioned fountain bar offering ice cream, floats, malts, sundaes, and homemade pies and cakes, and also serves traditional diner-style breakfasts, lunches, and dinners. For hours, call 520-366-5529.

CHAPTER 2

PALOMINAS TO HEREFORD

*Mammoth Steaks and Snake Stew: Paleo-Cookouts
on the River • Riparian Structure and the Wonderful Willow
Family • Life in the Flood Lane: Strand Ecology*

ALTHOUGH IT SHOULDN'T surprise me, it always does: human behavior can be remarkably predictable, bordering on atavistic. Like the human love of campfires. For perhaps millions of years, up to this day, most humans, urbanite and peasant alike, feel drawn to and comforted by the soft lick of flame, the smell of wood smoke in hair and clothes. Our genetic memory must tell us that campfires are safe havens from the nocturnal predators lurking beyond their warm glow. Likewise, a related genetic determination can be the only explanation for men's love of barbecuing, which approaches obsession in some. How else can one explain the $4,000 propane barbecue—a patio appliance, mind you, to be used perhaps twice a month—that I just saw in a lifestyle mail-order catalog?

So I was surprised, but I shouldn't have been, at what we found at the Lehner Clovis site, just south of Hereford in the San Pedro Riparian National Conservation Area.

IT IS A hot, hazy May morning, and only a few black-throated sparrows trill and twitter in the Chihuahuan desertscrub as we park the trucks by the BLM's National Historic Landmark sign and start walking northeast through an unsigned break in the fence. We skid down a bare, eroded bank of an arroyo that is about 40 feet wide and is choked with rocks and weedy, chest-high shrubs—rabbitbrush, acacia, and mesquite. Jane Pike Childress, staff archaeologist for the Bureau of Land Management's San Pedro project office, leads the way. Small and energetic in the taut, competent manner of field archaeologists, she crawls easily and quickly under two strands of a sagging barbed wire fence that crosses the dry wash, and my husband, Jonathan, and I follow.

We wade our way down the wash through the spiny river of mesquite and whitethorn on the south side of the arroyo as Jane talks about plans to build a real trail to the site. She admits her feelings are ambivalent because of what it will mean to the site, and I agree with her. Not many people visit the site, she says, a fact I am not surprised to hear, given the access difficulties. On the one hand, difficult and unmarked access protects places from overuse and increased vandalism—artifact digging, in the case of archaeological sites—but on the other hand, I tend to feel that history is alive only if it's available for participatory learning and that human history should be passed on by humans and by direct experience if at all possible. If a site as highly significant as Lehner fades back into the dusty desert in the next century because no one experiences it except in old scientific journals, the history might be lost as well. I think in this case it's worth the risk of overuse. I'm excited about seeing the site.

Jane stops at a spot where the arroyo sidewall is deeply undercut and about 10 feet high. Mesquite tree roots from a quarter of an inch to several inches thick dangle free of the eroded wall, like dozens of wires on an old-fashioned switchboard. At the base Jane scrapes at the dirt with her metal trowel. "Not deep enough," she says, indicating that she doesn't see the tell-tale line of black earth marking the layer called black mat that covered the Lehner artifacts 13,000 years ago and preserved them so well in situ.

"Black mat is usually found at about three meters," Jane says. "Paleobotanists think it might indicate algal growth from standing water—like pond scum. It's found at this level all over the valley."

I'm eager to get to the site, though, and not presently interested in black dirt and pond scum. I silently urge Jane to keep moving so we can get to the actual Lehner site; I keep craning my neck to see if I can catch a glimpse ahead of us. The arroyo leading to the site is less than idyllic, scattered with trash, and I realize I'm slightly disappointed. I was expecting a more dramatic lead-in, not pearled bottles of Jim Beam and Gordon's gin, pieces of Ready Rain irrigation sprinklers, plastic bags, an aspirin bottle, a tire, weathered boards, and cow bones. We walk a few

Clovis points are beautiful—long and slender, but definitely deadly looking.

more yards, and Jane points out a bulldozed trench leading south off the main arroyo—an exploration trench, she explains—then we step into a slightly elevated, sloping side drainage maybe 50 feet across and she says, "Here it is."

Here were found thirteen fluted Clovis projectile points, assorted animal butchering tools, flakes from spearhead-sharpening or tool-making sessions, and rem-

nants of fire hearths. Here were found the butchered remains, some charred, of twelve mammoths, a mastodon, a horse, a tapir, four bison, three camels, a grizzly and a black bear, a dire wolf, a gray wolf, a coyote, two rabbits, a garter snake, and three rattlesnakes (diamondback, Mojave, and ridge-nosed). Here is one of the most significant archaeological sites in North America, the first Clovis site found with definable fire hearths that could be radiocarbon-dated, and the first site where butchering tools were found with animal remains. Here, I realize as I look around the site, which barely shows signs it was ever disturbed by years of archaeological digging, is a 13,000-year-old barbecue site and trash dump.

I AM SURPRISED, although I shouldn't be. Having grown up in the arid Southwest, I've always known that modern humans use washes and creeks as trash dumps. Any place a back road bisects a wash, there are old tires, appliances, bottles, cans, and shotgun shells. Animal bones, firewood, chipped spear points—why should it have been any different for humans 13,000 years ago? Much of our behavior is atavistic, such as our love of campfires, so why not trash dumping? This arroyo most likely has been used off and on as a de facto landfill for thirteen millennia, up to and even after Ed Lehner, a rancher who owned the property, first discovered the mammoth bones in 1952. The RNCA's other famous Paleo-Indian prehistoric site, Murray Springs, 12 miles north of Lehner, was a favorite campsite of the Clovis people. It was found in the 1960s by archaeologists who had been camping near it for years as they searched up and down the San Pedro for artifacts. Everyone loves a scenic, well-protected camp, whether they schlep their household around in leather-and-fiber baskets or a Willys Jeep.

The radiocarbon dating of the charcoal found at the Lehner site set human activity there at around 10,000 B.C. Further soil stratigraphy studies by geochronologists pushed the date back another thousand years. From this work and from details of the few Clovis camps found in the Southwest, we know that between about 11,000 and 8,000 B.C. the Paleo-Indian people we call Clovis Culture hunted up and down the San Pedro River valley, to at least where the town of Naco is today at the Mexican border.

Evidence of Clovis people has been found in all forty-eight contiguous U.S. states and in Mexico. We don't know exactly when early hominids crossed the Bering land bridge and entered North America as successful predators—the oldest unquestioned human remains in the Americas, found in Alaska, are dated around 12,000 B.C., and recently scientists found human artifacts off the shores of the Queen Charlotte Islands that may be up to 20,000 years old (although the dating is controversial)—but we do know they were skilled, intelligent hunters who ate a wide variety of animals and plants and whose populations expanded rapidly. By the time Clovis people were having families and hunting along the San Pedro, humans had reached the other end of the Americas. In his excellent book *Guns, Germs, and Steel,* which tackles the question of why Europe and the Near East became the cradles of modern civilization (that is, science and technology) rather than Africa, Australasia, or the Americas, Jared Diamond makes the case that a thousand years would have been plenty of time for people to migrate to Patagonia. He believes that population pressures kept people moving (it's 8,000 miles from Canada to Patagonia, so expansion need only have been 8 miles per year); using a conservative growth rate of just 1.1 percent per year, which is far below many hunter-gatherer society growth rates, which have been as high as 3.4 percent, there may have been 10 million people in North and South America by this time.

Clovis people did not live in permanent villages but moved constantly, following the game animals and seasonal availability of fruits, seeds, greens, roots, and other foods. We think they lived in small groups, probably extended families of perhaps up to thirty individuals, and moved around in home ranges of several thousand square miles. They fashioned spearheads and tools from quartz, chalcedony, jasper, rhyolite, andesite, obsidian, and chert; the name Clovis comes from a site near Clovis, New Mexico, where this type of long spear point was first discovered. One intriguing Clovis Culture artifact found at Murray Springs is a tool thought to be a spear shaft straightener. Made of bone, possibly of mammoth, it is about 10 inches long; its shaft, or handle, is rounded and about an inch thick, and its head is a flat, 2¼-inch disc with a 1-inch hole bored through its center. The edge of the hole is beveled. The diameter of the hole matches the shaft diameter of spears used by Clovis hunters; it's possible a hunter would have drawn this repeatedly over a shaft to hew it to a uniform, smooth diameter to make a straighter, stronger, and truer spear shaft. This tool type is known from archaic Arctic Inuits and from Old World artifacts, suggesting that Clovis Culture had a link to Eurasia. No other example of this type of tool has been found in the New World, however.

There are four confirmed Clovis sites in the San Pedro River valley: Naco, the first to be discovered in the vicinity, in 1950; Lehner, discovered in 1952 and excavated from 1955 to 1956; Murray Springs, excavated in the 1960s; and Escapule, just south of Murray Springs, excavated in the 1970s. Six other site discoveries are possible Clovis sites, including two other mammoth discoveries near Naco, a bison site northwest of Hereford, two mammoth sites southwest of Charleston, and another "faunal" site by Benson. The Lehner excavation was an important dig, and it was special in that the landowners not only discovered the site and supported the work but assisted the work, hosting the scientists in their home, interpreting the site for thousands of visitors over three decades, and eventually donating the land to the Bureau of Land Management.

During the time Clovis people lived along the San Pedro River, the surrounding land was open savanna dotted with trees that today we associate more with mountain plant communities than with river valleys; archaeologists found pine, ash, and oak charcoal in the hearths at Lehner and Murray Springs. The climate was much wetter and cooler then, in summer averaging at least 12° to 14° F cooler than now because North America was in the waning years of the last of at least four major phases of glaciation, the end of the Pleistocene epoch (1.7 million to 10,000 years ago). Although glacial ice never reached the land we now call Arizona, the cooling effects on the continental climate—and their impact on species of plants and animals—were far-reaching. Most of the rain probably fell in winter because there was a stronger jet stream influence than there is today; the summer "monsoon" season had not yet developed, and desert plants were not around yet, either. The San Pedro River and its tributaries, such as the Babocomari, flowed year-round, and there were many small lakes and springs, which today we call ciénegas.

This lush savanna, much like the great plains of Africa, hosted an astonishing array and abundance of wildlife, some familiar, others exotic to us today. Several species of bison roamed the valley in large herds; *Bison latifrons* was the giant among them, with a horn spread of up to 10 feet. Camels, which evolved in the New World and probably crossed paths with early humans on their way over the Bering land bridge to the Old World, were also common along the San Pedro, probably in herds. *Camelops* was a large dromedary much like those of today's northern Africa, while *Hemiauchenia* was small and llamalike. Another familiar herd animal was the horse (*Equus* spp.), which evolved in North America 40 million years ago. There were most likely many different species in the San Pedro area. The little-known shrub ox (*Euceratherium* sp.) was also a member of the San Pedro fauna. Looking like a larger, less-hairy version of the musk ox, the shrub ox lived in mountain foothills. Elk (*Cervus* sp.) and pronghorn (*Antilocapra* sp.) were also around.

Much less familiar to us are the Pleistocene animals, such as the giant ground sloths and the tapirs. Although some North American sloths were larger than today's elephants, the San Pedro Valley sloth, *Nothrotheriops shastensis,* also called the Shasta ground sloth, was probably about the size of a black bear—6 feet long and 400 pounds. These lugubrious herbivores looked like giant versions of contemporary tree-dwelling South American sloths, but they were nonclimbers that foraged in the forested highlands for leaves, which they stripped with muscular tongues, or for roots, which they dug up with stout claws. Fossilized sloth dung excavated from caves in the Grand Canyon show that they ate globe mallow, Mormon tea, mesquite, salt bush, and yucca. Also living in forested areas were the solitary tapirs (*Tapirus* sp.), long-nosed relatives of horses and rhinos, which looked similar to today's javelinas but weighed in at around 200 pounds.

Of course, the most famous of the Pleistocene "megafauna" were the mastodons and mammoths, ancestors of modern elephants. When I was in grade school in Tucson, one of the obligatory field trips around third or fourth grade was a visit to the Arizona State Museum, on the University of Arizona campus. My favorite exhibit was a diorama tucked into an alcove in a back corner of the old, cool brick building—I think I had to stand on a stool or step to see it—which showed two "cave men" ambushing a mammoth at a water hole. One brave hunter stood off to the side, having just thrown a spear that was magically suspended forever in its powerful arc, while another hunter, standing on a cliff above the water hole, was about to launch a boulder down onto the mammoth's head. The mammoth's long trunk and huge, curving tusks were raised defiantly, as though in midtrumpet, a final warning to the rest of the herd before he did battle with those pesky little bipeds. The diorama is still there.

About twenty species of mammoth lived from about 4 million to 4,000 years ago on every continent except Australasia and Antarctica; several species ventured into North America about 1.5 million years ago. They lived in herds and grazed huge quantities of coarse grass. The mammoth that the Clovis people hunted in the San Pedro River valley was *Mammuthus columbi,* a relative of modern elephants, which was about the same size or a little larger than African elephants and similarly free, or mostly free, of long hair. The famous woolly mammoth (*Mammuthus primigenius*), most often depicted in children's history books, probably never came as far south as the San Pedro.

Mastodons were smaller than their distant relatives the mammoths. They sported trunks and tusks, but they had short legs and sloping foreheads, and their multicusped teeth suited browsing rather than the grazing habit of the flat-cusped mammoth; they lived in forests, along rivers, and in pine-clad mountains, where they dined on twigs, leaves, and roots.

With so many large grazers and browsers roaming the San Pedro area, there was also an abundance of large predators, including at least three species of big cats: relatives of the jaguar (*Panthera* sp.) and cougar (*Felis* sp.) and the 500-plus-pound lion (*Panthera leo atrox*), which lived much as African lions do today, in prides on the grassy savannas. Dire wolves (*Canis dirus*) were massive versions of gray wolves (*Canis lupus*), which were also around during the late Pleistocene. Coyotes (*Canis latrans*), grizzlies (*Ursus arctos*), and black bears (*Ursus americanus*) were also roaming the forests and savannas.

Although my favorite diorama depicts an adult mammoth under attack by presumably Clovis hunters, the reality of mammoth hunting during the Pleistocene probably was that most prey were juveniles that were ambushed or trapped at steep-sided water holes. Indeed, most of the kill sites contain the remains of only juvenile mammoths (it's easy to get carried away, even for scientists, guessing about early human habits; considering that we've only found a handful of prehistoric sites, we are still really only guessing). More commonly found at kill sites are bison, which no doubt were easier to hunt. However, judging from the charred animal bones found around the hearths—at Lehner, one pit was ringed by broken and charred bones of young mammoth, bison, jackrabbit, tortoise, and bear—Clovis hunters exhibited classic survivor habits: eat whatever is available, for tomorrow the tasty mammoth or bison steaks may be gone.

Which is indeed what happened. About 13,000 to 11,000 years ago, the global climate started to warm up. Along the San Pedro, summers became drier and hotter; rivers and springs became intermittent or dried up. Over the millennia, plant communities changed from species adapted to a temperate climate to those better adapted to desertlike conditions. The lush savannas became desert grasslands, much like those we know today. Trees such as oak, juniper, ash, and sycamore died off at lower elevations except along watercourses. This change in ecosystems meant one thing: adapt or perish. Species that could not cope with a changing habitat died off, to be replaced in the ecosystem by relatives or similar species; for example, dire wolves and lions could not adapt to loss of prey and were outcompeted by gray wolves and mountain lions.

A contentious debate rages among paleontologists about what role humans played in the megafauna extinctions, as the late Pleistocene die-off is called. Did humans become numerous, organized, voracious pred-ators, selecting too many juvenile and female prey, causing massive population crashes among the mammoths, mastodons, bison, and other large herbivores? Was climate change, which caused a large-scale ecosys-tem collapse and reorganization, the sole engine driving the extinctions? Or was it a combination of the two: animal populations weakened by cli-mate and habitat changes, coupled with slightly increased hunting pres-sure from humans? Jared Diamond makes a convincing argument for human-caused extinctions. Diamond cites the facts that the megafauna of North and South America had survived perfectly well for millions of years of climate changes, that they had evolved for millions of years with-out humans and were therefore unafraid of them as predators, and that there are virtually no megafauna left at all in the Americas, whereas in Africa and Asia megafauna remain, where they evolved as the prey of humans and are thus afraid of humans. Further, he argues, another megafauna extinction, in Australia, occurred nearly concurrently with the arrival of humans on that continent 30,000 years ago.

By whatever means, by around 10,000 B.C. most of the megafauna were gone and so was Clovis Culture, replaced by those we now call Cochise Culture. We do not know what happened to Clovis Culture: did they follow their prey as the herds dwindled and retreated north or south? Were Cochise people related, distantly, or did they, being more adaptable and technologically advanced people, conquer and kill off the less-organized Clovis Culture? Answers lie in the ancient mud of the San Pedro. Bones or spear points, a dwelling wall or pottery shards, a sandal fragment or a grinding tool. It will likely be just luck if we stumble upon them, as Ed Lehner did half a century ago.

BY THE TIME we climb back to the present and the parking lot, a hot wind is blowing from the south, where a line of hazy, gunmetal clouds wavers. Amazingly, I can smell rain on the breath of the wind, nearly unheard of for May, which is southern Arizona's driest month.

"Another gift from El Niño," quips Jonathan.

All winter we experienced higher-than-normal rainfall, a real-time lesson about the global climate change occurring thanks to the shifting warm-water current off South America's western shores. The current likes to act up around Christmas, so it is named for the Christ child, El Niño. Maybe this niño will keep sending us more rain to fill the arroyos and uncover more ancient mysteries.

In the meantime Jonathan and I say good-bye to Jane, who powers off in her full-sized BLM Bronco, a little figure in a big truck. We turn our truck north along Palominas Road, then east on Hereford Road a half mile to the BLM's gravel parking lot by the river. The bridge over the San Pedro is the last of the old single-lane, steel bridges spanning the river; the one at Charleston is now a simple pedestrian bridge, while a new concrete giant spans the river just a few dozen yards away. The Hereford parking lot is on the first river terrace, or flood plain, which is about a quarter to a half mile or more wide. Here on the east side near Hereford Road, some of the original sacaton grass survives.

The flat, grass-covered flood plain marches right up to the 20- to 50-foot-tall stand of riverside Frémont cottonwoods, Goodding willows, and densely packed understory shrubs, such as seep willow, desert broom, rabbitbrush, velvet mesquite, desert hackberry, catclaw acacia, wolfberry, buttonwillow, and desert willow. From the parking lot at the edge of the thicket, we can hear a soft trickle of water, dozens of birds calling and singing, and the first of summer's cicadas buzzing electrically. The wind here is cut by the tall trees, and the clear sky no longer tantalizes us with the scent of rain.

Several sandy paths snake through the understory toward the river; we choose one and step into the cool greenness, startlingly different from the sunny, hot, gravelly parking lot. Although I've logged hundreds of hours in riparian areas, the feeling of bodily transport upon entering the river habitat never diminishes for me—it's as definitive a transition as entering a building or diving into a swimming pool. The sensory changes combine to make you feel as if you are alone, much farther from the road or ranches or towns than you really are. It's the air on your skin: cool, moist, heavy. It's the strong smell: decaying plants, stagnant pools, wet dirt, tangy pollen. It's the view: dense shade, light filtered through shimmering, pale-green leaves, the curtain of green cutting off the view on all sides save for short stretches up- or downriver, only a sliver of blue sky above. It's the sound: burbling water, singing birds, humming insects, and muffled and filtered sounds from beyond the river. When photographer Jack Dykinga and I backpacked for four days along the San Pedro, from here to Fairbank, we stayed in the riverbed for most of the 40 or so miles, and I was surprised that I felt wonderfully isolated and immersed in wilderness even though at no point were we more than a mile from a house or moderately traveled road.

Jonathan and I walk along the 5- to 6-foot-wide shallow river about a mile upstream, about as far as the sandy riverside trail extends. Each year the river trails are partly or wholly wiped clean by high water, and it takes a few weeks or months for the feet of fishermen, hikers, birders, and picnickers to wear them back into the banks; the only permanent and officially maintained trail system in the conservation area is the San Pedro Trail, the system of old roads running from the border to the Terrenate ruins, mostly above the first river terrace. It seems that a mile is about as far as these "social" trails ever extend above or below an access point along the river. Beyond that, the only place to walk is in the ever-changing riverbed itself.

At the end of a 30-foot-long linear pool, where the flow of the water has slowed enough to create a temporary pond about 2 feet deep in the center, we sit down on a soft, sandy depression in the otherwise rocky gravel bar. A killdeer launches into histrionic shrieking and flapping, flying this way and that, scolding and scolding before settling at the other end of the pool. It is ten minutes before it stops complaining and the other birds, alarmed by the ruckus, begin to sing and forage in the trees around us once again.

Although to humans the vegetation along rivers in the Southwest seems long-lived and stable—the majestic, thick-trunked cottonwoods seem so unassailable—the habitats are surprisingly dynamic and short-lived, especially the cottonwood-willow galleries. Because flooding can be frequent in natural (undammed) river courses, trees are sometimes uprooted and washed away; large amounts of soil are eroded from upstream areas and deposited downstream, where new seedlings take root and grow rapidly; and the understories grow in succession from one type to another after being scoured by floods. Even the river course changes direction, moving in big S's from one side of a valley to another. If one hundred years in the life of a southwestern river such as the San Pedro could be compressed into a 20-minute film, you would see a river course whipping back and forth constantly like a snake, mesquite bosques growing and shrinking, oxbow ponds forming and filling with cattails and reeds, then silting in and disappearing, big cottonwood trees falling, sandbars zipping around, and water overflowing the banks and then disappearing. A similar movie showing the same time period for a desert habitat would show much less change and seem comparatively stable.

It would seem few plants could survive such a helter-skelter environment, but the Frémont cottonwoods and Goodding willows that make up the primary trees of the forest canopy are adapted to thrive along the banks of a free-flowing river. These plants are relicts of early Tertiary (65 to 5 million years ago) forests that covered much of North America during a mostly warm, wet climate. As a forest that has retreated to little pockets along rivers, the trees can't survive without such conditions—springtime high water, warm summers, and periodic flooding.

Cottonwoods and willows are both in the family Salicaceae, and both release their fluffy seeds in early spring, usually in March and April. The seeds survive for only one to five weeks, so they must land in perfect conditions in order to germinate. Perfect conditions occur during or just after the high sustained river flows of late winter and early spring, when rains fall and snow in the high mountains is melting. The high flows deposit thick, wet soils called alluvium along the first terrace slightly above and next to the river course. With sustained moisture, the little seedlings grow rapidly in the rich soil, get their taproots down into the water table, and begin to thrive. A huge 50-foot cottonwood tree might take fewer than 100 years to achieve its size. Cottonwoods are one of the fastest-growing trees in the world.

The cottonwood's close associate the Goodding willow (*Salix gooddingii*), named for botanist Leslie Goodding, who worked in southern Arizona from 1918 to 1944, is the other keystone plant of the southwestern riparian forest. While the cottonwood grows tall and spreading, this willow fills in the middle canopy with its upright branches and narrow, irregular crown of drooping, finely toothed, lance-shaped leaves. The leaves are pale green below and shiny darker green on top, which makes them shimmer when they blow in wind. Most Goodding willows grow to about 10 to 15 feet (30 to 40 feet is the maximum—the Goodding is Arizona's largest willow), and their bark is dark brown or blackish and deeply furrowed into scaly, forking ridges. They grow from California to west Texas and in northern Mexico below 7,000 feet. As a soil binder, perhaps no other shrub or tree provides so much for the riparian area, and certainly no other tree surpasses the willow for its insect productivity, especially when blooming in early spring.

Within a riparian area there are five major habitats where a dozen or more vegetation types grow: the aquatic, or submergent, zone of flowing water, ponds, and ciénegas; the strand, comprising sandbars or in-stream banks of soil that are often scoured by high flows; the marshland zone with areas of wet soil next to, not in, the river course; the woodland zone, including forests of larger trees and their understories of small to medium shrubs immediately adjacent to or on the first terrace above the river course; and the scrubland, with thickets or loose associations of usually thornshrubs on the second or third terraces along the river course or along tributary arroyos.

Typically, the zones are arrayed from bank to bank across the river, on stepped terraces that are remnants of historic river channel boundaries (rivers naturally incise the plains on which they flow, creating these steps, which can be miles wide). In exploring a "model" riparian habitat today, you would find the following: on the second terrace above the river, a mature woodland, a mesquite bosque; next, down a terrace, an emergent marshland forming in an old river channel or backwater, recently abandoned by the main river course; beside that, another woodland, a mature cottonwood-willow forest with a tall gallery and open, parklike understory; from the cottonwood-willow forest to the river, a succession of scrubland and strand, both of which are often inundated; then the river channel, then another succession of strand and scrubland. On the first terrace above that you would find an old, decaying cottonwood-willow forest being replaced by an emerging mesquite bosque. Beyond that, on the higher, older terraces, would be desertscrub upland (the same as on the other side). These associations are both static and dynamic: they change over time, one type succeeding another, but the basic structure is nearly always the same.

All the zones together form a complex, though physically narrow, association of plants and animals that is biologically very diverse. The plants grow closely together, and there is an intricate structure: ground cover, small shrub understory, medium to large shrub and sapling middle story, and a tall canopy of mature trees. This vertical layering and the "cluttered" conditions create many places for animals—especially birds—to feed, breed, and rest. Each of these places is called a niche and can be described in terms of which animals use it. For example, a couple of square yards of vertical riparian habitat can support a mallard feeding in the water of the pond; a willow flycatcher nesting in the Goodding willows on the banks of the pond; a Say's phoebe hunting above the pond from the middle canopy of the tall cottonwood over the willows; and a yellow warbler in the very tiptop of the cottonwood. Because each bird specializes in making a living in a particular part of a tree or place in the habitat—in its own niche—it competes less with the other birds for resources. The same is true for hundreds of other birds, mammals, reptiles and amphibians, fish, and arthropods.

The gravel bar on which we eat our lunch is part of the strand association in a riparian habitat, and there is a whole community of plants and animals dependent on this seeming wasteland of the riverbed, where floods roar through or high flows inundate for weeks on end. In the center of the strand is a 5-foot-high forest of dark green plants called seep willow (*Baccharis salicifolia*). Despite its name, seep willow is not a willow but a member of the family Asteraceae, formerly known as Compositae, and a native of California, Arizona, New Mexico, Colorado, and west Texas, as well as Mexico and South America. But it does look like a small, scraggly willow, with dark green and serrated, narrow leaves, and it grows in wet soil at elevations of around 2,000 to 5,500 feet. In Mexico seep willow is known as *batamote* or *yierba del pasmo,* which means "herb for chills." An infusion of the leaves was used as an eyewash, and the stems were chewed to relieve toothache. The roots of a European relative were used in ancient Greece to spice up wine, thus earning the name *Baccharis* after the god of wine and revelry, Bacchus.

Seep willow is a strand specialist along southwestern river courses. It forms big thickets up to 6 feet tall on sandbars and along the river's edge; after floods its flexible stems pop back up or just resprout from the buried parts. Many of the seep willows and other plants of the strands grow at about a 10- to 20-degree downstream angle. The effect is of a natural palisade, spiky branches substituting for pikes at a castle moat; seasoned river walkers always head downstream. But besides creating sometimes impenetrable thickets, seep willows and other strand-adapted plants are vital to slowing the flow of water, mitigating the rapid changes of the riverbed topography, and adding to the river water's decaying organic matter, which is one of the building blocks of aquatic life. It's no coincidence that there is a quiet pool just upstream of this thicket of seep willows and other strand plants, such as cocklebur (*Xanthium strumarium*) and cowpen daisy (*Verbesina enceloides*). Spiny softshell turtles bask on the moist edges of the strand and lay their eggs in the soft, wet sand, while black-necked garter snakes slip silently from the pools to hunt for toads among the seep willow stems. Great blue herons stalk the shallow pond spearing catfish or longfin dace, and shorebirds such as killdeer roost on the higher strands.

The strands near Hereford were covered by 4-foot-tall Verbesina enceloides *on an August visit; butterflies and bees mobbed the blossoms.*

Inconspicuous little flowers appear in the fall on seep willows, but looks are deceiving. Plants in the *Baccharis* genus are luscious nectar plants and are visited by thousands and thousands of insects: bees, butterflies, wasps, flies, bugs, beetles, and ants. A few years ago I was lucky enough to spend a fall morning with butterfly expert Robert Michael Pyle watching a dense stand of blooming seep willow and desert broom (*Baccharis sarothroides*). He counted more than fifty species of invertebrates—butterflies, moths, bees, wasps, flies, and bugs—visiting the shrubs, and was astounded enough to declare *Baccharis* among the most insect-productive plants he'd ever seen. The insects, of course, feed many birds and small reptiles.

But this strand where we enjoy our lunch and lie back, heads on our packs, to watch yellow warblers search for tiny insects in the cottonwoods 30 feet up, might be washed completely away in a flood this summer. For certain it will change: gravel will be whisked away or silt added, plants will be uprooted and others will resprout, animals will hunt or rest on its surface, or there might be a pool here where ducks dabble and fish swim. Change is the essence of a riparian area, of a southwestern river, but it's often a difficult trait for people to appreciate: embracing the necessity of floods and fire in natural habitats can be a difficult philosophical reach. Perhaps that's why protection for our last undammed, unchannelized rivers came almost too late. Our culture has for so long manipulated our rivers—with flood controls, irrigation projects, power-plant dams—that we are forgetting what a free river is like.

After having canoed the Colorado River below the big dams, hiked parts of the Gila River around Florence, where humans have siphoned water for farming for at least a thousand years, and grown up around the now-dead Santa Cruz and Rillito Rivers of Tucson, I know the costs of overuse: the eerie quiet of non-native tamarisk forests where willows and cottonwoods once stood, the cold sterility of dam-release water where only alien fish can survive, the bare and hot sand of an empty channel. I can understand that the change and uncertainty of a natural river might fill many people—especially those who need to control it—with a sense of unease, but as I lie on the warm sand with the river flowing beside and below me, the dynamic wildness of a free river fills me instead with a surprising sense of well-being and happiness.

☙ Exploration Guide ☙

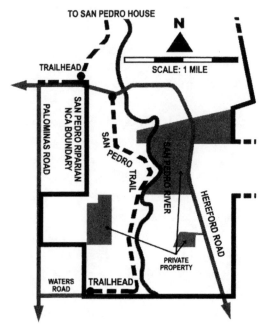

Palominas to Hereford San Pedro Trail and River Access Map

HIGHLIGHTS

At the Hereford bridge the riparian area is just a few feet from the parking lot, so this is an excellent section for people who have limited time to explore the riverside paths, have small children, or cannot walk long distances. This is also one of the best birding locations on the river for "rarities," as well as a fun bike-riding section if you plan a trip that includes a stop at the café in Palominas. For archaeology enthusiasts, the Lehner Clovis site can offer a memorable visit.

MILEAGE

19 miles to Palominas access point from the intersection of Highways 90 and 92; 17 miles to the Hereford bridge parking lot from the intersection of Highways 90 and 92.

DIRECTIONS

To get to the Palominas access point from the intersection of Highways 90 and 92, head south on Highway 92, which parallels the Huachuca Mountains, then curves east at about 13 miles; Palominas is 5 miles east of the turn-off to Coronado National Memorial (Highway 61). The RNCA is not contiguous at Palominas; the river land around this community is private. There is a small parking lot at the trailhead for the San Pedro Trail at the end of Waters Road (off Palominas Road, just north of Palominas).

To get to the Hereford bridge parking lot from the intersection of Highways 90 and 92, head south on Highway 92 to Hereford Road (about 8.5 miles) and turn left (east). Follow Hereford Road 9 miles to the river. The Hereford bridge parking lot is just after the one-lane bridge on the right (approach the bridge slowly, and yield to any cars already entering from the other side). There is a portable toilet at the parking lot, but no drinking water.

The parking area for the Lehner Clovis site is on Lehner Lane, which heads east off Palominas Road 1.5 miles south of Hereford Road; half a mile from Palominas, look for a dirt lot and a historical marker on the left.

ACCESS

Hiking is the only access on the riverside trails; bikes and horses cannot negotiate the low limbs and narrow passages. In this section the San Pedro Trail is on the west side of the river and runs along old ranch roads between the boundary of the RNCA at Waters Road, in Palominas, and Hereford (the RNCA is not contiguous between Hereford and Palominas).

To connect to the Palominas-border San Pedro Trail section, head west on Waters to Palominas Road, then south to Highway 92. Take the highway east to the Palominas access point.

If you are taking the San Pedro Trail south from Hereford Road, park in the official lot on the east side of the river and hike west on Hereford Road to the second dirt driveway on the left (south side of the road). The connection from Hereford Road south to the San Pedro Trail has not been completed to date. Check with the BLM's San Pedro office (520-458-3559) for current conditions, or be prepared to hike through tall weeds until you reach the completed portion of the trail.

This section is unique among all the RNCA sections in that there is access to the river from two private bed-and-breakfast operations, the San Pedro Inn on the east and the Casa de San Pedro on the west (for contact information, see "Accommodations," below).

HIKING AND BACKPACKING

The river trails that run north and south of the Hereford Road bridge are unofficial "social" paths that change yearly with floods and people's whims. The lengths of the paths are usually around a mile to a mile and a half, and they stay close to the river. If you want to hike the riverbed beyond the network of paths, be prepared to get wet during the spring and fall (it's not recommended to hike the riverbed during summer rains because of flash floods), so wear hiking sandals, river shoes, old running shoes, or waterproof hiking boots and gaiters. The going can be rough through the occasional thickets of seep willow and rabbitbrush; it's easier go with the flow north; if you try to hike south, you will run up against old flood debris that is nearly impenetrable. Park at the southern end of the San Pedro Trail at Waters Road and follow the road east to the river. To avoid problems with private property trespass, remain in the current river channel, below the high water mark.

BIRDING

The best birding along this section is from the Hereford bridge parking lot, along the riverside trails. Within 2 miles north and south of this area, some of the valley's most exciting birds have been sighted, including the neotropic cormorant, gray hawk, common black hawk, crested caracara, peregrine falcon, wild turkey, Montezuma quail, as well as the more common scaled and Gambel's quail, lesser and common nighthawk, plain-capped starthroat (accidental), elegant trogon (accidental), green kingfisher, thick-billed kingbird, scissor-tailed flycatcher, rufous-backed robin, Tennessee and Palm warbler, Baird's sparrow, rusty blackbird, and orchard oriole. If that's not enough, the southernmost U.S. record for a northern shrike occurred in the grasslands just to the southwest of the Lehner site in 1988. Northwest of the bridge, Cassin's and Botteri's sparrows are abundant in the summer rainy season (July through September); in winter as many as 20 species of sparrows and finches have been counted. In addition to the exciting rare birds, this area is also great for common residents of both riparian and grassland habitats.

MOUNTAIN BIKING

The San Pedro Trail is the only mountain bike route in this section. Bike riders must stay on established trails. The riverside trails are not open to bikes and are too sandy, narrow, and overgrown with low branches. This section of the trail is about 4 miles long and is best ridden from Hereford Road south to Palominas and back because of the excellent ice cream and homemade pie available in Palominas (see "Other Attractions Nearby," below); for the first mile and a half from Hereford Road, the trail heads straight south away from the curve of the river, but for the rest of the route after that, it snakes in closer to the river until Waters Road, where it turns west.

HORSEBACK RIDING

Horseback-riding access in this section is the same as for mountain bikes, although at publication the gate at Waters Road remained locked because of past problems with private property trespass between Waters Road and Highway 92. Contact the BLM for current access information before riding in this area and to find out about the status of the locked gate. The San Pedro River Inn (see "Accommodations," below) has barn and corral facilities for horses and riverside bed-and-breakfast cabins for riders.

ARCHAEOLOGICAL SITES

The Lehner Clovis site has no official trail or interpretation. Without a guide you won't know what you are seeing, if you can find it. The best way to experience this site is to join one of the organized hikes offered occasionally by the BLM, Friends of the San Pedro River, or an archaeological society or tour group (for contact information, see "Recreation in the San Pedro River Area" in the Appendix).

HANDICAPPED ACCESS

There is no developed access for low-mobility or wheelchair-bound visitors in this part of the RNCA. However, the Hereford bridge parking area provides the closest access to the river's edge. It is a good area for people who cannot walk long distances.

CAMPING

There is no car camping allowed in the RNCA. With a permit from the BLM, you can backpack and camp overnight anywhere in the RNCA except in Research Natural Areas (RNA); there are no RNAs along this stretch. There are two campgrounds—Townsite and Ramsey Vista—in the Huachuca Mountains, at the end of Carr Canyon Road (a narrow, unpaved 9-mile mountain road; vehicles over 20 feet and trailers longer than 12 feet are not allowed). There are toilets, and water is usually, but not always, available at Townsite. For help finding RV parks, contact the Sierra Vista Chamber of Commerce at 800-946-4777.

ACCOMMODATIONS

There are two bed and breakfasts with river access in this section: Casa de San Pedro Bed and Breakfast, south of Hereford on the west side of the river (520-366-1300); and San Pedro River Inn, in Hereford (520-366-5532), on the east side of the river. Ramsey Canyon Nature Conservancy Preserve (bed-and-breakfast accommodations; 520-378-2785) and Beatty's Miller Canyon Bed and Breakfast (520-378-2728) are in the Huachuca Mountains. There are many motels and hotels in Sierra Vista; contact the Chamber of Commerce (800-946-4777). Bisbee, with its famous Copper Queen Hotel and numerous bed and breakfasts, is also an option for lodging (see below).

OTHER ATTRACTIONS NEARBY

The Palominas Trading Post and Country Diner, at Palominas Road and Highway 92, is worth a stop after a hard hike or ride or morning birding excursion. It has a good old-fashioned fountain bar offering ice cream, floats, malts, sundaes, and homemade pies and cakes, and also serves traditional diner-style breakfasts, lunches, and dinners. For hours, call 520-366-5529.

Bisbee is a historic mining town with well-preserved Victorian buildings along narrow, steep streets reminiscent of San Francisco on a tiny scale. A stop here helps give one perspective on the massive mining operations that changed the face of this part of the West, including the San Pedro River, in the late 1800s and early 1900s. It's also a great art town. Contact the Bisbee Chamber of Commerce at 520-432-5421.

CHAPTER 3

HEREFORD ROAD TO HIGHWAY 90

Natural Succession • *Come Hell and High Water*
• *How to Poach a Trout and Other Desert Fish Stories*
• *Catching Hummingbirds*

JUST AFTER 1 P.M. my husband, Jonathan, drives off, waving, leaving me and photographer Jack Dykinga standing on the western bank of the San Pedro River at the Hereford bridge, adjusting our backpacks and drinking a few more liters of water. It is a beautiful November day, perfect 80-degree air ruffling the newly golden leaves in the cottonwoods. We are at the beginning of a 40-mile trek down the river to Fairbank.

The idea for this trip began one hot summer day as I stood on a bluff overlooking the river as it slithered across the desert valley like a bright green tropical snake. I thought of its near loss to overuse, its resurrection, as well as future threats. Right there I conceived a plan: I would backpack from the source of the river in Mexico, following its snaking form into the United States as far as I could through the RNCA. And along the way I would read its story and learn about its lives, and maybe something about myself and my culture. I sold the idea to *Arizona Highways* magazine, got Jack signed on as photographer, and then began the tedious preparations.

For more than a year I altered the plan several times as I gathered more information. Phone calls to biologist friends who had traveled in the Sierra Madre foothills where the San Pedro heads yielded the same exclamation: "You'd be crazy to go in there alone, or even with a whole army!" A call to the Border Patrol office confirmed their concern. The area is a hotbed of drug cultivation and transportation. If we didn't stumble into a drug operation, we might just as likely run up against the equally dreaded Grupo Beta, the Mexican equivalent of the Border Patrol. Not a good idea, I was told, to traipse around the Mexican backcountry wearing backpacks and heading north, to boot.

So to avoid the War on Drugs, I decided to start at the border, on the American side. Jack and I settled on a spring date in 1997, but that plan fell through, so we rescheduled for fall. We were set to go in October when a series of El Niño storms began to march across southern Arizona. We cancelled the trip once. The river rose. We waited. Then a window opened between storms in early November and we decided to go for it, but we had only four days free. So we started at Hereford, planning to cover the 40 river miles (more or less, since it's hard to measure all the meanders) to Fairbank, about 12 miles south of the RNCA border, in four days.

Packs adjusted, we drop down into the riverbed under the great green canopy, slosh our way across the foot-deep, 6-foot-wide river—the first of countless crossings—and settle into an easy pace on a well-worn riverside trail. Cars thump over the bridge with a metallic clatter. I see tracks of dogs, horses, people, some barefoot, some booted. Bits of trash dangle on the banks and in shrubs like holiday ornaments hung there by the high water. Then I begin to see tracks of raccoon, coyote, white-tailed deer. The trail and signs of people diminish, then disappear. Birds call and katydids whir like automatic sprinklers—now the only sounds. Meandering across the shallow river, following the clearest route on one bank, then the other, then the channel itself, we never leave the cool, cathedral-like canopy of cottonwoods and willows. Beyond the trees we see glimpses of bright sun, broad floodplains, faraway mountains. Jack comments that it's like canyon walking, giant trees substituting for rock walls.

From our starting point at Hereford Road to Highway 90, which is about 12 river miles north at the San Pedro House bookstore, the riverine canopy is an immense cottonwood-willow forest in its prime: magnificent 50- to 70-foot-tall Frémont cottonwoods and dense Goodding willows tower over a thick understory of young willows and cottonwoods, catclaw acacias, mesquites, buttonwillows, hackberries, and wolfberries. At midday many of the birds are quiet, but I can hear a ladder-backed woodpecker pecking with a staccato cadence that is different from the Gila woodpecker's drilling, which I hear a short time later, deeper and slower. A Bewick's wren trills out one of its many melodious calls, and lesser goldfinches whistle softly to each other high in the canopy top. Their shadows fly across the mud in front of me as I walk through a shallow pool.

We have followed the river for about 6 miles by the time the sun slides behind the Huachuca Mountains in the west; the river bends into several huge oxbows a quarter mile wide, and most of the time we stay in the shade of the big trees, although once or twice we cut across a bend through a tangle of shrubby mesquites and sacaton grass. We decide to set up camp at the southern end of one of the big oxbows. To the east of us are 50 acres or so of now-rare sacaton-mesquite grassland. The sacaton (*Sporobolus wrightii*) forms recliner-sized clumps with flower heads as much as 6 feet tall, and each clump is a foot or two from the next. Walking through the sacaton field, which is also dotted with rodent holes, is slow going and tedious because we can't see more than a few feet ahead and our feet occasionally collapse the roofs of the burrows. In the mid-1800s an explorer described the San Pedro bottomlands as "covered with the most luxuriant grass we had anywhere seen . . . our mules fed upon it as they traveled, for it was from three to four feet high in many places." It is thought to have been sacaton that the army and settlers later used as wild hay.

A predawn coyote chorus is my alarm clock the next morning, but I stay in my bag to fix tea, eat biscotti, and watch a nearby stand of fall-kissed adolescent cottonwoods flame in the golden dawn. It's cold, not quite freezing, but after the sun comes up, I tie my sweater to my pack and walk in a light linen shirt.

Not far from camp we come to a decaying cottonwood-willow gallery, a crescent-shaped grove of dying trees. Giant gray columns support bare branches that still reach to the sun, leafless, splattered with whitewash by numerous avian Jackson Pollocks, and full of woodpecker holes. The gallery, which had been growing along an old oxbow turn, was cut off from the main river channel when the river shifted its flow to the east. Sometimes trees can survive these channel shifts, as evidenced by the solitary giants now growing a half mile or more from the present channel. But more often the trees are past their prime anyway—cottonwoods and willows are not long-lived—and as the big tree canopies die off and the ground beneath them is flooded with more sunlight, mesquites crop up like weeds. There are hundreds of medium-sized mesquites jostling for space in this old gallery. Eventually a mature mesquite bosque, or forest, of large-trunked, 20- to 30-foot trees will completely replace the cottonwoods and willows here. In order for this natural succession to occur, certain events, besides the shifting of the river course, need to take place. One of these is flooding.

A river in flood sounds like an enormous freight train at full speed. It smells like a thousand acres of mud. It moves with a serpentine grace that belies its enormous power. A flood is truly one of nature's most terrifying and exciting events. When we witness one, it is often hard to realize, as stately cottonwoods topple and sweep away downstream and hundreds of animal homes are destroyed, that we are watching something not only perfectly normal but good for the habitat. Like the effects of a fire in a pine forest or grassland, the aftermath of a flood might not be seen in a puny human lifetime.

Flooding destroys and builds terraces next to the river course, deposits nutrient-rich debris, disperses plant seeds, wets the floodplain for their germination, and wipes out areas of plants, making way for other plant communities. In short, flooding creates and maintains riparian areas. The botanical "anatomy" of a southwestern riparian community is the direct result of flooding. The farther a terrace is from the current river channel, the higher it is and the farther it is from flood scour, as well as the water table. As a result, the soil is poorer and drier on the terraces farthest from the river, and the desert-adapted plant species that grow there represent the oldest communities because they are not wiped out by floods very often.

Of course, not all floods are big and dramatic. Usually they are small annual events. Along the San Pedro they occur in late winter and early spring when snow is melting in the mountainous watershed and spring rains fall. These flows are characterized by sustained high water. There are quicker flows of shorter duration following summer thunderstorms. In general, small floods are described in magnitude as less than ten-year floods, and they deposit more sediment than larger floods. Large floods are greater than twenty-five-year floods in magnitude, and they rework the floodplain by flattening terraces and widening the channel. Floods are rated by magnitude, such as a one-hundred-year flood, but this can be confusing. A one-hundred-year flood is not a flood that occurs only once every century like clockwork. A river can, in fact, have a one-hundred-year flood every year if the climatic conditions are right—or wrong, depending on how you look at it. The "year" designations are how hydrologists refer to the probability of occurrence of a flood of a certain magnitude; a flood with a one-hundred-year magnitude stands a one in one hundred chance of occurring in a given year. Southern Arizona experienced one-hundred-year floods in 1983 and 1993. In 1983 all the rivers spilled their banks, causing millions of dollars in property damage; parts of the lower Santa Cruz River were reportedly over a mile wide.

Riparian plants such as cottonwoods and willows establish more readily when a year of high flow—flooding—is followed by several years of low flow. The big flood event sets the stage by distributing seeds in thick, wet alluvial soil. Then a few years of low flow let the little seedlings get their roots under them before the next big flood. In one study along the Hassayampa River, an undammed river in the northern reaches of the Sonoran Desert west of Phoenix, survivorship was about 30 percent for riverside cottonwood saplings after a ten-year flood and about 60 percent for older cottonwood "poles." But in large floods, those greater than twenty-five-year floods, even the big guys go. However, as in every cycle, they are soon replaced by new saplings if the river system is healthy and not subjected to trampling by too many cows or humans.

In the same study on the Hassayampa River, scientists found that in order for successful, widespread mesquite seed germination to occur in bosque habitat there, summer floods of a five-year magnitude or greater must occur; only floods at those levels deposit enough nutrient-rich debris on the higher terraces, where mesquites flourish and get their roots down before the next flood. Also, mesquite seeds have a very tough coating that must be roughly scoured in the sand and gravel of floods or scarified in the digestive tracts of mammals in order to break open so the first roots and leaves can emerge from the inner seed.

A ladder-backed woodpecker whinnies in alarm and two white-tailed does sprint away as we struggle through the dense grove of young mesquites to find the main river course again as it S's west and north once more. I slosh through a shallow pool, and dozens of silvery inch-long fish shoot away from my feet like iron shavings repelled by a magnetic field. In the shadowy light of the cottonwood canopy, some of the fish look like they have dark stripes on their sides. They may be longfin dace (*Agosia chrysogaster*), one of only two native fish left in the San Pedro. The other is the desert sucker (*Catostomus clarki*). Historically, the San Pedro River was home to thirteen native fish. Besides the sucker and dace, both of which may become threatened or endangered, the vanished others are the loach minnow, flannel-mouth sucker, roundtail chub, spikedace, Gila top-minnow, Sonoran sucker, Gila chub, speckled dace, desert pupfish, and Colorado squawfish. The latter fish, *Ptychocheilus lucius,* grew up to 6 feet long and 100 pounds and was common in the 1880s along the San Pedro near Charleston, whose residents called it "salmon." Today introduced carp, rainbow trout, brook trout, green sunfish, mosquito-fish, goldfish, flathead minnows, channel catfish, bluegill, largemouth bass, threadfin shad, and red shiners pretty much rule the waters of the San Pedro.

The desert sucker is in the family Catostomidae, and the longfin dace is in the minnow family, Cyprinidae. Each is tiny—from about 1 to 6 inches long—making them especially susceptible to predation by the large introduced sport fish. But the suckers and dace are as tough as they are small. During the hot, dry early summer months, many desert streams retreat underground during the hottest, driest parts of the day, when evaporation is high, and resume flow again at night. This is not a good environment in which to be a fish, but the desert sucker and longfin dace both can survive hours of stranding under mats of damp vegetation when the streams dry up, as well as water temperatures that would poach a trout (over 90 degrees). The native little fish also can spawn rapidly and for extended seasons, allowing survivors to quickly recolonize a stream after a flood or drought.

Jack and I pass two hours mostly in silence, lulled to near somnam-bulation by the warm, humid air and soothing sounds of insects and birds. Sometime around four, we stop for a snack and Jack decides to shoot a linear pool reflecting a row of horsetails. He takes half an hour or more to set up his tripod, large-format camera, lens, hood, and film boards, then another half hour to wait for the wind to stop moving the trees or riffling the water. While waiting, I explore downriver a few hun-dred yards and find that we're just below Kingfisher Pond, one of the main "attractions" accessible from the San Pedro House at Highway 90. The pond is about a hundred yards long and half that wide, a former gravel quarry filled in by natural seepage from the floodplain aquifer. It is almost completely ringed by cattails. Beyond the cattails are young and old cottonwoods and willows and a thick tangle of shrubby trees and grasses.

These cattails are *Typha domingensis,* what we think of as classic marsh plants, growing with their roots underwater or in very wet soil. Cattails live at elevations from about 1,000 to 5,500 feet. These "aquatic emergents" often form dense thickets that are favorite habitats for many birds, especially red-winged blackbirds, which build their nests attached to the stalks.

The velvety brown "cattail" tops are the fertilized female (pistillate) flower parts; the male (staminate) flower parts appear at the very top of the stalks in summer, and the pollen rains down onto the female flower parts. The hot dog–shaped mass breaks open, and the mature seeds flow out onto the wind for dispersal. Cattails can also reproduce via their rootstocks.

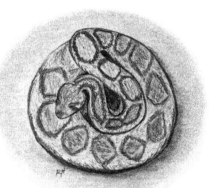

I ducked off a trail south of Kingfisher Pond to look for a shady spot to have lunch on a hot June day. I sat down and was taking my first bite when I noticed this little western diamondback rattlesnake not three feet away. He never moved, though I stayed for about ten minutes.

The protected and nutrient-rich habitats of ponds and ciénegas along the river are important nurseries for the seedlings of key riparian species such as the Goodding willow. Willow flycatchers and black phoebes hunt from and breed in the young woody vegetation, and bird-eating snakes such as whipsnakes hunt there as well. Eventually the pond or ciénega fills in with accumulated detritus, which forms soil, and in place of a marsh or pond grows a mature riparian forest, which will be replaced by mesquite bosque and eventually scrubland. If the water table rises again, a marshland will begin anew.

I sit at water's edge watching all the pond creatures scuttle around the surface, shore, and bottom of the pond. Inch-long water boatmen (*Arctocorixa* and *Corixa*) are conspicuous, zipping around as they eat up decaying vegetation and animal matter. They are slender, with paddlelike legs that jut out from midbody like oars. Giant water bugs (*Lethocerus*) are voracious predators with a venomous bite. Up to 3 inches long with grasping forelegs and piercing mouthparts, they capture and feed on insects, tadpoles, small amphibians, and fish. In the true bug family (*Hemiptera*), both water boatmen and giant water bugs fly and are attracted to lights. Predaceous diving beetles (*Dytiscus*) and whirligig beetles (*Dineutes*), members of the beetle family (*Coleoptera*), are equipped with thick forewings that cover membranous hindwings. Predaceous diving beetles often hang head down from the surface, watching for insect and small animal prey. Whirligig beetles are named for the circular paths they cut when swimming; the adults are scavengers, while the larvae are carnivores. Whirligig beetles' eyes are divided into two parts so that the beetle can see above and below the surface at the same time, although they find their prey using capillary wave echolocation.

Besides the visible invertebrates, there are also hundreds of species of freshwater microscopic, or nearly microscopic, animals that help make up the healthy "soup stock" of ponds and rivers. They include one-celled protozoans, multicelled hydras, and even a freshwater jellyfish. One of the more interesting micro-wildlife species is the rotifers, or "wheel animalcules." If I could scoop up a cup of pond water and strain it through a fine net, I'd find these tiny little animals that graze on algae or hunt other aquatic wildlife (I'd probably need a small field microscope or powerful hand lens to see them). Wheel animalcules are named for the rotating movement of the cilia, or hairlike projections, on the front of their bodies. Snails and worms feed on wheel animalcules and other micro wildlife and plants.

Among the larger crustacean inhabitants of ponds and rivers are the crayfish (*Pacifastacus* sp.), in the family Decapoda. They are an introduced species in southwestern rivers and streams, and when their populations are large, they drastically change the balance of the ecology, almost always detrimentally. Crayfish are nocturnal omnivores, scuttling along the bottom eating just about everything, from insects and small animals to large quantities of plants. In some ponds overrun with them, crayfish can literally take over, creating a nearly monospecific fauna. Raccoons, skunks, and other carnivores eat crayfish. If I had the energy to get up, I could look around and probably find scattered claws littering one of the pondside clearings.

All these little animals have to eat something. Besides each other, many eat plants, from the microscopic to the macroscopic, as well as bacteria and fungi. Bacteria are important reducers—they feed on dead plants and animals and return vital nitrogen, sulfur, and phosphorus to the nutrient cycle. The most common aquatic plants in the river and ponds are called thallophytes, a group that includes algae. Many of these lower plants are single celled and microscopic. Algae are nonvascular, contain chlorophyll, reproduce cell by cell, and are important as one of the primary base foods for the entire food pyramid, providing grazing fodder for the countless little animals that are eaten by larger animals, which are eaten by larger animals, and so on. Filaments of algae joined together in long, waving "beards" are often seen in the river; resembling miniature kelp forests, they are an important habitat for aquatic animals of all sizes. Thallophytes also contribute vital oxygen to the river water, which aquatic animals depend on. From tadpoles to grown frogs and toads, from insect larvae to flies and beetles, and from snakes and turtles to mammals and birds, thousands of species depend on the microscopic but complex aquatic forests of pond and river water.

Larger vascular plants that grow underwater or on the surface in ponds and ciénegas include water fern, poolmat, pepperwort, pondweed, and duckweed. Duckweeds are so named because they are a favorite food for waterfowl such as mallards, teal, pintails, and shovelers, the "dabbling ducks" named for their habit of dabbling in the water while they feed on the lush, floating carpet of small leaves. Duckweeds are among the smallest known flowering plants, but their tiny flowers are rarely borne; instead, duckweeds usually reproduce vegetatively (by parts of the plant budding off). Insects and their larvae and small vertebrates such as tadpoles take cover among and feed on the submerged stems, leaves, and roots of aquatic vascular plants. Amphibians such as bullfrogs and salamanders, as well as many birds, including flycatchers, warblers, and wrens, dine on the insects. Here at Kingfisher Pond I can see broad mats of pondweed, as well as several clumps of lily pads, which are not native to the Southwest. Rumor has it that some well-meaning person planted water lilies here to help "clean the water" and provide cover for the animals, but the only thing they do is reproduce and clog the pond; they may destroy the delicate pond ecology altogether by cutting off sunlight and altering the availability of nutrients and gases. With the river so close, a flood could also flush out the pond and introduce water lilies to the rest of the river.

A drawn-out wooden clacking calls my attention to the branches of a dead willow hanging over the pond. I don't see anything at first. Then a strange-looking little bird zips off a perch, skims the water, and returns to its perch, clacking like a castanet. It is a green kingfisher (*Chloroceryle americana*), one of the "stars" of the San Pedro RNCA, along with the gray hawk. Described accurately and with wit by bird expert Kenn Kaufman as looking like "a sparrow with the bill of a heron," the green kingfisher has successfully appeared in southern Arizona only since the early 1970s and bred here—only at the San Pedro River—since 1988, the year the conservation area was established. Since then about fifteen of the birds are known to live year-round along the river. The green kingfisher's larger and more widespread relative, the belted kingfisher, spends its winters along the San Pedro.

Kingfishers are "riparian obligates," meaning they need healthy riparian habitats along which to feed and breed. They perch on branches over standing or running water and scan the surface for small fish, which they dive head-first into the water to catch with their rapier bills. Kingfishers dig nest holes 3 to 6 feet long in vertical riverbanks; abundant livestock activity in the past may have degraded riverside banks to the point that nesting was disrupted. Too much recreation, including birdwatching, along the banks could also disrupt nesting and degrade the banks, so the BLM's biologists keep a close watch on the birds.

Twenty minutes later I hear Jack thrashing through the understory, muttering. The shoot hadn't gone well because of the wind, which causes blurry photos. We decide to take the main San Pedro House trail from Kingfisher Pond to Highway 90 to save a little time, since the riverbed in this area is piled with flood debris, making for slow going. The trail is well used, and it's a luxury after a day and a half of junglelike traversing. Across the broad floodplain, about a half mile away, we can see the small white San Pedro House, with its peaked roof, screened porch, and cheery American flag wafting in a slight breeze. The house, run as a bookstore and information center by the volunteer group Friends of the San Pedro River, is small, but it is dwarfed even more by the enormous cottonwood on its west side. For years I have been calling it Granddaddy Cottonwood.

One of the Friends of the San Pedro volunteers talked with a woman who was raised in the San Pedro House, who said her father had planted four cottonwoods around the house in the mid-1950s, one at each corner of a square with the house at the center, one tree for each of his children. Although this tree is huge, it is not the largest Arizona Frémont cottonwood. The largest Arizona cottonwood is near Patagonia, in Santa Cruz County; its trunk circumference is 42 feet, its height 92 feet, and its crown spread 108 feet. The San Pedro Granddaddy has a trunk girth of nearly 30 feet, and it may well be the second-largest known cottonwood.

Frémont cottonwoods (*Populus fremontii*), called *álamos* in Spanish, are in the Salicaceae, or willow, family. They grow from southern California east to Oklahoma and south into northern Mexico, at elevations from 2,500 to 7,000 feet. They are one of the most beautiful trees in the world: tall, with a gray trunk, they have lush leaves that shimmer in the river breezes. The leaves, which can be 2 to 3 inches wide, are broadly triangular and coarsely toothed. In fall they turn burnished gold before falling to the ground.

Cottonwoods are dioecious (male and female flowers on separate trees) and set their blooms in late winter. In early spring the fertile cottony, wind-borne seeds of female trees sail forth on the breezes, like seed snowstorms. The timing is crucial: the seeds form drifts on the moist alluvial soil of early spring high-water flows, the perfect potting soil for seedlings. Little taproots are quickly sent down to the water table, and within just a few years young cottonwood "poles" are established. One of the fastest-growing trees in the world, they can reach 100 feet in height in a century, although most don't grow that tall.

Although it is often said that the tree was named for its cottonlike seeds, the name actually comes from the wood's light weight and light color; explorer, soldier, and politician John C. Frémont (1813–1890) first described this tree. Despite its weak nature, the cottonwood is still widely used throughout the Southwest. In Sonora, Mexico, farmers plant cottonwood saplings as living weirs to trap stream sediment and enrich their fields; American Indians use the roots to carve kachinas and prayer sticks, and the trunks to make drums; and the wood is burned for fuel in rural Mexico. Saplings are also a favorite beaver repast.

Jack and I decide not to stop at the San Pedro House so we can get another couple of miles under our boots before the end of the day; we don't want to be too close to the highway when we camp. I think longingly of the cold Cokes for sale in the refrigerator in the back room. Some habits are hard to kick, even when backpacking. I sigh and keep walking toward the bridge.

SIX MONTHS LATER I visit the San Pedro House one Saturday afternoon as the sun is dropping behind the Huachucas. At a table under Granddaddy Cottonwood, a small group of nature tourists clusters around Sheri Williamson, who is preparing dozens of tiny aluminum bands that are carefully arranged in a box before her. The wind rustles the leaves of the giant tree above.

A rare violet-crowned humming-bird stopped by the feeders one May as I sat having lunch outside San Pedro House. It was gone before I could sketch it well.

"This is a very, very important area through which millions of birds pass in migration. Among the least studied are the hummingbirds," she says without looking up from her delicate work.

Sheri is codirector of the Southeastern Arizona Bird Observatory (SABO), which started capturing and placing the special bands on hummingbirds at this site in 1995. Each year SABO staff members band birds nearly every Saturday from spring through early fall. They banded more than 600 hummingbirds by early summer 1998, including black-chinned, rufous, Anna's, violet-crowned, calliope, and broad-tailed.

Sheri says the banders hope to learn something about the numbers and diversity of hummingbirds and the patterns of usage of the San Pedro riparian area. "Including," she explains, "how important it is to certain species for breeding and migration." For example, between 1997 and 1998 there was a perceived decline in the numbers of rufous hummingbirds (*Selasphorus rufus*). Aided by banding studies such as SABO's and that of the University of Arizona's William Calder, who bands and studies rufous hummingbirds at the Rocky Mountain Research Station in Colorado, scientists are gathering more information about why the little migrants declined. Possible reasons include weather pattern changes and habitat loss.

"In terms of conservation, what we hope to establish is the importance of riparian corridors for migration," Williamson says.

SABO is working on developing cooperative tourism and research projects in Mexico, where millions of migratory songbirds winter or pass through twice annually en route to and from Central and South America. Birds don't recognize international boundaries when they migrate, but too often the science that goes on north or south of the border isn't shared. SABO hopes to change that.

"We are hoping we can sit down together [with Mexican biologists] and say, 'These are our common concerns and problems,' and then get to work addressing them in a holistic way," she says.

While we talk, Sheri is preparing the tiny, flat aluminum bands that will be placed on a leg of each captured bird. Bird bands are sized for specific types of birds, and the hummingbird-sized band is the smallest; imagine a ring that will fit onto the small end of a toothpick.

Each band is stamped with a number code, and these are carefully recorded as each bird is banded. All bird banders are licensed and obtain their bands from the National Biological Service (NBS) Bird Banding Laboratory. Each banded bird has its "vitals" recorded on a card along with the band's code number: species, sex, age, feather wear, breeding condition (many birds develop bare patches on their bellies, called brood patches, when sitting on eggs; hummingbirds don't get brood patches, but Sheri says that a developing egg can easily be seen through a female's abdominal skin), physical measurements (bill, primaries, or main flight feathers, and rectricies, or tail feathers, among other things), and weight. The information is filed by the bander with NBS, which keeps the data on file. If, for example, a bird is re-netted by biologists during the winter in Mexico, the Mexican banders record the band's number and then contact the NBS. They receive valuable information about where that bird was during the summer it was banded, for example, and the original bander is told about the bird's whereabouts at the time of recapture.

After carefully filing any sharp spots off the bands, Sheri uses special pliers to bend the bands into a tiny C, ready to be carefully crimped closed around the legs of the birds that are captured in the nets set up nearby. Most banders I know use magnifying visors when manipulating the bands, but Sheri's eyesight is as keen as her subjects'. All birds have very sharp eyesight, but hummingbirds' vision is even sharper. Imagine the acuity needed to zip around at the speed those little birds do, to spot nectar flowers on the wing, and to avoid hazards such as branches and spider webs. This explains why only one hummingbird has been caught in the nets since Sheri and her volunteers and staff set up around 4 P.M.

We watch bird after bird zip up to the netting at full speed, stop a few inches away, stare for a moment, zipping this way and that as only hummingbirds can, then zoom away chittering, as if to say, "Well, I'm not that stupid!"

Two temptingly full nectar feeders hang on a metal pole. Four other poles are arranged around the feeder pole at the four corners of a square. Three four-tiered nets made of extra-fine-gauge black netting, called mist netting, are stretched between the poles to form a U around the feeders, leaving one end open for flights into the feeders and, hopefully, the nets. More netting is stretched across the top. When (or in this case, if) a hummingbird flies to the feeders inside the net "cage," one or more volunteers rush toward the feeder, waving their arms. The hummer turns to flee and flies into one of the net tiers, which are baggy and have "pockets" into which the hapless hummer drops. A volunteer carefully extracts the bird from the net, places it in a small net bag, and carries it over to Sheri's processing table, where its wings, tail, bill, and body fat are measured, its feather condition evaluated, and its body weighed. Before release each bird is held up to a feeder full of sugar water; nearly all will sit in their tormentors' hands and gratefully lap up the nectar before smoothing out their ruffled feathers and buzzing off.

Recaptures are not common, although one female black-chinned, which is the only hummingbird species that breeds along the San Pedro River, has been recaptured ten times in three years. This type of recapture provides the researchers with more insight into the life of one hummingbird: where she returns to breed every year, how many broods she nurtures, and when she leaves.

One of the visitors asks Sheri "how the hummingbirds know when to migrate." She says that scientists have learned that changing photoperiods trigger migration for hummingbirds and that their movements may be predictable to within three to four days every year.

Sheri explains that by early May the spring migration of hummingbirds is mostly complete. "Fall is bigger [in terms of numbers of hummingbirds] than spring. This is because April and May are historically dry and hot in the Southwest. Many species head north via the California coast and Sierras, where sea fog contributes to higher humidity. Migrating hummingbirds need flowers and small insects, things that are not abundant in southern Arizona until summer rains come." Flowers, especially ornithophilous blooms—those whose shape and color evolved to attract birds—begin in late June and early July, just in time for the first of the returning rufous hummingbirds. Mid-August is the peak period for diversity of hummingbirds along the San Pedro.

By six o'clock the SABO crew decides to pack up for the day, with only one hummingbird captured and banded. The tourists who have stuck around bid goodbye and drive off in search of dinner in Sierra Vista. The rest of us have the same idea.

"I think it's a pizza kind of night," someone says, and the group climbs into a van and a sedan and drives off.

As I point my truck west on Highway 90, a black-and-white flash crosses the road a few hundred feet ahead of me, then pulls up nearly straight to miss the barbed wire fence on the other side of the road. In a few seconds it is a dot in the sky soaring down the sloping river terrace toward the trees. I can't be sure, but it might have been a white-tailed kite—in the lexicon of birdwatchers, a really *good* bird.

≈ EXPLORATION GUIDE ≈

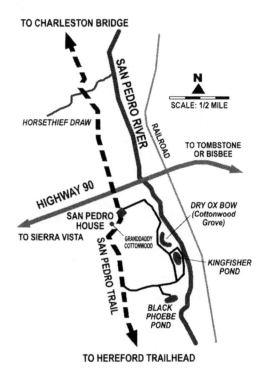

Hereford to Highway 90, including San Pedro House, San Pedro Trail
and River Access Map

HIGHLIGHTS

The San Pedro House trail system is excellent and offers a variety of habitats, from sacaton and mesquite grassland to old agricultural fields, as well as a good number of riverside and pond trails under a gorgeous full riparian canopy of cottonwoods and willows. The view of the river from both the road, where Highway 90 reaches the edge of the last river terrace, and San Pedro House is perhaps the best in the valley. The dramatic effect of the miles of tall green trees (in summer) is enhanced by the mile-or-more-wide flat floodplain. The old cottonwood next to the San Pedro House is one of Arizona's largest cottonwoods. This section provides birders with reliable sightings of the "target" species of the San Pedro: green king-fisher and gray hawk. Backpacking in this section is highly recommended.

MILEAGE

17 miles to the Hereford bridge parking lot from the intersection of Highways 90 and 92; 7 miles to the San Pedro House bookstore from the intersection of Highways 90 and 92.

DIRECTIONS

To get to the Hereford bridge parking lot from the intersection of Highways 90 and 92, head south on Highway 92 to Hereford Road (about 8.5 miles) and turn left (east). Follow Hereford Road 9 miles to the river. The Hereford bridge parking lot is just after the one-lane bridge on the right (approach the bridge slowly, and yield to any cars already entering from the other side). There is a portable toilet at the parking lot, but no drinking water.

To get to the San Pedro House, head east on Highway 90 for 7 miles; soon after the road drops down to the main floodplain, slow down and watch for the Bureau of Land Management sign and turn-off to the parking lot and bookstore on the right. There is a large graveled parking lot at the San Pedro House bookshop, with restrooms, picnic ramadas, interpretive displays, and free information. A site host lives here in an RV most of the year. There is no public parking on the north side of Highway 90, although cars do park there illegally.

ACCESS

For information on the Hereford bridge parking lot access, see chapter 2 "Exploration Guide."

The Highway 90 area is the most visitor-friendly access point along the river. The San Pedro House is run by the Friends of the San Pedro River and is open daily except Thanksgiving and Christmas, from about 9:30 A.M. to 4:30 P.M. (the center is run by all-volunteer staff; occasionally it may be closed during posted hours, but the bathrooms and the front porch, where maps and a bird register are kept, are always open). The gate at the entrance road is locked between sunset and sunrise. The bookstore and gift shop are excellent, and the volunteers are knowledgeable about the birds and natural history of the river. Pick up a free map of the San Pedro House trail system to avoid confusion in the baffling web of official and "social" paths. Beware if it has been raining: the trails turn to gooey muck.

HIKING AND BACKPACKING

There are about 5 miles of interconnected trails heading south and east of the San Pedro House across the abandoned agricultural fields and along the river. There are two ponds—Kingfisher and Black Phoebe, both popular for fishing on weekends—within the web of trails; about a mile and a half of trail is riverside. There are several benches along the trails leading to Kingfisher Pond. There is about a mile and a half of riverside trail north of Highway 90. The river is narrower and entrenched in this section, but the grassland to the west of the river is beautiful. The riverside trail ends at a linear pool. In 1998 a fire burned this section of the grassland and riparian area; the grassland and understory are thriving, but some of the cottonwoods and willows died.

The trail leading directly south from the San Pedro House, at the western edge of the floodplain, is the Old San Rafael del Valle Road bed, dating to the Spanish land grant of the same name in the 1830s. Now part of the San Pedro Trail, it heads south for 8 miles, to Hereford Road. For information on linking up with the Hereford Road–Palominas section of the San Pedro Trail, see chapter 2 "Exploration Guide"; for information on the Highway 90–Charleston section of the San Pedro Trail, see chapter 4 "Exploration Guide."

The Hereford Road–Highway 90 section is one of the nicest for through-hiking and backpacking; the cottonwood-willow gallery is in its prime, there is a lot of native grassland on either side of the river, and the stretch is isolated from roads and private property. An overnight permit is required, and there is one Research Natural Area, which is closed to overnight camping, about 2 miles north from Hereford Road. The San Pedro House, with its site host, is a safe place to leave cars overnight. Be prepared to get wet during spring and fall (it's not recommended to hike the riverbed during summer rains because of flash floods), so wear hiking sandals, river shoes, old running shoes, or waterproof hiking boots and gaiters. The going can be rough through the thickets of seep willow and rabbitbrush; it's easier go with the flow north; if you try to hike south, you will run up against old flood debris that points north like the pikes at castle fortifications. To avoid problems with private property trespass, remain in the current river channel, below the high water mark. For information on parking at Hereford Road, see chapter 2 "Exploration Guide."

BIRDING

The river habitat both north and south of Highway 90 is the largest and most diverse riparian zone in the RNCA. Some of the most spectacular bird sightings in the RNCA have occurred in the stretch of river from 1 mile north of the bridge to about a mile and a half south. These gems include black-bellied whistling duck, white-tailed and Mississippi kite, black hawk, gray hawk (nesting), broad-winged hawk, purple gallinule, ruddy ground-dove, groove-billed ani, chimney swift, green kingfisher (nesting), tropical kingbird (nesting), gray catbird, white-eyed vireo, yellow-throated vireo, 31 species of wood warblers, four species of tanagers, painted bunting, and Lawrence's goldfinch. A large percentage of Arizona's approximate 200 nesting pair of threatened (in Arizona) yellow-billed cuckoos breeds within the area from the Charleston bridge south to the Hereford bridge.

The Highway 90–Hereford bridge stretch of the river is also the only reliable area for nesting green kingfishers in Arizona. The Bureau of Land Management asks that birders not disturb this rare, shy bird during nesting season (March through October). If you chance upon a nest hole (they dig holes in banks), leave immediately. Occasionally an area will be closed if too many birders are harassing a nesting pair.

In winter gray, Hammond's, and dusky flycatchers are common in the riparian forest east of the San Pedro River in this section. During the late summer monsoon season, look for Botteri's and Cassin's sparrows breeding in the mesquite grassland immediately north of the San Pedro House, along the entrance road, as well as on the north side of Highway 90. The latter area is the best spot to find typical Chihuahuan Desert and grassland species.

Kingfisher Pond, about a half mile south of the San Pedro House on the west side of the river, is well named: in summer green kingfishers feed there. Other summer residents include the "usual" Arizona riparian species, such as green heron, mallard (sometimes Mexican duck), common moorhen, white-winged dove, yellow-billed cuckoo, black-chinned hummingbird, Gila and ladder-backed woodpeckers, northern and gilded flickers, western wood-pewee, vermilion flycatcher, brown-crested flycatcher, Cassin's and tropical kingbirds, crissal thrasher (which is easier to locate during early spring, when singing), Bell's vireo, Lucy's and yellow warblers, yellow-breasted chat, summer tanager, and northern oriole. In winter, look for great blue heron, common yellowthroat, occasional green kingfisher, song sparrow, and Lincoln's sparrow, and be sure to check the cattails at the south end for sora and Virginia rail.

Intrepid birders should consider hiking from the Hereford bridge along the river to the San Pedro House, about 8 miles as the gray hawk flies but more like 12 miles along the river. A car shuttle is recommended. See the "Hiking and Backpacking" remarks for more details.

MOUNTAIN BIKING

The San Pedro Trail's San Rafael del Valle section, which runs from the San Pedro House to Hereford Road, is a prime mountain bike trip. The old land grant road is 8.5 miles long and runs along the western edge of the first river terrace, in desert and grassland. The views are lovely and the ride is fast. Plan a car shuttle (use Moson Road, which parallels the river on the west side) or an out-and-back ride. You can also bike south from the San Pedro House on the del Valle Road about three-quarters of a mile, then turn toward the river on a road that parallels Garden Wash. At Black Phoebe Pond, turn north and head back to the San Pedro House along the river trail. (Bikes are not allowed on the paths immediately next to the river.)

HORSEBACK RIDING

The San Pedro House system of trails (see "Mountain Biking" section, above) offers excellent day trips for horseback riding. There are good parking and picnicking facilities at the San Pedro House; horses should be kept out of the visitor area. Horse access to the San Pedro Trail begins on the west side of the San Pedro House parking lot. With a truck-and-trailer shuttle, the San Rafael del Valle Road–San Pedro Trail ride would be a good day trip or, with side trips to the river, an overnight (permits are required for all overnight camping). Riverside trails are not open to horses.

ARCHAEOLOGICAL SITES

There are no archaeological sites with public access along this stretch of the river.

HANDICAPPED ACCESS

Many of the trails from the San Pedro House to the river area are flat, hard-packed dirt and navigable by wheelchairs and those people with limited mobility; however, trails that lead down to the river itself are not, so stick to the trails that parallel the river, such as the one to Kingfisher Pond. None of the trails are accessible if it has been raining. The San Pedro House now has a wheelchair ramp at the rear of the building. None of the trails on the north side of Highway 90 are accessible.

CAMPING

There are no car-camping facilities near the San Pedro House. The nearest commercial camping is at RV parks in Sierra Vista. For information, contact the Sierra Vista Chamber of Commerce at 800-946-4777. All overnight camping in the RNCA is by pack-in only, and permits are required.

ACCOMMODATIONS

Sierra Vista has many hotels and restaurants; contact the Sierra Vista Chamber of Commerce (800-946-4777). Bisbee, only 20 miles from the San Pedro House, has charming accommodations, from the historic Copper Queen Hotel to several bed and breakfasts. Contact the Bisbee Chamber of Commerce at 520-432-5421 for information.

OTHER ATTRACTIONS NEARBY

Bisbee is a historic mining town with well-preserved Victorian buildings along narrow, steep streets reminiscent of San Francisco on a tiny scale. A stop here helps give one perspective on the massive mining operations that changed the face of this part of the west, including the San Pedro River, in the late 1800s and early 1900s. It's also a great art town. Contact the Bisbee Chamber of Commerce at the number above.

CHAPTER 4

HIGHWAY 90 TO CHARLESTON

*Bird's-eye River View • A River of Birds • The River Pays
Its Keep • Swimming Snakes and Amazon Lizards
• How Fire Makes a River*

Dawn HAD BEGUN to stain the eastern sky a faint salmon, and
clouds squatted on the horizon all around. At the Genesis Aviation
hangar near Tucson International's Executive Terminal, Sandy Lanham
of Environmental Flying Service was giving her plane a preflight walk-
around—oil, flaps, controls, lights, tires. The air reeked of jet fuel and
vibrated with the whine of engines. Every few minutes we had to stop
talking while a roaring plane hurtled down a nearby runway.

Sandy's white-and-pumpkin Cessna is the oldest 182 still flying. In it
she's flown biologists, conservationists, politicians, and journalists over
the most remote wildernesses of the American Southwest and Mexico,
racking up thousands of hours under difficult conditions. Sandy is small
boned but strong looking, tanned and fit, with sparkling eyes and a voice
graveled from cigarettes, which she said she's trying to quit again. This
job was an easy one: fly photographer Jack Dykinga and me up the San
Pedro River so Jack could photograph the fall colors and I could get a
feel for the river's landscape two weeks prior to our November backpacking trip.

Working with the quiet competence that comes only from years of
experience, Sandy finished her flight check, then loaded us into the plane.
I climbed into the tiny back seat—just wide enough for me and a bag. It
took me a few minutes to adjust the seat belt and headset. Then Jack
jackknifed into the front passenger seat, literally; he's well over 6 feet tall,
and the plane is narrower inside than a compact car, with less foot room.

Sandy opened the window and locked it out of the way for photos. With Jack finally settled in, Sandy locked the door from the outside, then climbed into her seat and got herself strapped in. She checked in with the tower and taxied out to the runway; without more than a 60-second wait, we were cleared for take-off and zipping down the runway. Lift-off was quick, and soon we were heading straight east, just north of I-10, which we paralleled. The noise of the engine and wind hurtling through the open window was deafening, and the high-altitude fall air was cold. I snuggled into my down jacket, glad for the warmth.

Each time I fly out of Tucson, I am struck by how regularly the plants are spaced in the desert, as if each were marking an intersection on graph paper. In between the plants the rocky dirt is not brown but limestone white. The shrubs must be creosote or shrub-form palo verde; they don't look like mesquites to me, but it's hard to tell from several thousand feet up.

Soon we were flying over the Rincon Valley, then Mescal Road, and I could see the old movie set. Then there was grassland, where there weren't horrendous housing developments—those gruesome scraped lots, regular as a chess board, set with tattered trailers and prefabs as pawns and bishops. Some of the lots have no vegetation at all, only bladed dirt. Others are veritable horseman's paradises: arenas, barns fancier than the house, long drives planted with Italian cypresses. In places there are scores of ATV tracks scarring the land: donuts, straightaways, and curlicues. Over Benson we turned south over the short Chihuahuan mesquite-scrub desert that has invaded the grasslands here in the last century. We passed the nitrate plant on Apache Powder Road, where lots of arroyo incising is going on. From our altitude the incisions looked like tendrils of frost on glass. Far to the south I could see the emissions from Mexico's Cananea smelters—an oily brown stream that flowed up, then hit an atmospheric thermocline and spread out horizontally for miles and miles, an ugly brown puddle.

The light was playing hide and seek with us under the cloud cover, but it was lovely—thick and golden. We turned to gain the river and began to head directly along its course, a vibrant green path of tall trees snaking across the brown, short-shrub desert. Here and there, from the St. David ciénega south, some of the cottonwoods looked drought stressed, with leaves of brown rather than fall-kissed gold. There was no water in the riverbed. A few miles north of Fairbank, water appeared in the river, at first intermittently, then regularly. It shone like broken mirrors in the early light. Then we began to see lovely fall colors. The sun kept playing games—in and out—and Sandy had to chase it to keep Jack happy with the light as he hung half out the window with his medium-format camera. The result was a very green rear passenger, especially when we had to bank and drop altitude rapidly to dip the wing and wheel strut out of Jack's photo. Urk.

But I managed to enjoy seeing the wide and lazy meanders in the river, especially beautiful to me because I understood they represent the health of an undammed river. I recognized Fairbank and the Babocomari River coming in from the west and looked forward to seeing them on our upcoming backpacking trip. The mesquite bosque, or forest, near the Babocomari looked big. Then I saw Charleston Road. Then Highway 90. I was getting greener by the mile, but I recognized Granddaddy Cotton-wood next to the San Pedro House; it looked much smaller from my bird's-eye view. South of the San Pedro House it was obvious where the old agricultural fields lay: large squares with old canals marking their boundaries. They still looked sterile. Beyond the fields, stretching to the border, in the spicebush and creosote desert uplands that run from the river to the foothills of the Huachuca Mountains, we could see a shocking patchwork of housing, 10-, 20-, and 40-acre "ranchettes" cutting up the land. Hundreds of houses, each with its own well, their plots fenced off, often cleared of vegetation. I lost track of all the roads. I hadn't realized just how fragmented and damaged the open space had become between the river and the mountains.

Heading back north of Highway 90, we passed Escapule Estates, the inholding of private lots in the conservation area. Many of the houses sit surprisingly close to the river. The river had recently run quite high, flattening strand and bankside vegetation.

Mercifully, Jack proclaimed he had shot his last roll, Sandy pointed the nose of the sturdy little Cessna west, and we began zipping over the desert again. After the lush, wet, green river corridor, the desertscape looked markedly dry and harsh.

IT IS WELL after six o'clock by the time Jack and I make camp for the second night of our 40-mile backpacking trek down the San Pedro River. It took longer than we'd thought to get past the San Pedro House complex of trails, and once we crossed Highway 90 and started down the river past the bridge, it took more miles than we had hoped before we were free from the sound of cars on the busy road that connects Bisbee to Sierra Vista and Fort Huachuca.

We spread our sleeping bags at the end of a long, straight section of river that is lined by uniformly sized young cottonwoods. The effect reminds me of the long reflecting pools fronting the Taj Mahal. After stuffing ourselves with a dinner of chicken with cranberries and walnuts, we settle into our bags to read and write.

Just as a crescent moon presents itself over the reflecting pool, a large shadow passes a few yards over my head, silently, straight up the river over the horns of the moon. Twenty minutes later, just as I've convinced myself I had imagined a phantom overflight, the shadow returns, croaking the rusty call of a great blue heron as it passes overhead again, gliding on its 3-foot wings downriver.

The heron is not the only bird flying this night. As I lie next to the river, its waters flowing beside me and below me, above me flows an unseen river of birds. It is fall, the time of migration for millions of songbirds and waterfowl.

Riparian corridors like the San Pedro are vital to this great event. The reason has to do with geographic location, food, and shelter. Let's say you had to jog as quickly as possible from San Francisco to Washington, D.C. Would you head cross-country via roadless wilderness, having to carry all your own food and water, or would you stick to the interstate highways, which are lined with fast-food joints and safe overnight rest stops? Easy choice. So if you were a 1/3-ounce warbler flying from Central America north to Montana for the summer, and you had enough fat reserves laid on to last you to northern Mexico, what route would you choose? Over a harsh desert? Or along a lush green river corridor running conveniently north-south as you hit the border area, providing a life link from desert lowlands to the beginnings of the Rocky Mountains? I am reminded of my own flight down the river and the harshness of the desert in contrast to the green lushness of the San Pedro.

There are four major north-south "flyways" in North America: the

Pacific, Central, Mississippi, and Atlantic. Birds have been using these flyways for millions of generations. The San Pedro River is a critical link in the Central Flyway, providing a food- and shelter-rich bridge between the Rocky Mountains, which birds follow as they hit the north-central United States, and northern Mexico's Sierra Madre, which they follow down into Central and South America.

Bird migration evolved as an alternative to overwintering, a brutal

prospect for small creatures in some parts of the Northern Hemisphere. Some birds, such as jays and woodpeckers, took to hoarding food to last them the winter, but most insect-eating birds, including warblers, flycatchers, orioles, and many shorebirds and waterfowl, travel vast distances to maximize their chances of surviving winter and successfully reproducing.

A yellow-breasted chat "chatted" at me for about twenty minutes one morning, although I only saw him once as he darted around the thick riparian understory.

Although a mild winter with abundant food awaits in southern climes, the journey itself is only marginally less difficult than overwintering. Many birds die from the stress of the journey; some birds lose as much as half their body weight during migration or are eaten by predators. Defense measures for many birds include flying nearly nonstop throughout the night and stopping to rest and feed during the day, which is why riparian areas in the Southwest, many of which run north-south along flyway routes, are critical to migratory bird survival.

The migration spectacles don't go unnoticed. Hordes of humans—a peculiar breed called birdwatchers—flock to migratory "hot spots" throughout the country to catch glimpses of dozens of different warblers or hummingbirds, orioles and other songbirds, or waterfowl. According to the American Birding Association, 50 million Americans consider themselves birdwatchers; of ABA members responding to a poll, 85 percent travel outside their state to see birds. Southern Arizona's riparian corridors rate number one among the twelve top birding destinations in North America. The San Pedro was recently named by the American Bird

Conservancy as North America's first "Globally Important Bird Area."

Serious birders spend a great deal of money on their sport. A serious birder, which I define arbitrarily as one who competitively keeps track of, or "lists," number of species seen, may spend $1,000 on binoculars, another grand and a half on a spotting scope, several hundred on special outdoor clothing such as pocketed vest and brushed nylon sun shirt, and thousands on air travel, hotels, car rentals, and food while searching for target species. A serious birder goes to great ends to get a bird, even hiring hotshot guides and using electronics to call in birds. It's not at all unlike sport hunting, and although every birder you meet will deny that birding "takes" any bird life, the sport is not without sometimes significant impact. My husband and I spent nearly three years as naturalists and caretakers at a popular birding destination; we taught birding and natural history courses for our local Audubon Society for a year; and we managed a property that specializes in catering to birders in summer; so we're intimate with all types of birding activities and birders. I once watched, speechless with surprise, as a birding guide beat bushes for his clients so any shy species would be flushed into the open, regardless of the presence of predators. When an extremely rare species of gnatcatcher was reported nesting in a canyon south of Tucson, birders both local and from across the country descended en masse to the nuptial site; more than a hundred people a day crowded too close to the site, and the pair abandoned the nest. Many rare species in southern Arizona have become rarer because of this type of overbirding; the five-striped sparrow is an excellent example. Common birder practices such as mimicking owls or the alarm call of woodland birds ("pishing") flush birds off nests, exposing them to direct predation or leaving an opening for a cowbird to lay its egg in the unguarded nest. And if you add up the impact of millions—many, many millions—of people out pounding trails and disturbing habitat, the impact is not small.

Nevertheless, birding does much more good than harm for birds, their habitats, and the communities near birding hot spots. Most of the publicity about the San Pedro River, especially the conservation area, focuses on the value of the river as an ecotourism destination. One rarely reads about the San Pedro without a reference to the millions of tourism dollars it and other birdwatching hot spots pump into the coffers of Cochise County's hospitality and related industries.

Ten years ago neither *ecotourism* nor *riparian* was a common word in the vocabulary of most Americans. Today, because of the type of publicity generated by hot spots like the San Pedro, these words are now used commonly. The danger with such a strong focus on ecotourism and birds is that the value of a river like the San Pedro will become unidimensional. I would like to think that the San Pedro can be considered as more than just a pretty place to watch birds or a cash cow for its nearby communities.

The San Pedro River ecosystem is essentially a huge engine creating enormous amounts of usable energy for animals—mammals, birds, insects—as well as humans. At some point in high school science, most of us probably learned about the water cycle and plants' role therein. Plants lose moisture through their leaves in a process called transpiration, and they also release water vapor after breaking down carbohydrates to produce stored energy. Without plants pumping water up into the atmosphere, our water cycle would lose a link and falter. But plants are also important to humans and other animals in two other ways: they provide us with oxygen for breathing, and they provide the basis for our food chain. In order to process carbohydrates to make stored energy, plants must first manufacture them. They do this via the metabolic pathway called photosynthesis, which gets its energy from sunlight (the other by-product of photosynthesis is oxygen). Chlorophyll, the green pigment of plants, is the only known natural substance that can convert light energy into stable chemical energy. That stored carbohydrate energy, of course, is starch, which we eat either directly (plants themselves) or indirectly (animals that eat plants).

The food chains in healthy desert riparian ecosystems and their watersheds may produce as much as one hundred times more living matter—bacteria, plants, insects, vertebrates—than nearby desert areas. Some people think trees are water gluttons, especially in the desert Southwest, because of all the respiring and transpiring they do. These people think that if they remove trees and shrubs along river courses and in the watershed, the water level in the river will increase. At more than one public comment meeting on saving the San Pedro from a lowering water table, I heard someone, in all seriousness, suggest that removing the cottonwoods and willows would increase runoff and therefore increase the flow in the river. But such runoff is virtually unusable locally. Increased volume increases speed of flow, so the water simply keeps running off—out of the area—instead of seeping into the local aquifer or being taken up by plants to be transpired or respired into the local atmosphere where it can be recycled as rain. Decreased local groundwater eventually creates a more desertlike climate, killing off more plants and further decreasing rainfall and thus locally available water. For the people of the San Pedro River valley, the river is more than just a source of increased ecotourism cash in their checking accounts. It's an oxygen- and water-producing engine.

THE NEXT MORNING, our second on the San Pedro, I wake up with a sore throat and body aches. I wonder if I have caught a cold or if I just slept with my mouth open in the cold and damp river air and my 105-pound body is merely whining about hauling a 35-pound pack while trying to keep pace with a 6-foot-plus companion. My shoes are frozen bricks, and I have to thaw them over the camp stove before I can cram into them. My toes, preferring warm summer mornings over those of crisp fall, register their unhappiness with excruciating throbbing. This is not fun, I think. Three cups of tea, two ibuprofen, and a mile and a half later I am feeling better. I can even smile convincingly for the camera when Jack makes me cross the freezing river six times while he gets just the right shot.

This section of the river, from Highway 90 to the Charleston bridge, passes through the private property inholding I saw when we flew over the river a few weeks ago, Escapule Estates, which we are fast approaching. It is the least "wild" of the San Pedro sections we hike, with hardly a stretch of any length free of detritus from mining, agriculture, and cattle ranching; we see household garbage, horse manure, and motorcycle tracks, and soon we hear the noise of car traffic, chain saws, and barking dogs.

Our ingress to the private property is announced in no uncertain terms by multiple KEEP OUT signs and enough unleashed, snarling dogs that we move at a fast pace until we reach Sandy and Al Anderson's Gray Hawk Ranch, where we stashed extra food and film a few days ago. We relax in their yard, wolfing snacks, wishing glumly we had included beer in the stash, and chatting with Al and with John Porter, who lives at Gray Hawk as a caretaker.

Sandy and Al bought Gray Hawk Ranch, a former farm, in 1984. They moved from California onto the old homestead with the intent to resume farming using water pumped from the river. They soon learned of the river's tenuous nature and now work as advocates for its preservation. Sandy is a naturalist and tour guide, and Al works in construction and volunteers for the Huachuca Audubon Society.

I ask John, a full-time amateur herpetologist, about the reptiles and amphibians of the San Pedro, specifically whether he's ever seen any leopard frogs. A year before, in August, I spent a couple days exploring the river and ponds around the San Pedro House with friends from the Tucson Herpetological Society. We had hoped to find lowland leopard frogs, which were thought to be extirpated from the river but had recently been reported at Lewis Springs, a couple miles north of Highway 90. Bullfrogs and introduced sport fish decimate native frog populations. John says he has not seen any leopard frogs. His true love is the rattlesnakes; he has spent decades in the West studying their life histories. He tells us he is currently observing two western diamondback denning sites in the cliffs near the river.

Of the seventeen species of snakes found among the habitats of the San Pedro River, two are rattlesnakes: the western diamondback rattlesnake (*Crotalus atrox*), which is the largest rattlesnake in the West (second largest in the United States, after the eastern diamondback), and the Mojave rattlesnake (*C. scutulatus*). Rattlesnakes are well known because of their venomous bite and the namesake tails they use to warn off threats. Although they are widely feared by humans, rattlesnakes are not aggressive without provocation. Their venom evolved as a food-procuring tool, not as a defensive or offensive weapon, probably on grassland savannas much like those of the San Pedro Valley during the late Pleistocene. The hoofed feet of all the large browsers and grazers were hazardous for ground-dwelling, soft-bodied serpents. Somewhere along the evolutionary line, snakes whose tails could make a warning buzz lived longer than those whose tails could not. The bison and horses learned that the buzz was a strong "Leave me alone!" message that would be followed by a painful bite.

Rattlesnakes hunt when the temperature warms up to 70° F or so but retreat to cooler shade during the hottest part of the day. Rattlesnakes are members of the pit viper family, so called because they have a pair of pits between their eyes and nostrils. The pits are heat receptors that allow the snake to strike accurately at warm-bodied prey—even in complete darkness. Mice and kangaroo rats, two dietary staples of rattlesnakes, often succumb to the venom within minutes. The snake then tracks down the carcass by scent.

Different snakes specialize in different prey types and habitat types. Rattlesnakes are terrestrial specialists and stick mostly to rodents and bunnies. Most snakes are entirely opportunistic and will take what they can, including eggs. Aquatic garter snakes hunt tadpoles and adult amphibians, and riparian specialists such as whipsnakes take to the understories to ambush birds, as well as rodents and amphibians.

The checkered garter snake (*Thamnophis marcianus*) is the most common garter snake along the San Pedro; its relative the Mexican garter snake (*T. eques*) is at the northernmost portion of its range in the RNCA and is much more rare. The Sonoran whipsnake (*Masticophis bilineatus*) is long and very thin, its pale green and yellow body with thin green and blackish stripes providing excellent camouflage in the willows and hackberries where it waits for a bird or rodent to come within its strike zone. With lightning speed it snatches its prey and swallows it up. Once while watching a young black-headed grosbeak in a seep willow shrub, I was startled when a pale branch leaped to life and seized the bird by the head. The bird thrashed and spun, but the whipsnake held strong, its forebody swinging with the bird while its afterend clung to the branch. I took a step forward for a closer look, and the snake disappeared, bird and all, into the thicket below.

In all the time I've spent on the San Pedro, I have seen only a half-dozen snakes, including one huge, beautiful western diamondback that was killed by a couple of ignorant fishermen by Kingfisher Pond. Lizards are far more conspicuous than snakes along the San Pedro; they are easy to spot darting across trails, scrambling up tree trunks, sunning on rocks. Their small bodies (compared to those of snakes or turtles) heat up quickly, so they are often active on cool days when their larger relatives stay in their burrows.

The habitats of the San Pedro are home to sixteen lizard species. Whiptail lizards are abundant, especially in the strands and floodplains adjacent to the river. They hunt for insects in loose dirt and sand and in leaf litter; their style is unmistakable, a jerky start-and-stop movement as they listen for prey and then dart forward to dig furiously in the dirt. After the first of the summer rains brings out swarms of new ant and termite colonies, whiptails can be seen by the dozens darting around trails and roads, snapping up the mating arthropods.

The desert grassland whiptail (*Cnemidophorus uniparens*) is probably the most common of the four "cnemis" (pronounced NEH-mees) in the area. Eight of the thirteen whiptail species in the Southwest are parthenogenic, which means the females can reproduce without male sperm—they simply clone themselves. It is thought that this strategy allows the all-female whiptails to quickly reproduce and fill new, whiptail-suitable niches created when the habitat changes, such as after a long drought or severe overgrazing. Along the San Pedro the desert grassland and Sonoran whiptails (*C. sonorae*) are all-female species; Arizona desert whiptails (*C. tigris gracilis*) and giant spotted whiptails (*C. burti stictogrammus*) comprise males and females.

Spiny lizards are the kings of the lizard world. They are large—up to about a foot long—and are aggressive predators and defenders of territory. Spinies eat other lizards, including rivals, but round out their diet with flowers, buds, and seeds. Clark's spiny lizard (*Sceloporus clarkii*) lives along the San Pedro and can be found most often on tree trunks, where they declare their territory by pumping their bodies up and down push-up style.

The San Pedro RNCA is also home to Texas (*Phrynosoma cornutum*) and regal (*P. solare*) horned lizards and a few Gila monsters (*Heloderma suspectum*). The 2- to 3-inch horned lizards feed on ants and small arthropods—in summer they use ant holes as food dispensers, lapping up the bite-sized insects as the emerge from their colony. The Gila monster is the only venomous lizard in the United States; the related beaded lizard, in Mexico, is also venomous. Gila monsters are not aggressive and bite only when handled. They are large—up to 20 inches long or so—but they are slow, lumbering lizards that specialize in prey that can't run away: eggs, baby mammals, and nestlings. Gila monsters are most active later in the summer, usually in the daytime, although you are unlikely to see them because their black-and-orange pattern hides them well in the sun-dappled shade where they often hunt for nests and burrows.

On our quest for leopard frogs, my Tucson Herp Society friends Chris Wolner and Dennis Caldwell saw two Texas spiny softshells (*Trionyx spiniferus*), one of three turtle species along the RNCA. Texas spiny softshells are called spiny because the front of the carapace is sometimes dotted with spinelike tubercles. They are not native to Arizona and need permanent water, preferring shallow, quiet rivers with sandy or muddy bottoms. Their shells are soft, leatherlike, and oddly flattened. Spiny softshells eat snails, crayfish, insects, fish, frogs, tadpoles, and sometimes aquatic vegetation.

The western box turtle (*Terrapene ornata ornata*), sometimes called the ornate box turtle for its lovely yellow, brown, and black carapace, is a land turtle that prefers grasslands and areas of soft soil, such as the older river terraces along the San Pedro. They emerge in spring from winter burrows, which are sometimes co-opted and modified kangaroo rat mounds, and get busy finding each other to mate. Box turtles eat beetles and other insects, as well as berries, new plant shoots, leaves, and carrion.

The aquatic Sonoran mud turtles (*Kinosternon sonoriense*) are superbly adapted native Southwesterners. Small and mud colored, they can live in both high- and low-temperature water, and when water holes begin to dry up in late spring, they can survive in surprisingly small, turbid ones. Their coloring provides good camouflage, but you can spot them if you look carefully in calm pools, where they bask with their shells barely peeking above water. Mud turtles slowly search the bottom of ponds or streams for snails, insects and their larvae, small fish, and tadpoles.

Chris, Dennis, and I never did find leopard frogs. The only known frog, and by far the most abundant amphibian, currently living along the San Pedro is the introduced bullfrog (*Rana catesbeiana*), a voracious predator that eats whatever it can get its large mouth around. Leopard frogs (*R. yavapaiensis* and others) were once more common in the Southwest, but habitat alterations and introduced species of fish, crayfish, and bullfrogs have sent most populations spiraling toward threatened or endangered status. Introduced catfish and bass—both present in the San Pedro system—eat up frog tadpoles, and crayfish alter pond ecology by eating just about everything, from plants to tadpoles. Long ago the repeated flash flooding and drying out of most southwestern streams provided a harsh enough habitat that most introduced species could not survive. But damming and other controls, as well as the development of permanent water, allow non-natives to thrive and outcompete the natives. Along the San Pedro, where numerous permanent ponds allow non-natives to dominate, toads exist in smaller numbers than expected, but native frogs have disappeared.

Jack and I reluctantly break off our chat about San Pedro reptiles with Al and John. We top off our water bottles, shoulder our backpacks with groans, and turn downriver once again, our planned campsite for the night still many miles ahead.

IT IS THE last day of May in 1998, the summer after our backpacking trip, and it's a typical one: hot, hazy, dry. As I pull into the Murray Springs archaeological site parking lot off Moson Road, just over a mile north of Highway 90, road dust engulfs my truck and hangs in the still air. The entrance road sits atop the old railroad bed for an El Paso and Southwest Railroad line from Lewis Springs to Fort Huachuca, built around 1912. Low Sonoran-Chihuahuan desertscrub of creosote and blackbrush covers the mostly flat terrain, which just to the east begins to fall away to the broad river terrace several miles away.

A cactus wren scolds me as I shoulder my day pack and step through the stile in the fence. The trail parallels the fence to the south, then turns east at a little arroyo. Unlike at the Lehner archaeological site, there are well-made, hardened-surface trails here and sturdy wooden footbridges across the eroded arroyo. Murray Springs, dry on the surface now but with robust sacaton grass and big mesquite trees attesting to the presence of a high groundwater table, is one of the San Pedro RNCA's most important archaeological sites. From 1966 to 1971, with money from the National Geographic Society and the National Science Foundation, Vance Haynes and a team of University of Arizona archaeologists excavated this extraordinary 13,000-year-old Clovis Culture campsite, which yielded sixteen spear points, many extinct mammal bones, and a unique bone tool.

The tool is now on display at the Arizona State Museum in Tucson. It's an evocative object, about 10 inches long, with an inch-thick rounded handle and a flat head that is a 2¼-inch disc with a 1-inch hole bored through its center. The edge of the hole is beveled. The diameter of the hole matches the shaft diameter of spears used by Clovis hunters; it's possible that a hunter drew this repeatedly over a shaft to hew it to a uniform, smooth diameter, making a straighter, stronger, and truer spear shaft. Some archaeologists link this tool to similar ones used in Eurasia—a tantalizing suggestion of Clovis man's origins or trading habits.

Perhaps it is the midday heat, but my enthusiasm for being on-site at Murray Springs wanes quickly. Without anyone to interpret the site for me, as did archaeologist Jane Childress at the Lehner site, I can only stand in the miserly shade of a mesquite, guess where the camp was, where the bone tool was found, what the mammoths were like, and otherwise muse on man's life here ten millennia ago. (By early 2000 the BLM had installed interpretive signs at the site. Vance Haynes hopes to construct a re-creation of the dig and the fascinating life of Clovis man so that visitors can better appreciate this dusty, quiet place.)

Back at the truck I crank up the air conditioning and head over to the nearby San Pedro House to eat my lunch under Granddaddy Cottonwood. Despite the heat, a fair number of nature tourists—mostly birders—come and go from the bookstore and river trails, drawn by the migratory bird activity in May. Most of them are on the southern Arizona "circuit": Madera Canyon, Patagonia, Ramsey Canyon, San Pedro River, and Cave Creek Canyon. I hear several ask the volunteers if there are any "good" birds, and while I talk to an acquaintance, we have to pause while a hired birding guide loudly owl-calls and makes *pishing* noises a few feet away, trying to lure a warbler from the top of the cottonwood for his two power-birder clients.

The fascinating bone tool found at Murray Springs is on display at the Arizona State Museum in Tucson. I thought it was very enigmatic.

Half an hour later, sipping my second Coke, I think I see smoke by the entrance road, on Highway 90. I pass it off as dust from a departing car, then I realize there are heat waves. It *is* a fire. By the time I run to the San Pedro House just 50 feet away, I can see flames.

Using a cellular phone, one of the volunteers calls in the fire, and we watch from the steps as the wind whips up the flames and the fire really takes off. Moving northeast faster than a person could run, it jumps from clump to clump in the big field of sacaton grass from the San Pedro Trail to the river. In less than four minutes it has crossed over a mile of grassland and is leaping up into the hackberries and acacias of the river understory, lapping at the trunks of the cottonwoods and willows.

We can hear a siren approaching from Sierra Vista, and a lone, absurdly tiny tanker truck arrives. The two firefighters get out and stare for a moment, then one runs back to the truck and grabs the radio, presumably to call for backup. By this time the fire has jumped the river and is rapidly spreading through the riparian area. By the time this cigarette-caused fire burns out three days later, it will have burned more than 750 acres of the RNCA, including several miles of one of the finest cottonwood-willow galleries along the river, from Highway 90 to Lewis Spring. A slurry plane will be necessary to help put out the blaze as it bears down on Escapule Estates. Dot Rhodes of the Friends of the San Pedro River tells me later that six weeks after the fire, volunteers working at a bird-banding station in the burn area found the still-smoldering root ball of a burned-out cottonwood.

I leave after watching for about half an hour, on my way to Palominas. As I drive slowly toward the bridge, a tongue of fire is still burning in the sacaton grass along the road. The heat is so intense I can feel it through the door of my truck, scorching hot; I even pull off the road to see if the paint is blistered. I can see that the broad field of sacaton on the northwest side of the river is reduced to smoldering black humps, like hundreds of burned pineapples.

In some riparian systems, such as in the Mojave Desert, fire has probably never been a very common event. But fires, both natural and human caused, most likely were once common in the upper San Pedro Valley. Native Americans used fire to hunt game during fall in the grasslands. Anthropologist-author Henry F. Dobyns recounts Spanish explorers' fascinating tales of Apache hunting parties that formed burning circles 15 miles in diameter to drive game to a preselected location, and fire-driven hunting most likely predated the Apaches in the Southwest by many thousands of years. The winter-season native grasses not only tolerate such fires but thrive because of them.

One of the West's most respected botanists, Raymond M. Turner, recently retired from the U.S. Geological Survey, believes that a combination of frequent grass-fed fires and marshy conditions along southwestern riparian areas prior to the turn of the century maintained a riverine habitat much different from the woody galleries we know, love, and are trying to protect and restore today. Turner, in an as yet unpublished revision of his famous book *The Changing Mile,* writes: "The encroachment of woody plants into riparian areas follows much the same timing as their encroachment into adjacent grasslands. Before the turn of the century, channels of the San Pedro River and other regional streams, such as Ciénega Creek, were largely free of trees and shrubs, covered instead by grasses, such as sacaton and tobosa."

Turner has found that the Santa Cruz River, which flowed from near Nogales north past Tucson, was marshy prior to a large flood in August 1890, and that early photos of the grasslands in the valley did not show old trees or stumps from woodcutting. He explains that the seasonally flooded plains adjacent to the rivers promoted lush grasslands but were too waterlogged for woody species to take hold. But with the severe period of down cutting and the subsequent drop in the water table at the end of the nineteenth century, woody species such as mesquite moved in. The newly opened mineral soil, a by-product of the down cutting, was ideal for colonization by cottonwoods and willows, and eventually the river channels continued to widen and support large gallery forests as we know them today. Turner writes that by the middle of this century, the banks of southeastern Arizona's rivers were "densely covered by forests of mesquites, willows, and cottonwoods and, in general, remain densely covered today. Yet, it is the opposite trend that has been emphasized. . . . The perception that the health and vigor of regional riparian habitats has declined is supported by wildly inaccurate reports." Turner goes on to describe how, as recently as 1994, writers were still passing on false stories of steamboats on the San Pedro and Gila Rivers.

Turner admits that dams, water diversion, and groundwater pumping have altered the hydrologic regimes of our rivers and caused severe losses of aquatic species. However, the new habitat has become a refuge for hundreds of bird and mammal species. Is fire, then, a danger today to those refugia, which were created by a combination of natural and human-caused events a century ago? Scientists David E. Busch and Stanley D. Smith, of the Bureau of Reclamation and the University of

Nevada, respectively, believe that fire increased dramatically in some riparian areas after the introduction of European tamarisk trees, which not only thrive after fires but may, because of their flammability and leaf litter characteristics, increase the frequency of fires in habitats not prone to frequent burning. Also, hot fires destroy soil nutrients, increase concentrations of minerals such as boron, and reduce the availability of moisture for native plants; tamarisk, apparently, can withstand these harsh conditions and regrow without the competition of the natives. So it's a losing battle for cottonwoods, willows, and mesquites in riparian areas where tamarisk has taken root. Only time will tell how the Highway 90 fire, caused by a cigarette tossed from a passing car, will affect this section of the San Pedro's riparian habitat.

Nearly four months later, in September, I return to the San Pedro House to visit the burn area. The BLM has closed the whole area from Highway 90 to Lewis Spring because of the danger of dead branches falling from the burned cottonwoods or whole trees toppling over, so I can walk only the fence and scan with my binoculars. There are at least a dozen large cottonwoods I can see from the road that appear fully dead; their blackened trunks and brown leaves look like scabs in the otherwise continuous green canopy. But the summer monsoon rains were good, and there is lush, bright green regrowth all over the riparian understory. Fortunately, tamarisk has not invaded in significant numbers in the upper San Pedro, although it has begun to take over north of the St. David cienega and dominates much of the lower San Pedro to its confluence. Postfire regrowth here is mostly native, except for a stand of Johnson grass on the east side of the river; the sacaton grassland west of the river looks like it not only was never burned but grew back more robust and healthier than ever and in full bloom. And most intriguingly, San Pedro biologist Dave Krueper reported that a study station located in the fire-burned habitat yielded the highest number of migratory birds ever recorded there, a tantalizing look at the potential for a return to natural fires in the riparian area.

Sacaton (*Sporobolus wrightii*) is an intriguing and increasingly rare component of riparian areas, most likely because of the decrease in fires and the encroachment of woody species. A member of the grass family (Poaceae), sacaton looks more like a large ornamental shrub than what we think of as classic prairie grass. It is a perennial, bunch-forming grass that thrives along terraces next to southwestern rivers, from west Texas to southern California and south to central Mexico, at middle elevations (2,000 to 5,500 feet). In the moist, sandy-soiled, alluvial floodplains, sacaton forms nearly monospecific, 3- to 6-foot-high grasslands, sometimes sharing space with mesquite, catclaw, and graythorn shrubs. Sacaton is summer adapted, flowering after the monsoons begin. By fall the tall seed heads are nodding on cool breezes, and sparrows and rodents feast on the seeds. Several southwestern grassland sparrow species, such as Botteri's, depend on such native grass stands for their winter food.

Sacaton grass has long been important to people as well, as food for themselves and for their prey, such as mammoths, and later for their livestock. The seeds of big sacaton were collected and eaten as a grain, and the whole plant was harvested and used as fodder. During the 1800s wildgrass hay was an important resource for the army posts in the area—nearly all their stock feed came from grasses such as sacaton and tobosa, especially along riparian areas.

Heartened by the regenerating grassland and news of the postfire bird migration, I head over to Bisbee for lunch. Afterward, on my way back to Tucson, I decide to swing by the river at Charleston Road to see what the summer floods have done there, where past floods have drastically altered the vegetation and river channel.

A sedan and a pickup truck are in the parking lot—nearly deserted for a Saturday afternoon. Most of the power birders stop coming to southern Arizona after the main hummingbird migration ends in August, although there are still many wonderful birds, butterflies, flowers, and reptiles to enjoy in the fall.

On the bridge an old Hispanic gentleman wearing dark suit pants, a powder blue *guayabera* shirt, and a fedora stands at the rail watching the river upstream, his hands clasped in front of him on the metal top rail. By the river below I can hear the happy chatter and laughter of a half dozen or more people. As I approach, he tips his hat and bids me good afternoon. I stop and assume the same comfortable stance as he, forearms on the bridge rail, hands clasped, gazing upstream at the river.

Isn't it beautiful, I say. I love this river.

The San Pedro slides fat and muddy under our feet, full of water and sediment from the summer rains. Plants 10 feet up the banks lean down-stream, their crowns full of debris from a recent high flow. Nearly black, wet soil, newly deposited, covers the banks. Young willows and cotton-woods are thriving here now, after years of flood scouring.

If the water ran like this all year, says my bridge companion, there would be big fish in it.

He looks surprised, almost dubious, when I tell him there used to be really big fish here—three-footers. Before settlers came to the valley in the 1800s, Colorado squawfish (*Ptychocheilus lucius*) were common on the San Pedro River. An unlikely member of the minnow family, Cyprinidae, at up to 6 feet or more long and 80-plus pounds in the bigger rivers, squawfish were the top-of-the-food-chain predators on the big rivers of Arizona. These behemoths preferred silty rivers with deep pools and strong currents. Overfishing for commercial markets and the damming and overpumping of rivers led to extinction of the squawfish in Arizona. Only a few populations are left in the upper Colorado River.

Where I am from, says my companion, who introduces himself as Manuel, on the Gila River near Winkelman, there are huge catfish. We used to fish for them there and up the San Francisco.

Manuel calls the Gila the "Great River" and tells me he was a miner for thirty years. There are large open-pit copper mines at Winkelman and Clifton-Morenci and a smelter at San Manuel; mining companies are the highest-volume water users on the upper Gila and lower San Pedro water-sheds. Manuel moved to Sierra Vista to be closer to his grandchildren, many of whom fish and play in the San Pedro below us. We walk to the downstream side of the bridge and he calls to his family; a chorus of greetings drifts up to us. There are five adults and two teenagers lounging around the muddy banks, some in lawn chairs, some on coolers, all drinking sodas or beer, chatting and laughing. The men all have cheap fishing rods equipped with red and white bobbers drifting in the current. Several little boys dash up and down the banks, laughing and shouting, while two boys and a girl fish with great seriousness. The two teenagers, probably a granddaughter and her boyfriend, apparently see no need to don special outdoor clothes for their fishing outing: she is classic His-panic music diva, hair pulled severely up to a wide-banded ponytail sprouting from the top of her head, her face painted with black eyeliner and shadow and black-cherry lipstick, body bedecked in a bustier and super-baggy hipster pants; her boyfriend is classic black inner-city gangster, buzzed hair covered in a black stocking with a funny ball on top, black shirt, and impossibly huge, baggy pants. But there they sit with their bare feet in the mud, their arms around each other, laughing as her uncle or brother tries to show them how to bait a hook.

I call down to them, Have you caught anything?

Everyone answers in unison, NO! And they erupt in raucous laughter.

We're just here to have fun, says Manuel, lifting his hands and shrugging his shoulders eloquently. He smiles down fondly at his family, leans again on the rail with his hands clasped, and resumes his peaceful musings of the San Pedro River in late summer.

EXPLORATION GUIDE

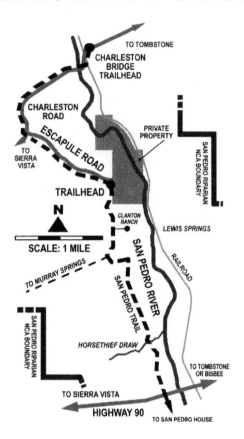

Highway 90 to Charleston San Pedro Trail and River Access Map

HIGHLIGHTS

The trails around the San Pedro House north and south of Highway 90 are well traveled and fun to hike, bird, and bike. The San Pedro Trail section north of Highway 90 passes the ruins of the historic Clanton Ranch (of Shootout-at-the-OK-Corral fame). Just a few miles from the San Pedro House is the prehistoric Clovis Culture archaeological dig at Murray Springs, which has new, excellent interpretive signing. The Charleston Road area offers a unique view of the river on the old bridge, which is now a pedestrian walkway, and good birding south of the bridge at Escapule Wash.

MILEAGE

7 miles to the San Pedro House from the intersection of Highways 90 and 92; 9.5 miles to the Charleston Road parking area from the intersection of Highways 90 and 92.

DIRECTIONS

To get to the San Pedro House from the intersection of Highways 90 and 92, head east on Highway 90 for 7 miles; soon after the road drops down to the main floodplain, slow down and watch for the Bureau of Land Management sign and turn-off to the parking lot and visitor center on the right. There is a large graveled parking lot at the San Pedro House visitor center and bookshop. There is no public parking on the north side of Highway 90, although cars do park there illegally. The entrance road gate is locked between sunset and sunrise.

To get to the Charleston Road parking lot from the intersection of Highways 90 and 92, take Charleston Road (about half a mile north of the 90/92 intersection, at the Wal-Mart) east to the river. The Charleston Road parking lot is on the east side of the river, on the south side of the road. It is large and graveled. There are no facilities.

ACCESS

For details on the San Pedro House facilities, see chapter 3 "Exploration Guide." The easiest way to connect to the river trails north of Highway 90 is to follow the main trail from the San Pedro House east to the river, then north to the bridge and under the bridge. After about a mile the river trail degrades, then disappears; there is a trail that connects the river trail to the San Pedro Trail at Horse Thief Draw. The San Pedro Trail begins opposite the entrance road to the San Pedro House and connects to Escapule Road in 3.6 miles.

The river at Charleston Road has in the recent past been deeply incised after years of flooding. But the river is now aggrading—the banks and riverbed are building back up—and the cottonwood-willow gallery has regenerated rapidly. There are no official trails along this stretch.

Stay in the riverbed for the first half mile to avoid private property trespass.

HIKING AND BACKPACKING

There are about 2 miles of hiking trails north of Highway 90, but the river is less scenic here than south of the highway. However, the San Pedro Trail–River loop passes through nice sacaton grassland. Backpacking or through-hiking from Highway 90 to Charleston Road is not recommended because of the private property at Escapule Estates. There are no established hiking trails at the river south of Charleston Road.

BIRDING

For more on birding around the San Pedro House, see chapter 3 "Exploration Guide." North of Highway 90, in the mesquite and sacaton grassland, look for Botteri's and Cassin's sparrows breeding during the late summer monsoon season, as well as plenty of resident Chihuahuan and Sonoran Desert species, such as cactus wrens, black-throated sparrows, black-tailed gnatcatchers, and verdins. At Charleston Road, park at Escapule Wash and walk down to the river along the wash; this stretch has been home to gray hawks, green kingfishers, and varied buntings in summer, and harbors the only known stand of yew-leafed willow in the RNCA.

MOUNTAIN BIKING

For more on mountain biking around the San Pedro House, see chapter 3 "Exploration Guide." The San Pedro Trail from Highway 90 north to Escapule Road makes a great ride and passes the ruins of the historic Clanton Ranch. Ride north from 90 to Charleston Road—it's dirt all the way—and then back for a total of 7.2 miles, or arrange a shuttle; Moson Road, which parallels the river on the west, connects Charleston Road to Highway 90. At Charleston Road, leave the shuttle car at the RNCA parking lot by the bridge; it is 1.6 miles up to Escapule Road from the parking lot.

HORSEBACK RIDING

The best riding is along the San Pedro Trail; see details above, in "Mountain Biking." You will need to contact the BLM prior to a ride if you plan to use the Moson Road access point, which has a locked gate.

ARCHAEOLOGICAL SITES

Murray Springs is a Clovis Culture site northwest of the San Pedro House. To get to the parking area, take Moson Road from Highway 90 north 1.1 miles to the closed gate on the east side; close the gate after entering. The parking lot is at the end of this short gravel road. There is a network of well-made trails through the archaeological site, which is southeast of the parking lot, across the fence. The trails and site are in Curry Draw; Murray Springs, which has several large cottonwoods and perennial water, is about half a mile down the draw from the archaeological site, toward the river. The San Pedro Trail intersects the lower end of the arroyo (Curry Draw). The main site has interpretative signs, installed in 1999. Check with the Friends of the San Pedro for a schedule of guided walks at the site. The entrance road gate is locked between sunset and sunrise.

HANDICAPPED ACCESS

For more on San Pedro House accessibility, see chapter 3 "Exploration Guide." There is no wheelchair or low-mobility access north of Highway 90. At Charleston Road the old bridge is accessible but river trails are not. Murray Springs is wheelchair accessible for some types of chairs; call ahead to the BLM for details before visiting.

CAMPING

There are no car-camping facilities near the San Pedro House. The nearest commercial camping is at RV parks in Sierra Vista. For information, contact the Sierra Vista Chamber of Commerce at 800-946-4777. Tombstone, about 9 miles east of the river at Charleston Road, has a KOA campground. All overnight camping in the RNCA is by pack-in only, and permits are required.

ACCOMMODATIONS

Sierra Vista has many hotels and restaurants; contact the Sierra Vista Chamber of Commerce at 800-946-4777. Tombstone, about 9 miles east of the river at Charleston Road, has hotels and restaurants. Contact the Tombstone Chamber of Commerce at 520-457-9317.

OTHER ATTRACTIONS NEARBY

Tombstone is the famous site of the gunfight at the OK Corral. This "town too tough to die" is a well-preserved remnant of late-1800s mining boom times in southern Arizona. There are museums, shops, saloons, and plenty of special events throughout the year. Contact the chamber of commerce at 520-457-9317.

CHAPTER 5

CHARLESTON
TO FAIRBANK

*The Mighty Mill Towns • Entrenching and Aggrading
• Railroads Then and Now • Bugs, Bats,
and Limestone • Corridors*

"TIMBER DEPREDATIONS IN southern Arizona are becoming so extensive that there is just cause for alarm. Even the palo verde trees are being stripped from the mesa lands."

So exclaimed an editorial in the *Arizona Daily Star,* March 7, 1884, describing the woodcutting in southern Arizona. According to Tellman, Yarde, and Wallace, authors of *Arizona's Changing Rivers* and researchers at the Water Resources Research Center at the University of Arizona, in Tombstone alone 120,000 to 130,000 cords of wood were cut between 1879 and 1886. Most of it was taken from the evergreen woodlands of the Huachuca, Whetstone, and Dragoon Mountains, as well as along the San Pedro and Babocomari Rivers. One cord equals 128 cubic feet, so 130,000 cords, if stacked 4 feet high in 4-foot lengths, would stretch 200 miles—from Sierra Vista to Phoenix. During the mining boom of the 1880s, Tombstone teemed with a population of 15,000, while Charleston and Fairbank housed 1,000; in the surrounding mountains there were fifty mines and twelve steam hoists; and along or near the river and its tributaries there were 150 ore processing stamps at seven milling sites—all using wood for fuel, heating, and cooking. This does not include some twenty-six other mining centers in southeastern Arizona, sixteen of which were within 25 miles of Tombstone. Researchers believe that nearly 900,000 cords of wood were cut from the woodlands of southern Arizona over a one-hundred-year period beginning in the early nineteenth century.

Ironically, I discover that I can't find the remains of Charleston when Jack and I pass by on our 30-mile backpacking trip down the river from Hereford to Fairbank. While Jack goes on up the river to The Narrows, a site he hopes to photograph, I poke around in the dense thickets on either side of the river. The trees have reclaimed the land from the town that, from 1879 to 1889, included a school, church, post office, meat market, livery stables, restaurants, retail stores, hotels, and saloons. At their peak the mills of Millville, across the river from Charleston, processed nearly $1.4 million in bullion from 1881 to 1882. Mill operators built a dam across the river here, siphoning the water into a wooden flume to power the mill. A 160-foot-long bridge spanned the river so that the frequent floods would not delay any ore shipments and processing.

But the wood of the buildings and bridges was carted off to other mining towns, has rotted, or was burned for firewood by squatters in the early twentieth century, and the adobe walls are melting back into the earth, nourishing the roots of the thriving mesquites, cottonwoods, and willows.

Although today the river here seems lush and healthy, the San Pedro Valley of the late nineteenth century, when Charleston was booming, was vastly different. The riverbanks and valley within 50 miles were treeless except for a few uncuttable giants; grasslands were grazed down to bare dirt or cut for hay. Smoke from the thousands of households, mines, and mills must have hung heavy in the air. Dust from thousands of livestock, sources of food and transportation, added to the pall. Their grazing stripped the hills of grass and shrubs. And the noise must have been horrendous: the giant stamp mills along the river ran day and night and could be heard all the way across the valley, in the Huachucas. It was during this time that the San Pedro River underwent massive physical changes.

Explorers in the eighteenth and nineteenth centuries described the San Pedro as flowing perennially, with extensive ciénegas along its banks and rich grasslands in the riverside terraces. Only a few reports were made of intermittent flows, and these were on the lower San Pedro, downstream from Benson. Richard Hereford, who has researched exhaustively the changes along the San Pedro, writes that the river was "once a narrow, unentrenched stream with extensive marshes, beaver ponds (referred to as ciénegas), and abounding in fish." Around the 1880s, after decades of extensive cattle grazing, mining-related uses, and a combination of weather events, the San Pedro began a dramatic period of incision—the stream cut down deeply on the riverbed—and its tributary arroyos became severely entrenched. This erosional activity was not unique to the San Pedro; most of the Southwest's rivers and arroyos began erosional cycles at this point. The series of events that led up to these erosional cycles are complex and poorly understood, but their outcome is well studied and easily observed.

Forces of weather and gravity constantly work away at topsoil, removing it grain by grain. Since it takes approximately five hundred years of ideal conditions for an inch of topsoil to form from decaying plants, animals, and bedrock minerals, the balance between normal erosion and soil building is indeed delicate. Plant roots are important soil binders, slowing or preventing erosion. Without plant cover, rates of water flow increase to the point where more topsoil is swept away and little water sinks into the ground, causing plants to die off. Rivers that are not entrenched—incised—have more ciénegas and oxbow ponds and more bankside vegetation, so the water's velocity is reduced. This in turn increases the amount of sediment deposited by the river—there is more soil building—and there is far more seepage and recharge into the local water table.

After entrenchment of a river's floodplain, the velocity of the water's flow increases, causing decreases in soil building and groundwater recharge. In the floodplain aquifer the water table drops, along with overall soil moisture, and rapid vegetation changes commence: ciénega vegetation, such as cattails, bulrushes, sedges, and sacaton grass, dies out and is replaced by woody species, such as cottonwood, willow, and mesquite. If the water table drops more dramatically, the woody species become more desert-associated thornshrubs, such as desert hackberry and wolfberry. Today the San Pedro runs from 3 to 30 feet below its former floodplain in a broad channel lined with trees.

River entrenchment and rebuilding, or aggrading, are natural events, albeit infrequent. The last erosional cycle for the San Pedro and other southwestern rivers began about 1,200 years ago. By dating samples of fossil pollen imbedded in floodplain sediments, scientists have determined that the closest previous cycle of erosion began about 8,000 years ago. No doubt vegetation changes along the rivers occurred during these erosional cycles. We don't know for sure what caused the period of entrenchment that lasted from about 1880 to 1926, but the suspects include removal of native riparian and surrounding grassland vegetation—by livestock, by people needing fuelwood to power mining equipment and heat homes, and by settlers converting the land to agriculture; increased construction of roads, railroads, trails, and irrigation ditches adjacent to or in the river floodplain, which restricted the width of the floodplain and concentrated runoff; and a series of El Niño–fueled high-rainfall years resulting in very large floods in the 1880s, 1890s, and early 1900s that, coupled with loss of vegetation and alteration of the natural floodplain, encouraged severe entrenchment.

But after nearly a half century of entrenchment, the San Pedro began evolving a new dynamic equilibrium of water flow, soil deposition, and riparian vegetation establishment; the continuous tall-gallery forest of riparian trees that we see today is a new habitat along southeastern Arizona's river courses, having become established after the entrenchment period. Scientists with the U.S. Geological Survey have been monitoring floodplain changes, surface flows, and vegetation changes on the San Pedro since the 1930s. They have found that the river has reestablished deep meanders—looping bends in the watercourse—thus widening the main river channel substantially. The rate of channel expansion has been decreasing since about 1955, while the density of riparian vegetation has increased steadily, suggesting that the river channel may be stabilizing. The result is that peak flow rates during floods have decreased because there is more riparian vegetation and more "sinuosity" and width in the channel; also, the oxbow pools within the meanders act as reservoirs to contain and slow down flood peaks. An additional plus is that low-intensity rainfall was more common between about 1957 and 1967, which provided excellent growth conditions for riparian as well as upland vegetation. Reestablishment of the sacaton grasslands is more problematic, since frequent fire is necessary to keep the grasslands free of trees such as mesquite. With urban development so close to the RNCA and with so many species—including endangered and threatened birds such as the willow flycatcher and gray hawk—now utilizing the thick riparian understory of the riverine tree canopy, which would be diminished by regular burning, a return to natural fire regimes is probably not possible.

Establishment of the Riparian National Conservation Area in 1988 was crucial to continued regeneration of parts of the river. But the threats are not gone; in 1990 a report by University of Arizona hydrologists predicted that if groundwater pumping rates continued along the San Pedro, the aquifer would be sufficiently depleted after two decades to begin to affect surface flow. In 1995 the conservation group American Rivers named the San Pedro as one of three most endangered rivers in the Southwest. And finally, as if more proof were necessary, in 1998 the multinational Montreal-based Commission for Environmental Cooperation, part of the North American Free Trade Agreement, concluded that groundwater pumping, mainly agricultural and municipal in both the United States and Mexico, will continue to decrease surface flows and lower the water table. Wells pump up to 7,000 acre-feet of water per year *more* than goes back into the aquifer from rain and other recharge. The report states that unchecked urban growth and agriculture will cause a water deficit of 14,000 acre-feet per year by 2030, a situation that will most definitely permanently kill the riparian forests, the remaining sacaton grasslands, and the river, a fate already *accompli* for most of the rivers in southern Arizona.

"I CAN MAKE it across," Jack says with more confidence than the situation warrants. We have come to what I call a bank-out: when following a meandering river, hikers cross and recross the river dozens of times, but eventually they will come to a section where the water has cut a bank too steep to climb down or where the pool at the base of the bank is too deep to cross. We stand on such a bank, only about 5 feet high, but the pool at its base is wide—about 6 feet—and deep. Dark. Jack proposes jumping from our bank to the opposite side of the pool. Taking into account the distance, the weight of our backpacks, and the presence of surprisingly deep quicksand along this stretch of the San Pedro, I opt to bushwhack around the pool and climb down a less steep bank an eighth mile downriver. Call me a wimp, I say to Jack, but I'll be a dry wimp.

As I am fighting my way through a dense web of mesquite branches, trying not to lose my balance and fall off the bank into the deep pool, I hear a wet thunk and then an exclamation of colorful language. I turn to see Jack thigh deep in quicksand at the edge of the pool, struggling like a figure from some dramatic Greek mythological tale that is caught from below by a giant sand-dwelling river monster. His pack, full of thousands of dollars of photographic equipment, not to mention images shot over the last day and a half, is just inches from the water. Briefly I wonder what I will do if he keeps sinking, but I see that he is slowly extracting himself from the powerful suction of the sand.

By the time I reach him, Jack is standing on dry land, his legs mucky brown and gritty, and he is still muttering. I opt not to proclaim the obvious merits of my own choice to go around the pool; instead, I mention that the quicksand we're finding in this section of the river is a good physical example of aggrading—the river building up again after incising. Not ready to be impressed by the forces of nature, Jack stalks off downstream, dribbling muck and sand.

The day is warm—in the mid-80s—and the cottonwoods are less numerous, so we walk mostly in the sun. The cottonwood-willow gallery is younger than upriver sections and has not yet formed an unbroken gallery. Riverine strands are wide and long and full of rabbitbrush and other shrubs, through which we have to bushwhack every couple of miles.

The rabbitbrush is just past blooming, and a few butterflies still flounce around them: sulphurs, sleepy oranges, and what look like a few hackberry butterflies. On a midmorning break I am surprised to see a big monarch butterfly charge past us, but it is flying high and strong almost directly upriver. Monarchs (*Danaus plexippus*), also called milkweed butterflies for the food preference shown by their larvae, or caterpillars, are famous for their migratory habits, and this one appears to be heading directly toward its wintering grounds in Mexico. Butterfly scientist and author Robert Michael Pyle, who visited Jonathan and me in Brown Canyon in 1996 while on a 9,000-mile North American driving tour following migrating monarchs for his book *Chasing Monarchs*, believes that monarchs may use southwestern riparian areas as migration corridors, but he has not amassed proof. My sighting is among his first reports of San Pedro migrants.

Hoping to camp at a scenic site that Jack can shoot in the golden evening light, we push on much farther than we feel like after a long day of hiking. Finally, as dusk is closing in, he endorses a site at a sharp bend in the river, and I collapse on a sandbar and start pulling food and stoves out of our packs while Jack stalks up and down the river picking out just the right shot.

A strange sound interrupts my culinary preparations, and a minute passes before my brain places it: a train. I forgot about the tracks that still run along the east bank of the river, although we walked along them for about a quarter mile south of Charleston when the river became too deep to walk and the banks were choked with understory shrubs. Chuffing and straining up a grade, a small engine and five or six open-top cars full of something obviously heavy come into view just across the river, its cyclopean eye throwing an eerie cone of light across its path. In our hurry to find a camp, we did not notice that the tracks came so close. Later, a couple of phone calls reveal that the San Pedro Southwestern Railroad, out of Benson, still runs trains on these very old, historic tracks. The company has a contract to run Mexican ore from Naco, just south of Bisbee on the border, to Benson, and it runs a weekly tourist excursion train from Benson to Charleston and back. SPSR is the last of many historic railroads that ran tracks along the San Pedro, dating back to 1881 when the New Mexico and Arizona Railroad built a line from Benson to Fairbank, where the tracks turned abruptly west toward Nogales, its destination on the Gulf of California at Guaymas. A wye was built at Fairbank to turn the locomotives. In 1888 this line was extended to Bisbee, then to Douglas in 1901, primarily to serve the smelters and mines. A second line from Benson to Fairbank was built for the Arizona and Southwestern Railroad in 1894. Spur tracks were built from Fairbank to Tombstone in 1903 and from Lewis Spring to Fort Huachuca in 1912. Over the years several railroads owned the tracks, including the Southern Pacific, and today the only tracks still continuous and running trains are from Benson to Naco. The rest have been removed or are slowly crumbling away.

That night we go to bed early and do not use our flashlights for reading. Because we are camped so close to the railroad tracks, we don't want to attract the attention of anyone walking the tracks. Fall is harvest time for the massive plantings of marijuana and poppies grown in the Mexican Sierras, and many thousands of tons of dope, heroin, and cocaine move across the border day and night, but especially at night, and especially along such natural corridors as the San Pedro. The night is cold— well below freezing—and I sleep fitfully, every sound of a skunk passing or rodent scritching in the leaf litter becoming a band of drug runners descending upon us. Around 10 o'clock I find myself yet again lying on my back watching the stars, trying to sleep. By the light of the moon sliver and countless stars, I am astonished to see the tiny forms of bats darting through the sky above me. They are probably western pipistrelles, hardy little bats that stay active most of the year in southern Arizona.

Although the San Pedro RNCA has become famous for its bird population, even more astounding but less well known is the diversity of its mammals. Out of a possible 137 mammal species that occur in Arizona, 86 species, 12 of which are federally or state listed as threatened or endangered, live along the San Pedro. The reason so many different species can live in such a relatively small place is the highly productive food chain, which starts with the thick, moist soil in which many plant types grow, the abundant insects that thrive on the surface water and very nutritious plant types, and then the multitude of animals that eat insects and the animals that feed on animals that eat insects. Twenty-four species of bats have been identified during surveys on the San Pedro and its surrounding habitats; Arizona's entire known bat species number 28, a total second only to that of Texas.

Each evening in the spring and summer, a natural wonder takes place in the mountains surrounding the San Pedro Valley. It begins as a trickle and slowly builds until thousands of soft wings putter in the dusk, flooding out into the valley from the limestone caves. Most are cave myotis bats, and as they feast on the millions of insects that fill the sky above the river corridor and valley, these tiny mammals connect the river with its ancient past, as well as its future.

Nearly all bats are insectivores, and a few are nectivorous and frugivorous—they eat flower nectar and fruit. Most insectivores pursue their prey in flight, using echolocation to target insects, then swooping down and either grabbing them directly in their mouths or scooping the insects up using their wings and tails to funnel them into their mouths. To minimize competition, different bat species hunt at different altitudes above the ground—some high, some medium, and some right above the surface. A few specialize even more. The pallid bat, for example, hunts on the ground for arthropods such as katydids and scorpions; unlike its relatives, it listens passively, as we do, rather than using echolocation (pallid bats do use echolocation for orientation).

In the United States most bats mate in the fall. The females store the sperm during hibernation, and when hibernation is broken, the sperm fertilize the eggs. After several months, usually in mid-June, each female gives birth to one baby in warm maternity caves shared sometimes with thousands of other female bats. The young bats mature in about four to ten weeks, during which time they accompany their mothers on feeding forays.

In the fall many bat species head south to Mexico for the winter, while others, such as silver-haired bats (*Lasionycteris noctivagans*), move from summer forest homes down to desert areas for the winter. These small bats feed on insects along the river in the evenings, then use the tall cottonwoods as roosts in the daytime. Many other bat species hibernate in Arizona in caves that bat scientists have dubbed hibernacula. In the Huachuca Mountains cavers were causing significant disturbance in several important hibernacula and roost caves on Fort Huachuca; the U.S. Army worked with cavers to mitigate their impact, and populations of cave myotis increased in one study cave from a low of 1,000 to more than 9,000 today.

The cave myotis (*Myotis velifer*) is the most abundant bat living in the San Pedro watershed. Roost caves in the Huachuca and Whetstone Mountains, including the soon-to-be-famous Kartchner Caverns, a state park, house tens of thousands of bats. The caves are in limestone deposits and represent an important page in the valley's geological and ecological history book.

Beginning about 570 million years ago, in the Cambrian era, a series of seas flooded and receded from what was to become the American Southwest (although at the time it straddled the equator) until 63 million years ago, during the Cretaceous period, when the last ocean drained off. During those 500 million years, layers of

Cave myotis bats like this one are very common in the limestone caves of the San Pedro River basin.

calcareous sediments formed from the remnants of sea creatures, and the pressure and resulting heat of all that weight turned them into stone—

what we know as limestone. Other rocks formed in similar ways include sandstone and shale.

The basic landscape we see today in the upper and lower San Pedro Valley—north-south trending mountains separated by broad valleys, the mountains thus dubbed "sky islands"—formed between about 8 and 15 million years ago. Most people assume that mountains are thrust up by pressure; that's the classic scene in grade school geology videos. But during this last period of mountain building in the Southwest, called the Basin and Range Orogeny, huge chunks of the earth's surface dropped down to form vast linear depressions, or valleys. Even as the valleys dropped, erosion of the mountains continued to fill them in, so that today the sediment in the valleys is many thousands of feet thick. This period most likely marked the birth of the San Pedro River, which became one of the major forces carving the landscape into what we see today. Over the millennia, the San Pedro River's base level—the elevation at its mouth, in this case at the Gila River 100 miles to the north—fluctuated, either because of tectonic uplift or changes in the worldwide sea level. The result of these fluctuations is the wide terraces that the river cut in the valley sediments. Several of these are visible today as bare, eroding escarpments just east of Benson on either side of Interstate 10 as the highway begins to climb out of the current river valley.

The limestone caves in the Huachucas, Whetstones, and Dragoons formed around 365 to 330 million years ago. Bats first show up in the area's fossil record around the Oligocene era, about 37 to 24 million years ago. Of course, geology and caves and bat evolution would mean nothing without a vital link along the river: insects. All those bats have to eat something. But one important question is, How do insects that are dependent on water for reproduction—that is, part of their life cycle includes an aquatic larval stage—survive the harsh conditions of the desert stream: long droughts, horrendous floods, high summer temperatures, low winter temperatures?

The answer lies in two important adaptations, both of which laid the foundation for the productivity that is the hallmark of desert riparian oases. The first is the very fact that insects have a number of life stages. If at some time of the year a particular environmental event, such as a flood, kills off all the aquatic eggs and larvae, there are still plenty of flying adults left around to lay new eggs that develop into larvae and eventually adults. Or if a severe cold kills off all the flying adults, there are still eggs and larvae lying dormant in or near the water, waiting for a warmer spell.

The second important adaptation insects have developed in desert stream environments is the ability to crank up the reproductive rate. Because the environment is harsh, the insects of desert streams produce a lot more offspring than their temperate relatives, and they do so a lot more rapidly. In as few as seven days an insect can develop from egg to flying adult to beat the heat or flood or cold.

As a result, desert riparian streams are always bursting with insect life. Studies have shown cottonwood-willow forests to be the most insect productive of all forest types in the United States. It's not surprising, then, that riparian habitats have such high numbers of migrating and breeding songbirds and bats, both of which dine on insects as their primary food source.

THE NEXT MORNING my sleeping bag's outer fabric is frozen and crinkles like cellophane, and I feel like a lozenge of hard candy. It takes Jack and me three cups of hot liquid and nearly two hours to get going in the cold morning air that lies thick over the river. We talk little.

This is our final leg, a 7-mile walk to the 1880s ghost town of Fairbank, where we left Jack's truck and, more important, a cooler full of beer. After years of working in the field, we've both learned that such carrots are vital to getting through the last, usually hardest day. Like horses returning to the stable, we quicken our pace.

Cold early morning gives way to a warm late morning. The river channel continues to widen, the river gets shallower, the sand deeper. By early afternoon warmth gives way to heat, and we slog on, sweaty and determined. We lose track of the meanders and don't know where we are on the map. At lunch on a sandbar in the skimpy shade of a young cottonwood pole, we finally orient ourselves on the topo: we are still several miles short of the beer. Our spirits flag, so we conjure an additional carrot, a dinner at a great Italian restaurant we know in Sierra Vista.

By the time I realize we are nearing Fairbank—I recognize the huge, rare mesquite bosque at the Babocomari River—I am too tired to admire anything but the trail that leads from the river to the parking lot. We drop our packs gratefully in the dirt, and Jack does the honors with the beer; cheap but cold, it is nectar to our parched throats.

Bob McNab, the friendly site host who has looked after Jack's truck during the trek, invites us to visit for a while, but our stomachs, already promised a date at Delio's, urge us to decline politely. We take turns cleaning up in Jack's camper, then head to town.

Delio's is decorated like a Chicago bistro. Like nearly all the 40,000-plus Sierra Vistans, the owner comes from beyond the Southwest and tried to recreate something from "home," in this case an Italian restaurant. We order up big plates of lasagna and tall glasses of water, fresh from the aquifer. I sip and think about the new university study that shows Sierra Vista's wells are already drawing from the aquifer below the San Pedro. It may be only a matter of time before we drink it all up or pour it onto lawns and into swimming pools. I order a beer instead and we offer a toast to the wild San Pedro.

IN A SMALL canyon in the northeastern flanks of the Huachuca Mountains, a group gathers each June for three days. Many are biologists, some are teachers and writers, several are professional animal trackers, a few are hunters, a handful are animal rights activists, and all are conservationists. For a decade they have volunteered their time to survey the roads and trails of the Huachucas for the tracks of large carnivores, primarily mountain lions and black bears, trying to amass data on their movements and distribution in the face of increasing human encroachment from Fort Huachuca and Sierra Vista. When I heard that the group planned to begin a track-searching transect on the San Pedro River in 1998, I packed up my truck and joined them at their mountain campsite.

As I pull up, I recognize several people sitting around the headquarters camp: Harley Shaw, founder of the track count and Arizona's foremost mountain lion researcher; David and Christine Coblentz, longtime volunteers with the Sky Island Alliance, a group that strongly supports track counts; and Sue Morse, one of the original Huachuca track count volunteers and an animal tracking expert who helped develop many of the survey techniques used by the group. David and Christine introduced Jonathan and me to mountain lion tracking when we lived in Brown Canyon in the Baboquivari Mountains; they also introduced us, via e-mail, to Harley, who answered many of our questions about the mountain lions we encountered. Harley's book, *Soul Among Lions,* about his many decades radio-collaring and studying mountain lions for Arizona Game and Fish, is one of the finest natural history books I've read. And Vermont-based Sue Morse started an organization called Keeping Track, which teaches children and adults the skills necessary to observe, interpret, and record evidence of wildlife in their communities. The goal of Keeping Track is to foster community-based wildlife habitat conservation; the Huachuca track count is a perfect example of one of the many programs the organization has started from California to Vermont. I had read extensively about but never met Sue.

After setting up my camp, I join the group for dinner. Other people have wandered in from a day in the field, including Kevin Hansen, author of the excellent book *Cougar: The American Lion,* and Christine Haas, a freelance biologist working on coatimundi research on Fort Huachuca. After a few beers the conversation turns a little more animated, with no-holds-barred critiques of several books about mountain lions—writers are always hitting on Sue and Harley for help, without compensation, on their projects. One book we all agree leaves much to be desired romanticizes the cougar, dwelling overly much on American Indian symbolism. When it comes to human reactions toward them, large carnivores seem to attract extreme as well as polar emotions: on the one hand is New Age spiritualism, and on the other is old West kill-all-the-predators. Then there are those who jump on the large carnivore bandwagon for political or environmental reasons. One well-known Southwestern environmental group repeatedly claims the jaguar as a member of the San Pedro River fauna, citing its presence—or potential presence, since there has been no physical evidence or photographs of jaguars on the river—as one of the primary reasons to increase protection of the river and its habitats, including limiting growth in Sierra Vista and Fort Huachuca.

The organization certainly has the right idea, just the wrong species. Large but secretive carnivores, such as mountain lions and bears, as well as their smaller mammal kin, such as bobcats and coatis, use thickly vegetated river habitats as corridors for moving around the Southwest. Biologists and conservationists talk a lot about riparian areas being important because of their biological diversity—especially in terms of migratory songbirds—but the understory, the physical cover, of a riparian area is also a vital component of the "big picture" when you consider a riparian area's value to wildlife. To animals such as bears and lions, crossing a 20-mile-wide valley in a night, from one mountain range to another, or moving down a valley for a hundred miles is not a big deal. Or at least it wasn't in the recent past. But nearly every valley is filled with growing towns and cities, their suburbs spreading like metastasizing cancers—Sierra Vista, Sonoita, Green Valley, Tucson, Oro Valley—so that it is next to impossible for large mammals to move around unharassed or even make it through the mazes alive. Imagine a lion trying to move from the Huachucas to the Mule Mountains, threading its way through the fences and floodlights of all those ranchette parcels between the river and the mountains. I remember all the barking dogs chasing Jack and me down the river at Escapule Estates. I remember all the roads and speeding cars I saw when I flew over the valley. Obviously, undeveloped and protected corridors, such as the river itself and its tributaries that thread from the surrounding mountains, are increasingly vital to the survival of large mammals. If the cats and bears can't mix their genes from one mountain to another, they will die out, as they have in several ranges in southern California where housing developments marooned them as effectively as if they had been on an island surrounded by water.

So Harley Shaw, Sue Morse, and the rest of the track count steering committee decided to set up transects on the San Pedro River to collect data on any large mammals using the river and its tributaries to move around the valley, from mountain to mountain as well as up and down the river. Their first choice was fairly easy: the Babocomari River at the ghost town of Fairbank, by Highway 82. The Babocomari is the largest tributary of the upper San Pedro River. Draining the northern slopes of the Huachuca Mountains, it snakes diagonally across the valley, through Sierra Vista's sprawl, to meet the river at the Fairbank bridge. It is a narrow creek—the water is no more than a couple of feet wide in a 20-foot-wide channel that is incised 5 or so feet from the surrounding land—and little traveled by humans.

The next morning we caffeinate, fuel up with quick breakfasts, and then head out toward the Babocomari by 7 A.M. Sue rides with me and tells me how she got started tracking animals. She learned her woodswoman's skills from her grandfather, hunting and exploring on his 2,000-acre Pennsylvania farm. One of the only women in forestry school at the University of Pennsylvania, she excelled but found that the career choices for a forester at that time were limited. She transferred to the University of Vermont and majored in English instead. But the wilds still spoke strongly to her, and in the 1980s Sue became interested in tracks and contacted Harley Shaw, who was studying mountain lions in Arizona. She learned about lion tracking with Harley and soon became involved with the beginnings of the Fort Huachuca track count, which became the model for Sue's countrywide tracking programs and Keeping Track.

"I hope that folks [on these tracking weekends] will take something back home with them and make a difference in their own communities," Sue tells me.

At the rendezvous we greet a dozen other volunteers and head south on a dirt road that parallels the river. About a quarter mile down the road at Walnut Gulch, a wide side drainage coming in from the east, we turn toward the river. I've walked track transects before, in the Baboquivari Mountains, but never with so many people. By necessity it's a casual affair. Harley, Sue, and some of the veterans lead the way, which helps reduce the chance of passing up a track and obliterating it with our own.

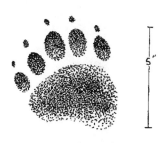

Within a few minutes someone calls out. The group crowds around in the sandy wash, and the experts confer. Yes, a single lion track. Fairly old—at least a couple of days. The walls of the track have caved in, spread out, so it's hard to measure with any accuracy or interpret the sex of the animal by the size of the pads. The animal was moving down toward the river.

The discovery buoys the volunteers, some of whom have walked

This beautiful bear track, in the thick mud where the Babocomari River joins the San Pedro River, was found by a group of us doing the first track survey of the river (part of the annual Huachuca Track Count). He was heading up the Babocomari, toward the Huachuca Mountains.

half a dozen transects without seeing any lion or bear tracks. In a few hundred feet we find tracks of coyote, dog, raven, and cow. I am impressed with the way Sue works in the field. She makes no shoot-from-the-hip identifications or interpretations. She always sizes up the track scene from as many angles as possible, not only from each cardinal direction but also from standing and squatting heights. And she's not afraid to say "I'm not sure" or "I think it might be." To me, careful qualification is always the mark of a true pro. Amateurs are the ones who are sure of everything. Harley Shaw is even more reserved than Sue, although I'd be willing to bet, because he is at least twenty years her senior and has twice the field experience, his knowledge of the language of tracks is even deeper.

At the river we turn upstream. The water is at a typical early summer low, about 6 to 8 feet wide and half a foot deep. By now we are split into three or four small groups, meandering along studying the soft mud along the shallow river. Stories are written everywhere: killdeer foraged here, according to dozens of little hashmarks scribed in the mud; a raccoon caught a crayfish there, its surprisingly humanlike paws showing where he dined, the claws of the hapless meal discarded at water's edge; a coyote patrolled along this bank, while a ringtail came down that bank and drank its fill; and a great blue heron stalked through this pool, spearing fleeing tadpoles.

By 10 A.M. the sun is beating down and we turn downstream, discussing jaguars and their recent incursions back into Arizona, documented on film once in 1996 in the Peloncillo Mountains, by the Arizona–Mexico–New Mexico borders, and twice in 1997 in the Altar Valley and Baboquivari Mountains, southwest of Tucson. Many people would like to believe the great spotted cats are attempting to return to Arizona, while others believe it is more likely that the animals were wandering males, possibly displaced from their natural ranges in Mexico by development, logging, drug trafficking, or hunting. There are no records of permanently established, regularly breeding jaguars in Arizona. A female and cubs were reportedly killed near the Grand Canyon sometime between 1885 and 1890, so some biologists count them among the state's breeding fauna (although in *Mammals of Arizona* Donald Hoffmeister writes of this information, "I cannot verify the dates for these . . . reports and am not certain that any are correct"). Most relevant for our neck of the woods, there is as yet no proof the elusive spotted cats are using the San Pedro River as a corridor. For that we'd need perfect sets of tracks or a photograph.

As we slowly approach the Babocomari River, several of the volunteers ahead of us cluster around a large mud hole that stretches across the mouth of the river. One calls out, "Bear!" We rush over, and there in the mud, as true as can be, is a perfect set of bear prints heading up the Babocomari toward the Huachucas. Sue photographs and measures the prints. Everyone gets a good look at the elongated rear pad, similar to a human foot, and the smaller, rounder front pad. The tracks are deep and perfect, and after everyone has their fill, I make a plaster cast of the rear foot; I don't have enough plaster in my pack to capture both front and rear. After about 40 minutes I dig up the cast and hurry to join the departing group.

I am elated. No words could more clearly write the story that large mammals such as bears and mountain lions use the riparian corridors as lifelines across mountains and valleys. Track counts like this will hopefully let the animals write their own future in the face of development pressures.

❧ EXPLORATION GUIDE ❧

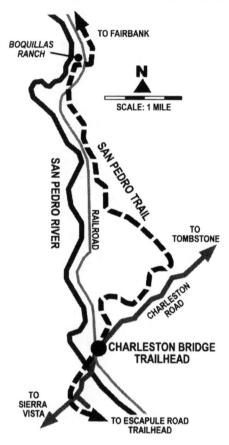

Charleston to Fairbank San Pedro Trail and River Access Map

HIGHLIGHTS

This is a beautiful stretch of the river, with an especially scenic portion near Charleston called The Narrows, excellent for hiking and backpacking. The ghost towns of Charleston, Millville, and Fairbank are popular destinations for history buffs; Fairbank is the most accessible and best preserved. The San Pedro Railroad tourist train excursions stop at this ghost town and feature special picnics and Western musicians.

MILEAGE

9.5 miles to the Charleston Road parking area from the intersection of Highways 90 and 92; 10 miles to Fairbank from the intersection of Highways 90 and 82.

DIRECTIONS

To get to the Charleston Road parking lot from the intersection of Highways 90 and 92, take Charleston Road (about half a mile north of the 90/92 intersection, at the Wal-Mart) east to the river. The Charleston Road parking lot is on the east side of the river, on the south side of the road. It is large and graveled. There are no facilities.

To get to Fairbank, take Highway 82 east from the Highway 90 intersection; the turn-off (on the left) is immediately after the railroad overpass—slow down as you pass the top of the bridge. The Fairbank parking lot is large and graveled. There is usually a site host present. Facilities include a portable toilet and nonpotable water (a faucet).

ACCESS

The river at Charleston Road has in the recent past been deeply incised after years of flooding. But the river is now aggrading—the banks and riverbed are building back up—and the cottonwood-willow gallery is regenerating rapidly. The old bridge is open to foot traffic and is accessible to wheelchairs. North of Charleston Road there are several unofficial trails and roads that lead to the ghost towns (or remnants) of Charleston and Millville. The San Pedro Trail begins on the east side of the river (east of the railroad tracks), north of the parking lot, and follows a dirt path (old road) north 8 miles to Fairbank; along the way it passes Millville and circles Charleston Peak on the southeast side, then drops down into an arroyo before following an old road to Boquillas Ranch.

At Fairbank, access to the river is via a quarter-mile trail that leads west from the information kiosk through the mesquite bosque. There are no riverside trails at this section, south of Highway 82; the road to Boquillas Ranch, across from the parking lot, is open to foot and bike traffic, and there is side drainage access to the river at Walnut Gulch. The riverbed is wide and flat at Fairbank and easily hiked (see below).

HIKING AND BACKPACKING

This is an excellent section for hiking and especially for backpacking. Just 2 miles north of Charleston Road is The Narrows, a beautiful section of cliffs where water flows most of the year; hikers will get wet passing through here. From Charleston Road to Fairbank, the river flows about 12 miles, which makes an excellent and easy two-day backpack. The river between The Narrows and Fairbank is aggrading—filling in with sediment—and is wide and fairly easy to walk, at least compared to the more mature gallery forest sections between the San Pedro House and Hereford. South of Fairbank, about half a mile up the river, is a popular section for day visitors where the river passes over a series of rock slabs and shallow pools. The Babocomari River meets the San Pedro just south of the Highway 82 bridge. The Babocomari is densely vegetated but rarely traveled and makes a nice day hike for hikers inclined to bushwhacking.

BIRDING

The river north of Charleston Road is not often birded, but green kingfishers, black hawks, gray hawks, and varied buntings have been seen here. The rocky hillsides near the old Millville site are reliable for rufous-crowned sparrows.

The habitat around Fairbank is primarily mesquite bosque, or forest. In the ghost town proper, around the old mercantile, is a mix of mesquites, soapberries, and ash trees—excellent breeding habitat for a variety of birds. In spring and summer, check the mesquite bosques for ash-throated flycatcher, northern beardless-tyrannulet, Gambel's quail, white-winged dove, vermilion flycatcher, Bell's vireo, Lucy's warbler, summer tanager, and blue grosbeak. A yellow grosbeak visited the townsite for a few hours in 1992. The habitats south of Fairbank are extremely good for varied buntings in summer; males sing from sunrise to around 8 A.M. In migration, lazuli, indigo, varied, and painted buntings have all been seen on the road to Boquillas Ranch (the ranch itself is not open to visitors). Also check these habitats in summer for foraging gray hawks.

In winter gray flycatchers are common in the mesquite bosques, and many wintering sparrows fill the grassland and mesquite habitats.

MOUNTAIN BIKING

The San Pedro Trail from Charleston to Fairbank (see "Access," above) is a great mountain bike ride, looping first (if you are riding south to north) up into the desertscrub and then dropping down close to the river around Boquillas Ranch.

HORSEBACK RIDING

This is one of the most beautiful rides on the river. There is plenty of room for trailers at the Charleston Road parking lot, and access is good on the east side of the river for riding north (see "Access" and "Mountain Biking" sections, above). Riders should be prepared for river crossings, sections of possible quicksand, and passing through thickets, and should be on the lookout for trains. South of Fairbank the road to Boquillas Ranch makes for good riding; several side drainages offer access to the river for a loop ride. The riverbed south of Highway 82 is wide and sandy, not good for riding because of quicksand. Do not park trailers in the Fairbank parking lot; there is room across Highway 82 at the gated entry. If you plan a trip south from Fairbank, call the BLM to check on whether or not the gate is locked.

ARCHAEOLOGICAL SITES

The only public historical sites in this section are the ghost towns of Millville and Charleston, a mile north of Charleston Road, and Fairbank. See "Highlights" for more information, as well as chapter 6 for more on Fairbank.

HANDICAPPED ACCESS

At Charleston north of Charleston Road, the trails are wide and sandy, not suitable for wheelchairs. The old bridge at the road, now closed to traffic, is accessible.

At Fairbank the trail to the river is packed dirt but is not suitable for wheelchairs because of the steep, sandy approach to the river. The ghost town itself is accessible for most wheelchairs.

CAMPING

Tombstone, about 9 miles east of the river at Charleston Road, has a KOA campground. All overnight camping in the RNCA is by pack-in only, and permits are required.

ACCOMMODATIONS

Sierra Vista has many hotels and restaurants; contact the Sierra Vista Chamber of Commerce Convention and Visitor's Bureau at 520-458-6940 or 800-288-3861. Tombstone, about 9 miles east of the river at Charleston Road, has hotels and restaurants. Contact the Tombstone Chamber of Commerce at 520-457-9317.

OTHER ATTRACTIONS NEARBY

Those folks interested in the valley's geology should visit French Joe Canyon in the nearby Whetstone Mountains. The turn-off is just north of milepost 300 on Highway 90, between Mustang Corners (intersection of 90 and Highway 82) and I-10. The road is rough dirt, best for trucks and sport utilities. The Huachuca Audubon Society sometimes leads hikes into this interesting canyon (write to P.O. Box 63, Sierra Vista, AZ 85636).

Also in the Whetstone Mountains is the new Kartchner Caverns State Park, home of many of the cave myotis bats that hunt insects along the river. For information, contact the park at 520-586-2283.

Train buffs will enjoy a four-hour, 54-mile roundtrip ride on the scenic San Pedro Southwestern Railroad, which offers excursions most Saturdays throughout the year. The train departs from Benson and wends its way along the river corridor to Charleston, with a stop at Fairbank on the way back for a barbecue and live music. For information, contact the railroad at 520-586-2266 or 800-269-6314.

Another nearby attraction is Tombstone, the famous site of the gunfight at the OK Corral. This "town too tough to die" is a well-preserved remnant of late-1800s mining boom times in southern Arizona. There are museums, shops, saloons, and plenty of special events throughout the year. Contact the chamber of commerce at 520-457-9317.

CHAPTER 6

FAIRBANK TO
ST. DAVID CIÉNEGA

Spanish Vanity Meets Apache Resistance · Mosquitoes
and Beavers · Looking North into the Future

IT WAS 1775 when Irish soldier of fortune Colonel Hugo O'Conor, in the employ of the King Carlos III of Spain, stood on the western bank of the Río de San Pietro a few miles north of the Río de Babocomari and declared it the perfect site. Unlimited fresh water, high ground from which to keep an eye on enemies, abundant game, and river terraces for growing crops—indeed, it seemed like an excellent site for a royal *presidio,* or fort, from which Spain's soldiers could conquer new territory and expand the northern frontier.

But just four years later the Spanish commander of the frontier ordered the unfinished Presidio Santa Cruz de Terrenate abandoned and its soldiers and settlers recalled to the safer environ of Las Nutrias, in present-day Sonora. Don Teodoro de Croix wrote in a 1781 report of "the terror instilled in the troops and settlers of the presidio of Santa Cruz that had seen two captains and more than eighty men perish at the hands of the enemies in the open rolling ground at a short distance from the post, and the incessant attacks which they suffered from the numerous bands of Apaches, who do not permit cultivation of the crops, who surprise the mule trains carrying effects and supplies, who rob the horse herds and put the troops in the situation of not being able to attend their own defense, making them useless for the defense of the province."

The original plan for the presidio was grand: a large square compound surrounded by 12- to 15-foot-high walls, big enough for three hundred or so people; a main gate and guardhouse in the east wall, the structure having a second floor protected by a wall with weapons loops; spacious commandant's quarters and troop barracks along the west wall; a small chapel along the south wall; workers' huts, called *jacales,* throughout the interior; and at the southwest corner a large bastion with four bronze cannons and a powder magazine.

When they arrived at the beautiful site, the grassy plains rolling away to dramatic mountains in the south and east and the lush river just below, the three hundred soldiers, workers, and their families must have had hopes as big as their future presidio. Likewise the Apache bands that certainly watched the arrivals from their strongholds in the Dragoon Mountains to the east must have been excited: their livelihood increasingly depended on raiding the rich stores and livestock herds of the new Europeans, who despite their guns, cannons, and armor were woefully ill equipped and ill trained to fight the Apaches (European warfare was based on age-old troop maneuvers and elaborate rules of battle). New meat had arrived, and the Apaches wasted no time in beginning frequent raids on the new presidio.

In just a short time it must have become painfully apparent to the Spaniards that this was not an ideal site after all, and life became a terrible struggle. The presidio's layout did not defend well against the Apaches, who scaled the walls or undertook sneak attacks while people worked in their fields, gathered water, or tended their herds. An additional encumbrance for the Europeans was their traditional clothing, which was stifling hot and restrictive in the harsh climate: wool jackets, breeches, and capes with black hats, neckerchiefs, and leggings, and seven-layer buckskin tunics.

In four years the Apaches killed two commandants and one priest; the remaining priest applied for and was granted retirement soon after his assignment; eighty soldiers were killed; and the vital and expensive oxen that were to be used to haul the rocks for the fortifications were captured and most likely eaten by the Apaches two months after their arrival, along with most of the cattle and horses.

The raiding caused much-needed supplies and food to become scarce. Construction of the grand presidio took a second seat to daily survival. A survey of the bastion recorded that the ceiling leaked and most of the gunpowder was wet. Morale plummeted and crime soared;

records from the presidio show that many residents took leave at any opportunity and often applied for reassignment to other presidios.

Sitting on a new metal bench overlooking the San Pedro River and the rocky outcrops we now call Cochise's Stronghold in the Dragoons, I find it easy to imagine the Apaches streaming out of the canyons on their newly acquired European mounts and causing panic among the ill-protected settlers at the fort just behind me. My bench is near where the main gate would have been, and I can almost hear it banging closed, the bolts shooting home. Today only the stone foundations of the presidio wall and a few of the adobe walls of the chapel, commandant's quarters, and bastion stand. Peaceful and quiet in the hot summer sun, they are now favorite basking sites for numerous tree lizards that hunt for insects while black-throated sparrows trill and tinkle in the creosote that is overtaking the fort.

Nearly two and a quarter centuries after being abandoned and forgotten by the Spanish, Presidio Santa Cruz de Terrenate has been declared a site on the National Register of Historic Places, and the Bureau of Land Management has installed trails and bronze interpretive signs throughout the compound. It is one of the best-preserved presidios in the New World, and study and excavation of the site in the 1950s by Charles DiPeso of the Amerind Foundation provided an excellent look into our area's Spanish history. Although DiPeso found many wonderful artifacts at the site, much had already been removed during the first part of this century—Spanish coins, buttons, and religious artifacts have always enjoyed popularity among illegal collectors. Even recently, BLM archaeologist Jane Childress told me, someone broke into the site with a small bulldozer and destroyed part of the chapel walls looking for collectibles.

Walking back to the truck through the hot Chihuahuan thornscrub, a smooth object, out of place in a mound of rocky soil recently excavated by a ground squirrel, catches my eye. It is an Indian potsherd, about an inch square and slightly curved. Its inner surface is dull brown, and the outside a smooth, rich red just beginning to fade with exposure to the sun after many centuries underground.

The shard reminds me that man's presence in the San Pedro River valley has stretched most likely unbroken for at least 13,000 years and that the Spanish were barely a drop in the ever-changing tide of humanity. Clovis Culture disappeared around 11,000 years ago, supplanted by Cochise Culture. During their early occupation, the Cochise people built temporary brush- and skin-covered huts, hunted game, gathered wild plant foods, and made baskets, manos and metates, and mortars and pestles, as well as spears, hammer stones, scrapers, projectile points, bone and horn tools, awls, and pendants. Later this intriguing culture began to build pit houses and grow corn.

Sometime shortly after A.D. 1, the people we call Mogollon and Salado arrived in the San Pedro Valley. Like the Cochise people, they were hunter-gatherers and also dryland and floodplain farmers who lived in pit houses. They made pottery and bows and arrows, and left burial sites and cremations. Dryland farmers called the Hohokam most likely migrated north from Mesoamerica around A.D. 500, and shortly thereafter a few Mimbres and Anasazi people lived in the valley. There are at least a dozen rock art sites, most in the Hohokam style, along the San Pedro, concentrated north of Charleston near The Narrows.

By A.D. 1400, though, the distinct cultural group in the valley was the Sobaipuri, who shared some traits of the Hohokam, Salado, and Anasazi people. The Sobaipuri spoke a language in the same family as today's Piman, or O'odham, Indians, and they farmed the river bottomlands using irrigation canals. They hunted, traded with Pueblo Indians from the north, and later acquired cattle from the Spaniards, who showed up in the sixteenth century. There may have been around 2,000 Sobaipuris in the upper San Pedro Valley during this time. Charles DiPeso believes that the Presidio Santa Cruz de Terrenate was built on top of an old Sobaipuri village called Quiburi, although some archaeologists dispute this, saying DiPeso's Indian huts were just workers' temporary quarters.

Like the Spaniards, the Sobaipuris could not withstand the violent attacks of the Apaches, who migrated into the Southwest sometime in the seventeenth or eighteenth century. Their numbers dwindling and their people suffering, the Sobaipuris went to the Spaniards for protection. In the mid-1700s the Spanish moved the Sobaipuris out of their homeland in the San Pedro to presidios along the Santa Cruz River to the west, where they merged culturally with the Papago, or Tohono O'odham, people.

I place the potsherd back in the earth and wonder about the hands that made it: were they Hohokam or Sobaipuri? Or did a Pueblo artisan from up north make a pot to trade for beads or art? Did someone drop it while running from Apaches, or was it part of a household garbage heap? Whoever made it belonged to one of the many cultures that, over thirteen millennia, shaped the San Pedro River into what it is today, and I am part of the culture that will shape it in the future.

THE PRIMARY THOUGHT in my mind as I struggle knee deep in the foul-smelling black muck of the St. David ciénega is, *Why did I wear my new socks?*

My friend Chris Wolner laughs as the muck sucks off one of her sandals—a slightly better choice than boots—and she teeters dangerously close to losing her balance and falling fully into the ooze. Chris and Dennis Caldwell, both members of the Tucson Herpetological Society, are exploring the ciénega with me in hopes of seeing some interesting herpetofauna—snakes, lizards, frogs, toads, salamanders. It is August and already steamy at 8 A.M. When we drove in, a heavy mist, nearly as thick as fog, shrouded the ciénega and surrounding desert for a few hundred feet but lifted as the sun heightened. I was just beginning work on this San Pedro project and had looked forward to exploring the ciénega, a foreign habitat to me, its soggy, green character so different from the desert in which I grew up. When Jonathan and I worked on the Buenos Aires National Wildlife Refuge, I often visited the refuge's Arivaca ciénega, but with its tidy boardwalks and viewing platforms to keep visitors' feet dry and canned interpretive signs to make sure visitors didn't miss The Ecological Point, I felt I hadn't really gotten to *know* a ciénega.

Well, I was certainly getting to know one now. The smell in the muck that oozes into my boots and coats my pant legs is the product of thallophytes, a group that includes algae, bacteria, and fungi. Many of these lower organisms are single celled and microscopic, and they form the building blocks of a marsh. The bacteria are important reducers—they feed on dead plants and animals and return vital nitrogen, sulfur, and phosphorus to the nutrient cycle—hence the smell. Many microscopic organisms feed on the thallophytes, and larger ones feed on those, and so on up to tadpoles and fish fry. In addition to being important nutrient composts and oxygen producers, ciénegas are also nurseries for fish, amphibians, and insects, providing calm water that is cooled by shady aquatic plants. Surrounding the pools of the wetland are dense thickets of water-loving plants, beginning with the sedges, rushes, and cattails with their feet in the water, followed by ranks of young willows and buttonwillows, a shrub that is not a willow but likes the same habitat, and ending with mesquites, cottonwoods, acacias, and various thornshrubs.

Today the buttonwillows are in full bloom, and hundreds of butterflies crowd around them as though they were competing at a fire sale: monarchs, queens, red admirals, snouts, duskywings, and sulphurs. I

can hear Bell's vireos counting in the mesquites—to me they seem to be calling "One-two-three-four-five-six! Six-five-four-three-two-one"— and black-throated sparrows twitter and tinkle while vermilion flycatchers, common yellowthroats, and varied buntings dash brightly through the thickets. We see no fish or snakes, and the only amphibians are non-native bullfrogs in the many rush- and cattail-lined pools, but we are the recipients of ample attention from mosquitoes as we free ourselves from the mud and then thrash through the tangle of thorny brush. Although tiny, the mighty mosquito has accomplished much to change

When my friends Chris and Dennis joined me for a summer survey of the St. David ciénega, dozens of butterflies like this two-tailed swallowtail were swarming the blooming buttonbush.

the course of natural and human history around the world.

Along the San Pedro mosquitoes were a primary cause of the extirpation of the beaver. In the 1800s the San Pedro River had many ciénegas along its snaking route—explorers described the river bottom as marshy and nearly impassable except around Palominas or north of Benson. Most of the ciénegas were the product of beaver dams, which created standing water, a benefit of which was tremendous recharge to the aquifer but a drawback of which was mosquito production. In the 1820s beavers were so numerous along the San Pedro River that trapper James O. Pattie called it Beaver River. By the end of the nineteenth century and beginning of the next, the army became so alarmed about mosquito-borne malaria outbreaks at Fort Huachuca (an 1879 *Arizona Daily Star* said the San Pedro "might well be called the valley of the shadow of death" because of malarial outbreaks) that they dynamited the dams and destroyed most of the ciénegas. Thanks to this scheme, as well as intensive trapping, beavers had disappeared permanently from the river by the 1920s.

Beavers (*Castor canadensis*), in the family Castoridae, are the largest rodent north of Mexico and have been around since the Oligocene epoch, roughly 37 to 24 million years ago. An adult may be from 25 to 36 inches long in the body and have a paddle-shaped tail that is about 6 inches wide by 15 inches long. They tip the scales at a surprisingly heavy 30 to 60 pounds. Their brown fur has a dense and insulative undercoat covered by long, silky, and water-resistant guard hairs; their tail is unfurred, almost scaly. Beavers were trapped for both their fur and for the oil of their anal glands, called castors.

Most beavers live in family colonies consisting of the parents, yearlings up to about age two, and the young of the year. Colonies establish territories with central and secondary lodges, and they defend them vigorously from each other. All members of a colony participate in building and maintenance of the dams and lodges, which they construct with sticks, rocks, and mud, creating a still water, or "beaver pond," along the river. The entrance to a lodge is underwater. In Arizona beavers also have been known to dig dens with underwater entrances into riverbanks, with the sleeping ledge well above high water and thus dry.

Beavers dine on tubers and the bark and stems of woody plants; they especially favor cottonwood, willow, mesquite, cattail, aspen (at higher elevations), and even tamarisk and pond lilies. A pair will have two to four, sometimes eight, kits per litter in the spring.

In the 1940s Arizona Game and Fish reintroduced beavers to the San Pedro River as part of an ambitious effort to place five hundred beavers on waterways throughout the state. A 1955 *National Geographic Magazine* article enthused that "in the wild Mogollon Rim country, the animals have not only survived, but prospered. Where seeps trickled in springtime, beaver dams now store water. Where topsoil washed away during heavy rains, lush meadows now grow. Where grass previously was parched by midsummer, the water table has risen and keeps the sod wet. Where wildlife and livestock once watered at stagnant pools, they now drink from natural streams." Although by the early 1990s about 40,000 beavers could be found elsewhere in Arizona, there were none left on the San Pedro River.

Nearly eighty years after their extirpation from the San Pedro, beavers are once again going to get to work damming its waters, beginning in the Riparian National Conservation Area near Hereford. Never a simple process, the reintroduction hit a snag in the mid-1990s when the Bureau of Land Management discovered that there were nesting southwestern willow flycatchers along the river. The southwestern willow flycatcher is an endangered subspecies of willow flycatcher that is dependent on cottonwood-willow habitat. Beavers harvest cottonwood and willow shoots and saplings, so the U.S. Fish and Wildlife Service and the Arizona Game and Fish Department, the agencies coordinating the reintroduction, could not just let loose the beavers without first conducting extensive environmental impact statements, despite the fact that in the long run beavers create more and better cottonwood-willow and marsh habitat because the dams widen riparian channels and decrease the effects of floods. Rather a case of hoist by their own petard, the agencies finally completed their environmental assessment in 1998.

On March 3, 1999, near Hereford, a lone 57-pound male beaver from the lower Colorado River near Yuma was released into the San Pedro. Biologist Mark Fredlake, BLM coordinator for the reintroduction, Mike Pruss of Arizona Game and Fish, and other staff and volunteers plan to release nine more beavers along the river. Fredlake said that the team had to make sure that the transplants are all lodge-building beavers rather than bank-denning beavers, since managers hope the beaver lodges and dams will help slow the river and return it closer to its early "marshy" character. Beaver number one lived up to his species' reputation and began building dams right away; using bulrushes at first, the male first dammed the main channel and then, as the water level in the new pool rose and a side channel filled with water, dammed that channel and then another and so on, creating a series of deep pools. The team hopes the beavers will pair up and establish numerous healthy colonies along the river—as many as fifty would be great, according to Fredlake.

This latest beaver reintroduction hasn't been without the usual controversial baggage attached to species reintroduction in the late nineties.

Why spend so much money on just one species (the beaver reintroduction will cost around $25,000)? Private landowners worry about the presence of a listed species on their property (beavers are not listed, but the southwestern willow flycatcher, which biologists hope will increase with the beaver lodges, is endangered). The issue is sensitive and complex.

While reading up on beavers and other lost species in Arizona, I found an interesting story in a 1994 issue of the *Arizona Daily Star*. Two biologists had completed a study that found biodiversity in Arizona today to be greater than it was one hundred years ago. I was not surprised to read such a statement from one of the authors, Dave Brown, an adjunct professor of zoology at Arizona State University and well-known biological iconoclast. He was quoted as saying, "There has been a lot of hand-wringing by a lot of people" who presume that the number of species is declining.

Because Brown is a man who likes to stir things up, I did not pay much attention to the article until I read that the other author of the study was a friend of ours, Russell Davis, professor emeritus of ecology and evolutionary biology at the University of Arizona and hardly a gad-fly. I perked up. But their message disturbed me. Do we want developers, corporate ranches, and agricultural empires to grab onto this new finding and use it to beat down such things as beaver reintroduction?

What Davis and Brown found was that nine species of birds and mammals disappeared from the Southwest in the past century and an additional thirty-four species declined significantly (they did not include aquatic species, or the numbers would have been much higher). But fifty-five species moved into the Southwest or expanded their range over the same hundred-year period.

Davis told the reporter, "If you asked almost anyone who's interested in the out-of-doors, including ecologists, what's happened in the Southwest in the past hundred years, most would say that it's gone down-hill in terms of the numbers of species. So this is sort of a lesson to be cautious with letting our emotions guide our science. Another lesson is that things are pretty dynamic, always changing."

Among the species that have disappeared from Arizona's fauna are beavers, jaguars, grizzly bears, and Mexican wolves. Species that have moved into Arizona or significantly expanded their range here include opossums, hog-nosed skunks, Inca doves, and several species of rodents. Declines and disappearances were caused by loss of habitat and by persecution by humans. But it's unclear why other species expanded their ranges; possibly a gradual warming trend allowed Mexican species such as opossums to move north, or more disturbed habitat opened up new niches for species such as Inca doves.

"For example, when you overgraze an area, everybody feels this is very bad," Davis said. "But that view might be a little myopic. It's true that people have changed the environment by overgrazing livestock and that some of the species that lived there when the grass was tall are gone.

"But while there are losers, there are also winners—species that move into the area because they prefer low grass. Various kinds of mice, for example, might move into that kind of area."

I winced. After having walked most of the San Pedro RNCA, I could hardly endorse grazing along riparian areas and adjacent grasslands because species lost are balanced by species gained.

Fortunately, Brown and Davis also said that an increase in the number of species doesn't imply that environmental conditions are improving.

"All we're saying is that . . . biodiversity should not be the ultimate goal of ecologists," Davis explained. "I would rather have less biodiversity and a more natural fauna. I'd rather have a grizzly bear out there than an opossum.

"You get into some questions of value. Is a wolf more valuable than a coatimundi? Is a squawfish the equivalent of a small-mouth bass? You may have a decrease in the quality of the fauna even though the biodiversity is increasing."

Quality of fauna. Value of an animal. What *is* the value of a beaver? A jaguar? What good is the last wild river in the Southwest?

CHRIS AND I find our way out of the ciénega thicket and join Dennis near a giant Goodding willow at the edge of a meadow of lush grass dotted with flowering *yierba mansa* (*Anemopsis californica*), the only species in its family, Saururaceae, in Arizona. To early people it was an important medicinal plant. The meadow is scarred by the recent presence of cattle, pockmarks and feces and broken plants. The rickety fence that marks the northeastern boundary of the preserve is a few feet away from the big tree.

The St. David ciénega is a severely degraded habitat in the first stages of repair; it has not healed as fast as other parts of the RNCA because of recurring problems with cattle. Although officially cattle have been banned in the ciénega since the RNCA was established, the BLM has not had the money or personnel to regularly check the fences at the site, and cattle still roam the rich and delicate habitat, mowing down the grass and young shrubs and trees. This annihilates cover for animals and increases evaporation, beginning a drying cycle that tips the ecological balance away from wetland and allows more desert species to invade. With permanent exclusions and careful monitoring, it does not take long for this moist habitat to recover from cattle degradation, as evidenced at the Arivaca ciénega, as well as the Bingham ciénega farther downstream on the San Pedro.

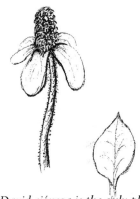

St. David ciénega is the only place along the San Pedro where I have found Mexican hat (Anemopsis californica). *Also called* yierba mansa, *it is the only species in its family, Saururaceae, found in Arizona and is a useful medicinal plant.*

We eat our lunches under the giant willow and listen to red-winged blackbirds clang and clatter in the cattails beyond the mesquites. High above, a red-tailed hawk searches for a hapless bullfrog. I sit facing the fence, wordlessly studying the river north of the ciénega. Its character changes drastically. There are few cottonwoods here, and most of them are old, scraggly, and dying next to the waterless, shadeless river channel that is lined by rabbitbrush, seep willow, and the beginnings of a tamarisk invasion; young willows and cottonwoods are struggling to compete. Cattle browse in the riverbed and on its banks. Beyond my vision, upstream a few miles, a diversion dam and irrigation ditch suck what little water is left out of the river and shunt it over to the many alfalfa and grain fields, lawns and private ponds in the lush hamlet of St. David, a few miles northeast of the ciénega. Beyond St. David the river goes underground most of the year. At Benson more farms extract water from the floodplain aquifer for green fields struggling to survive in the harsh Chihuahuan Desert climate. The river has begun a new cycle of downcutting there, and rarely does it flow continuously past Benson, except in summer and spring floods. The cottonwood-willow gallery is broken, sometimes nonexistent in places, as tamarisk invades. The river is a ghost of its former self, a sickly patient struggling to survive a life-sapping cancer.

I get up, dust off my grass-damp pants, and walk over to the wobbly, partially collapsed fence. My boot swings on the slack bottom strand, and I look north from the end of the Riparian National Conservation Area, hoping I'm not looking into the future of the San Pedro River.

❧ EXPLORATION GUIDE ❧

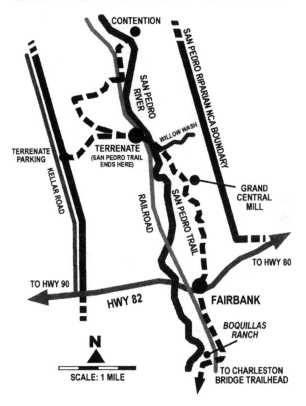

Fairbank to Terrenate San Pedro Trail and River Access Map

HIGHLIGHTS

Fairbank and the ruins of the Grand Central Mill, Boston Mill, and Contention City are exciting for western history buffs. The river around Fairbank is easily explored and good for picnicking and dayhiking. The varied habitats around Fairbank—Chihuahuan desertscrub, mesquite bosque, cottonwood-willow riparian—make for excellent birding year-round. The Spanish ruins of the Presidio Santa Cruz de Terrenate, northwest of Fairbank, is the best-preserved example of a royal Spanish presidio left in the United States. The St. David ciénega is a rare wetland habitat in the Southwest, well worth the time to explore.

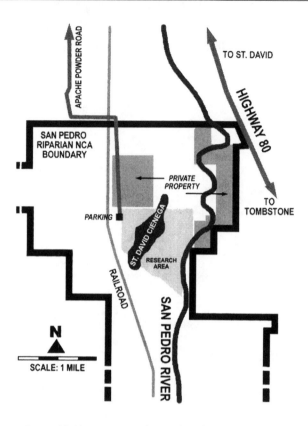

St. David ciénega San Pedro Trail and River Access Map

MILEAGE

10 miles to Fairbank from the intersection of Highways 90 and 82; 10 miles to St. David ciénega from Benson.

DIRECTIONS

To get to Fairbank, take Highway 82 east from the Highway 90 intersection; the turn-off (on the left) is immediately after the railroad overpass—slow down as you pass the top of the bridge. The Fairbank parking lot is large and graveled. There is usually a site host present. Facilities include a portable toilet and nonpotable water (a faucet).

To get to the ciénega from Benson, take Highway 80 south for 4 miles to Apache Powder Road (if you get to the river, you've gone too far); turn right and continue on this road 4.6 miles to the railroad track, then turn right on the road that runs south along the tracks for 1 mile to the parking lot. (Note: This last mile can be impassable during periods of heavy rain.) The ciénega parking lot is large and dirt, with a portable toilet and a trash can. There is no water.

To get to the parking area for the ruins of the Presidio Santa Cruz de Terrenate, take Highway 82 east from its intersection with Highway 92 and watch for Kellar Road on the left after about 8 miles. Look for the parking lot on the right 1.8 miles from the highway. There is a portable toilet near the Terrenate ruins but no water or other facilities.

ACCESS

At Fairbank, access to the river is via a quarter-mile trail west from the information kiosk through the mesquite bosque. There are no riverside trails in this section, south of Highway 82. The road to Boquillas Ranch, across from the parking lot, is open to foot and bike traffic, and there is side drainage access to the river. The San Pedro Trail runs from east of Charleston to Fairbank on this road. The riverbed is wide and flat at Fairbank and easily hiked north and south of the bridge. North of Highway 82 the final segment of the San Pedro Trail leads from Fairbank north 2 miles to Willow Wash on an old road, then loops back to Fairbank. From Willow Wash it is a short walk to the Presidio de Terrenate ruins (see "Archaeological Sites," below).

There are two access trails into the St. David ciénega. From the parking lot, follow the old dirt road south along the railroad tracks for about .2 mile; look for a dirt trail heading into the ciénega through a mesquite thicket (it can be hard to locate). Or keep walking south on the road, taking the left fork at each possible turn. At about .7 mile from the parking lot, there is another access trail into the ciénega. If you continue south on the road, you will come to the river.

HIKING AND BACKPACKING

From Fairbank the San Pedro Trail runs north for 2 miles along an old road to Willow Wash, with a side trail to Fairbank Cemetery. It is easy walking through desertscrub habitat. Willow Wash is a small riparian habitat. The trail loops back to Fairbank following the river. River walking in this section is easier than in more southern sections, since the river is wider and the riverbed more open, but there are sections of quicksand. A good one-night backpacking trip is from Fairbank to the Contention City ruins via the San Pedro Trail and the river, then back to Fairbank via the trails through Terrenate. There is an easy 1.2-mile trail to Terrenate from the Kellar Road parking lot. It winds through Chihuahuan desertscrub, and views from the bluff overlooking the river are lovely.

Hiking around the ciénega is more like bushwhacking except for the main road/trail that heads south from the parking lot to the river. A bushwhack up to the top of the small tablelands near the river provides excellent views of the valley. Backpackers should check with the BLM about the status of the Research Natural Area near the ciénega.

BIRDING

For information on birding around Fairbank, see chapter 5, "Birding."

Birding at the ciénega can be exciting because of the potential for specialty species. Near the parking lot, look in the creosote desertscrub for sage thrasher in the fall and winter, as well as sage, black-throated, white-crowned, lark, vesper, chipping, and Brewer's sparrows in winter. Residents include Abert's and canyon towhees, northern beardless-tyrannulet, and curve-billed thrasher. In the ciénega, keep your eyes high to spot white-tailed kite or prairie falcon, and look in the thickets for Lawrence's goldfinch and brown thrasher in migration. In winter, look for northern harrier, red-tailed hawk, Virginia rail, sora, song sparrow, Lincoln's sparrow, and eastern meadowlark. During summer, as many as seven breeding birds per acre are busy in the productive habitat of the ciénega; common yellowthroats are the most common breeder.

MOUNTAIN BIKING

The San Pedro Trail heads north from Fairbank for 2 miles to Willow Wash. This section is good out-and-back riding. Trails around Terrenate are not appropriate for mountain bikes. The road south from the ciénega to the river is a fast ride, about 3 miles one way.

HORSEBACK RIDING

Except for the ciénega (see "Mountain Biking," above), this section is fairly difficult for riding unless you know your way around or have access to gate keys. The Ironhorse Ranch (520-457-9361) offers trail rides and guides in this section of the RNCA. Contact the BLM for more information about access for horses in this section.

ARCHAEOLOGICAL SITES

The Grand Central Mill ruins are 1.5 miles north of Fairbank on the San Pedro Trail. This once-bustling ore mill was one of several that processed silver for the Tombstone mines, operating from about 1876 to 1886, when the mines flooded and were shut down. The mill, comprising fifteen iron stamping rods, is now reduced to only its stone foundation. The ore was ground into powder and mixed with river water and mercury; the silver adhered to mercury and was heated, causing the mercury to vaporize. Contention City, 4 miles north of Fairbank (follow the trail to Grand Central Mill ruins, then the river to the ruins, which are on the east side of the river), was one of six towns along the San Pedro where the mill workers lived. Contention City had two mills and a railroad depot. Many hundreds of people lived along the San Pedro around Fairbank and Contention City.

The Boston Mill ruins are about 2 miles south of Boquillas Ranch, on the old road running from Highway 82 south. There is an old diversion dam near the mill as well; the rock work is lovely—look for a petroglyph on one of the larger rocks.

The Presidio Santa Cruz de Terrenate is a well-marked, well-interpreted ruin perched on the western bank of the river. Begun in 1775 and abandoned four years later because of Apache Indian raids, the Spanish fort is a fascinating piece of American history. The views of Cochise Stronghold are beautiful.

Friends of the San Pedro River occasionally lead interpreted hikes through all of the archaeological sites along this section of the river (for contact information, see "Conservation Groups" section in Appendix 2, "Resources").

HANDICAPPED ACCESS

At Fairbank the trail to the river is packed dirt but is not suitable for wheelchairs because of the steep, sandy approach to the river. The ghost town itself is accessible for most wheelchairs. The trail to Terrenate is very rocky and eroded in a couple of places and not negotiable by most wheelchairs.

At St. David ciénega, during dry weather a sturdy motor-driven wheelchair with wide tires could navigate the main road south from the parking lot, but the ciénega is not accessible.

CAMPING
Tombstone, about 9 miles east of the river via Charleston Road or Highway 82, has a KOA campground. All overnight camping in the RNCA is by pack-in only, and permits are required. Camping is not allowed in the ciénega.

ACCOMMODATIONS
Sierra Vista has many hotels and restaurants; contact the Sierra Vista Chamber of Commerce Convention and Visitor's Bureau at 520-458-6940 or 800-288-3861. Tombstone, about 9 miles east of the river at Charleston Road or via Highway 82, has hotels and restaurants. Contact the Tombstone Chamber of Commerce at 520-457-9317.

OTHER ATTRACTIONS NEARBY
Train buffs will enjoy a four-hour, 54-mile roundtrip ride on the scenic San Pedro Southwestern Railroad, which offers excursions most Saturdays throughout the year. The train departs from Benson and wends its way along the river corridor to Charleston, with a stop on the way back at Fairbank for a barbecue and live music. For information, contact the railroad at 520-586-2266 or 800-269-6314.

Another nearby attraction is Tombstone, the famous site of the gunfight at the OK Corral. This "town too tough to die" is a well-preserved remnant of the late 1800s mining boom times in southern Arizona. There are museums, shops, saloons, and plenty of special events throughout the year. Contact the chamber of commerce at the number above.

Across the valley in the Whetstone Mountains is the new Kartchner Caverns State Park, home of many of the cave myotis bats that hunt insects along the river. For information, contact the park at 520-586-2283.

CHAPTER 7

BENSON TO THE GILA RIVER

Say No to Ecotourism, Yes to Mesquite · Resurrecting
Bingham Ciénega · How Phoenix Saved a Piece
of the San Pedro

I was intrigued by its title, "Mesquite: Regarding a Resource (A Workshop on the Ecological and Socio-Economic Values of Mesquite Trees and Their By-Products)." But when I called one of the organizers in the tiny community of Cascabel, on the lower San Pedro River about 25 miles north of Benson, and told her I was a journalist interested in writing about the event and the community, a definite chill translated over the fiber optics.

Barbara was honest with me: We don't want to be a destination for ecotourists, she said. We're a community of farmers and tradespeople and ranchers, and we don't want to develop a service economy for weekend warriors from the cities. Not long ago, she explained, the state's well-funded and powerful Off-Highway Vehicle Program planned to designate Pomerene, Cascabel, and San Pedro River Roads as an OHV trail and tried to romance the residents with descriptions of the riches they would reap when they built convenience marts and motels and cafes. Horrified, Cascabelians rallied, lobbied, and stopped the plan. They took the issue into their own hands and began to control their own future.

With the mesquite conference, a unique combination of talks by people who study as well as make their livings with—or despite—this intriguing plant, the community of Cascabel, nestled in one of the largest remaining mesquite bosques on the river, began another chapter in charting their future and the future of the San Pedro River.

I assured Barbara that I was interested in the conservation and natural history stories to be told at the conference, and she became excited and enthusiastic. So on a hot Friday in late September 1994, I head for Cascabel down the dusty, washboard-from-hell Cascabel Road, which parallels the river on its eastern side. As I near the community center, a few saguaros begin to show up on the hillsides—ambassadors of the southern edge of the Sonoran Desert. These columnar cacti around Cascabel, dipping their roots into the edge of the Chihuahuan Desert, can just barely tolerate the cold winters here, and many are spotted with the crusty black scabs of bacterial necrosis from past brushes with frozen skin.

I pull off to the right side of the road, which is lined by stark desertscrub and the steep, eroding slopes of an old downcut floodplain; smooth river rocks look back at me from the hills. On the left is a dense forest of huge mesquites, the size of which I have seen in only a few places in Arizona: here, and along the Gila River by Winkelman and a few parts of the Tanque Verde Wash east of Tucson. Several loitering Lucy's warblers trill their plaintive song. The Lucy's and its eastern cousin the prothonotary warbler are the only cavity nesters in their large family of wood warblers; the Lucy's is a desert specialist, found almost exclusively in mesquite forests. I hear a covey of Gambel's quail whistle and chitter and fuss, and two mule deer does bound across the road fifty feet up the road and crash into the dense understory thicket of wolfberry and acacia, running toward the river a quarter mile away.

The mature mesquite bosque, with its large trees and dense canopy, is an important component of the present riparian system. Like the continuous cottonwood-willow forests, the mesquite bosques are relatively new as habitats along the San Pedro, developing mostly after the last period of downcutting. But now bosques have become increasingly rare not because of weather and erosional events but because of woodcutting, land clearing, water pumping, and damming. Even here in Cascabel large swaths of bosque have been cleared for pecan orchards and alfalfa fields. The river from Benson to Cascabel runs intermittently, partly because of subsurface geologic features and partly because of agricultural pumping of the once-shallow floodplain aquifer. Along the river there are no long stretches of cottonwood-willow gallery forest, and there are quite a few non-native tamarisk groves.

The large Cascabel community center sits on a hill overlooking the bosque. Nearly a hundred people are already registering and taking their places at the rows of tables. I recognize some of the Southwest's foremost botanists and ecologists; there are also ranchers, land agency staff, conservationists, and writers; and pitching in at check-in and fixing food are community members and lots of kids. Many views are represented here, from those who would protect habitat at any cost to those who work to eradicate mesquite as an invasive pest.

Community activist Carlos Nagel, of Tucson and the International Sonoran Desert Alliance, opens the workshop by explaining that he works to help people find common ground. "We are in an unprecedented time," he says. "More and more 'different camps' are finding themselves more and more close, especially environmental vs. business people.

"The problem with communication is the illusion that it has occurred," he quips. "Today, we are going to use mesquite as a symbol, as a way of finding common ground together."

First up is the respected field botanist Ray Turner, formerly of the U.S. Geological Survey and author of *The Changing Mile,* a pictorial survey of habitat changes in the Southwest over the last century. Turner tells us the trees of the San Pedro bosques and surrounding deserts are velvet mesquite (*Prosopis velutina*), like all mesquites a member of the Pea Family, Fabaceae. The mesquite is a signature tree of the Arizona desert, but it thrives throughout the southwestern United States, and relatives of *Prosopis* grow all over the world. Velvet mesquites grow from southern Kansas to southeastern California and south well into Mexico, preferring elevations up to about 5,000 feet. Velvet mesquite was once considered a variety of the western honey mesquite (and is still thought to be so by some) but enjoys its own species status today. A relative newcomer to the Southwest, mesquite has been around Tucson for about 12,000 years and around the Big Bend area of Texas for about 40,000 years, Turner says.

Mesquites are distinctive, with very rough, peely dark brown, almost black, bark, many-forking trunks that can twist and droop in beautiful forms, spiny branches, and long leaves with many little ¼- to ½-inch-long paired leaflets called pinnae. In most of the Southwest but especially in areas with cold winters, such as in the San Pedro Valley, mesquites are deciduous. Their 4- to 8-inch-long yellow bean pods ripen in late summer, weighing down the branches like weeping willows.

Velvet mesquite can grow, in shrub form, in the hottest, driest deserts where scant rain falls, or it can enjoy abundant moisture along rivers, where it can grow up to 40 feet tall with a broad, spreading crown. Mesquite is famous for its long taproot—50 meters (about 150 feet) is the record—but a mesquite will also have an extensive lateral root system.

In May mesquites put forth long pale yellow catkins of fragrant flowers, which are visited by hundreds of insect species: bees, wasps, flies, ants, and butterflies and their caterpillars. Even hummingbirds will take a taste. Turner tells us that over 160 species of native solitary bees have been recorded as visitors at mesquite flowers, which offer a very high "nectar reward" (averaging 800 stamens per inflorescence, or catkin). A large mesquite tree may have hundreds of thousands of individual little flowers, but only an average of 26 flowers in 10,000 actually set fruit on a tree. That still means there are about 142,000 seeds—as much as 35 pounds—produced per tree per blooming period; occasionally, with well-timed rains, a mesquite will bloom twice per year.

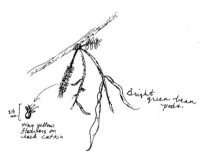

By summer the mesquites along the lower San Pedro droop, heavy with the 3–5-inch-long tawny beans; if you look closely at the flower catkins, you'll see little bean pods forming.

The mesquite beans, when ripe in mid- to late summer, provide food for many different types of wildlife, from insects to rodents to coyotes to javelinas. The seeds themselves are encased in the pod's starchy and sugary center; around the seed is a layer that is hard and leathery and impermeable to water. This coating must be broken in order for the seed to germinate. First the pods must be abraded, a process usually accomplished by being rushed along in a flash flood or run through the acid-rich digestive tracts of mammals. A substance in the pod that is released by the abrasion is believed to actually trigger germination. Along the upper San Pedro River valley, mesquites are subject to periodic deep freezes that kill younger trees and damage even the larger ones, which will drop dead limbs by the dozen.

According to riparian expert Julie Stromberg of Arizona State University, who speaks next, mesquite is a very important component in desert ecosystems because it has a symbiotic relationship with bacteria that grow on its roots. The bacteria, which also grow on roots of other plants in the legume family, produce nitrogen, a vital nutrient for most plants. So, a healthy mesquite bosque can be extremely important for enriching the soil along a river.

Bob Ohmart, also of ASU, next speaks of the tree-form mesquite (in the desertscrub, it rarely grows larger than a shrub) as being extremely important to wildlife. In a riparian area, the bosque provides vital herbaceous ground cover, a dense midlayer in the overall canopy, as well as patchiness in the habitat—that is, spaces of both open space and cover, which is more useful to more types of animals. A study comparing the mesquite bosques of the San Pedro River to the now-tamarisk-dominated lower Colorado River found that equal-sized study plots yielded 34 Bewick's wrens on the San Pedro versus 2 on the Colorado and 254 versus 38 Lucy's warblers. The only birds that came up with higher densities on the Colorado were mourning and white-winged doves.

"[Riparian areas] are an essential link for long-distance neotropical migrants and are important breeding habitat," Ohmart explains. "A 10-gram orange-crowned warbler puts on 5 grams of fat in a mesquite bosque, then flies almost 2,000 miles."

Mesquite was also one of the most important sources of living materials for early people of the Southwest: grocery, pharmacy, hardware, cosmetics, building materials, even sporting goods. In his talk ethnobotanist Richard Felger, founder of the Drylands Institute, calls the mesquite "an early K-mart for desert peoples." No other single plant provided so much for them. They used branches and trunks for building and fires, they made bows from the straightest limbs, croquetlike balls from thick branches, and baskets and medicine from the inner bark. The sap from the inner xylem provided black dye for baskets and hair (for men, not women), and the white gum was used as an eye medication. And of course the highly nutritious seedpods were a vital food resource, ground into a flour with a higher protein content than soybeans. Stone gyratory crushers many thousands of years old have been found in the Southwest.

Felger predicts that mesquite flour could become one of the world's most important food sources. A managed grove can yield as much as 1,000 pounds of beans per acre, he says. Few companies are currently exploiting mesquite as a food resource, however. Carlos Nagel has been trying for years to locally produce or import mesquite flour for sale in the

United States; only in 1998 did he finally find success, after tremendous wrangling with the Food and Drug Administration, importing the nutritious meal from South America under the name ProMez. I have baked with the flour, and it has a very strong taste that I find intriguing but my husband finds too sour. If used sparingly, mesquite flour can be an excellent protein supplement.

Cookbook author and desert foods specialist Carolyn Neithammer speaks about the structure of the mesquite bean pod and why it's so difficult to make the flour. The outer shell is tough fiber; the second layer is mostly sugar and has the most flavor; the third layer is the outer seed coat; the fourth, another very tough seed coat; and finally the fifth element is the true seed, where most of the protein is stored. The only way to get at that protein is with a commercial grinder. Still, she says, if you want to make your own flour, cook the beans at 150 to 160 degrees—a long and low heat—then cool them and grind them in the best grain grinder you can find (the seeds will chew up your blender or food processor blades); or break up the beans, boil them for half an hour, then mash them up and use the pulp like a gravy base.

The most common commercial use for mesquite is unfortunately the manufacture of charcoal. Over the last decade mesquite-flavored grilled meats have become *de rigueur* for yuppie gourmands, even those who send monthly checks to environmental organizations. As uneducated consumers, they do not realize that much of the supply for U.S. mesquite charcoal comes from Mexico, where mass harvesting of mesquite for charcoal has destroyed half a million acres of Sonoran Desert in Mexico, says speaker John Tuxill of Conservation International's Ironwood Alliance program. Speculators in Mexico buy up huge swaths of desert, have it bulldozed completely bare, sell off the mesquite and other woody trees (including ironwood) to charcoalers, then plant the bare land with South African grasses for grazing high numbers of cattle, which are sold as beef to U.S. consumers.

Over 160 species of Sonoran Desert plants, from saguaro cactus to night-blooming cereus, depend on mesquite and ironwood trees for regeneration. Additionally, ironwoods take between 100 and 500 years to reach full maturity. Ever eloquent when it comes to expressing conservation topics to the public, author and scientist Gary Nabhan recently said,

"Trees that germinated before Columbus arrived are being cut down for steakhouses.

"Although Sonora and Baja have the slowest rates of growth of anywhere in North America, over 95 percent of Mexico's charcoal exports to the U.S. and Canada are coming from these two states. It is more like mining than forestry, for these populations cannot recover during our lifetimes."

But with mesquite going for about thirty dollars a cord, the incentive in Mexico to curtail cutting just doesn't exist.

Ken Millhiser, of Lazzari Fuel Company in San Francisco, bravely takes the podium next. His company imports mesquite from Mexico as fuel for charcoal and chips. Recently Lazzari changed its harvesting policies and now works only with more ecologically balanced charcoal producers in Mexico; under scrutiny of Conservation International, Millhiser says his company is "looking for sustainability."

Among the last workshop participants to speak is Jan Wegenast of Cornville, Arizona. Wegenast has the perfect solution to the problem of mesquite clearcutting just for a cooking flavor. She discovered that a handful of dried mesquite bean pods soaked in water and then tossed onto a heat source just before barbecuing provides an even more intense mesquite flavor to foods than charcoal. After much trial and error getting her product packaged and marketed—the first batches she did not oven-dry, and the little bruchid beetle larvae hatched in the packages while on store shelves—the product is doing well at several dozen stores in the Southwest and West.

Wegenast says, "There is no way we can continue to keep meeting the demand for all the mesquite [charcoal] flavorings in all the different foods. Down the road there's going to be a problem of shortage."

Around Cascabel, there appears to be no shortage yet of mesquite. The conference ends with a delicious dinner, including some mesquite-flour muffins and cookies. I eavesdrop on a few nearby dinner conversations; several people are helping Jan Wegenast with some new marketing ideas; Richard Felger is describing a possible federal project to introduce a European insect to the Southwest that kills tamarisk trees, which are a threat to riparian forests; and four ranchers compare notes on what is the best herbicide for killing mesquite.

Leaving the conference and heading back to Tucson over Redington Pass the next morning, I drive through the heart of the bosque and I remember my childhood spent building forts in the scratchy arms of mesquites, the way the light filtered through the feathery leaves, the sticky dark sap on my clothes, the tangy taste of beans chewed while we lay on our backs and watched puffy late-summer clouds soar overhead.

FOUR YEARS LATER, in mid-November, I drive through Cascabel on my way to Bingham ciénega, a Pima County–owned preserve comanaged by the Nature Conservancy. More people have moved to Cascabel; a number of families have bought weekend homes here, and it is becoming popular for the young, socially and environmentally conscious. Nearby a Quaker-oriented sustainable living community is slowly gaining steam; founders of the Saguaro-Juniper Project bought a cattle ranch, continue to grow organic beef, and are selling off highly deed-restricted parcels to like-minded people, some of whom are building homes in the high desert on the eastern slopes of the San Pedro watershed.

Near Redington the road crosses to the west side of the river on a big concrete bridge. Although well into November, frost has only just touched the river bottom and the trees are just now showing faint yellow-gold leaves. Just past the bridge is a row of battered mailboxes and a small driveway disappearing into a mesquite bosque. I turn here and after winding through the bosque come upon an old shotgun-style, well-kept ranch house surrounded by barns and sheds and the trappings of farming and ranching. This is the old Bingham homestead, the home where Lois Bingham Kelly grew up and now lives, after raising her children, with her husband Jack Kelly. Lois's family has worked the land in the San Pedro valley since 1927; family members still farm and ranch down the river from the Kellys. In 1989 the Nature Conservancy helped the Pima County Flood Control District negotiate the purchase of the 285-acre property, including Bingham ciénega and adjacent agricultural fields, from the Kellys, who kept their homestead and cattle leases. The Nature Conservancy worked out a twenty-five-year management agreement and restoration plan with the county.

I park my truck next to a well-used tractor, say a wary hello to a large and silent rottweiler mix who is eyeing me from the shed, and walk to the kitchen door. The Kellys meet me at the door, and introductions are made. With them is Kim Fox, TNC's restoration coordinator, whom I arranged to meet for a tour of the ciénega. Kim is fair of complexion and hair, is quite tall, and has a bright, open, competent demeanor that must go a long way toward acceptance in the communities where she works on sensitive habitats amid sensitive feelings toward urban-driven conservation programs.

As we walk out into the yard, Belle the rottweiler is transformed into a silly, wriggling bundle of joy at seeing Kim. The bounding dog joins us as we head off toward the ciénega through an old wire gate. Kim tells me the property harbors at least five distinct habitats: the wetland-ciénega, the cottonwood-willow gallery forest, sacaton grassland, and mesquite bosque, as well as true Sonoran Desert with mesquites, creosote bushes, triangle-leaf bursage, and saguaros. We walk northwest from the house, stepping into a shady grove of tall, mature trees—walnuts, velvet ashes, cottonwoods, netleaf hackberries—and an understory of saplings of the same species along with shrubs such as Goodding willow and buttonwillow. Underfoot is a spongy layer of decaying leaves and drooping, red-kissed rumex and *yierba mansa*. Cattle have been successfully excluded here for ten years, unlike at St. David ciénega where there is frequent cattle trespass, and the structure of the wetland is more natural. There is a sweet, sharp smell in the cool and damp air.

Kim stops at a small spring, one of several sources of water for the ciénega. The small pool is only several inches to half a foot deep and bubbles for ten feet before going underground again, to surface elsewhere in the ciénega, which is sandwiched between San Pedro River Road and the agricultural fields along the river. The whole property here is just over ⅜ of a mile wide; the ciénega about ⅛ of a mile wide. Duckweed floats on the top of the water, and around the edges are native cattails, rushes, sedges, and dense thickets of Goodding willows. The smell here is of mild decay—the signature smell of a ciénega.

We follow the flow of the water north about 100 yards out to the main ciénega, which comprises about 27 acres of pools that are obscured from our view by cattails and rushes. This is one of the original, pre-entrenchment ciénegas on the San Pedro River; it is far enough away from the main river flow, on an ancient floodplain terrace, that it escaped subduction during the period when the river ate deep at its own roots over a century ago. At one time during the early part of this century a large berm held the ciénega back closer to the road, near the pool where we stood, but ten years ago a breach let the wetland "escape" and it reclaimed a large part of the agricultural fields that have been cultivated here for about one hundred years. The plan, Kim explains, is to further that expansion with an impressive restoration plan.

As we speak Jim Kelly arrives on the old tractor, which is equipped with a mowing blade. He gets to work in the field adjacent to the ciénega, taking down the invading shrubs and chopping up the bermuda grass so that willows and other wetland vegetation can take root. The Kellys help a tremendous amount with the restoration, Kim explains. Even their grandchildren pitch in.

The restoration plan for the property is ambitious, to say the least. In the last decade natural reclamation has advanced about as far as it can in the wetland. As we pick our way across an old agricultural field to the first replanting site, Kim explains that exotic weeds such as bermuda grass and Johnson grass, the lack of natural overbank flooding, and reduced water availability at the surface have prevented natural reestablishment of the sacaton grassland, mesquite bosque, and cottonwood-willow forest habitats.

Using a University of Arizona study that, among other things, mapped soil moisture and groundwater gradients in the preserve, Kim drew up a replanting plan based on surface-to-ground-water needs of the keystone plants of each habitat. Julia Fonseca, project liaison with the county, studied an 1879 General Land Office survey of the area to determine the extent of preclearing habitat types. For the first phase of the restoration, three planting zones were chosen, one each for sacaton grassland, mesquite bosque, and cottonwood-willow deciduous riparian forest. The plan prescribes every action in the process, from growing out the seedlings (including evaluating which methods work best, so that future restorations on other preserves can benefit) to pest control and irrigation to monitoring plants, animals, groundwater, and climate.

The 23 acres of new grassland will be planted with 80,000 sacaton seedlings (*Sporobolus wrightii*) as well as 500 seedlings each of knotgrass (*Paspalum distichum*), saltgrass (*Distichilus spicatum*), sideoats grama

(*Bouteloua curtipendula*), vine mesquite grass (*Panicum obtusum*), and sand dropseed (*Sporobolus cryptandrus*).

The broadleaf deciduous riparian forest area, comprising 11 acres, will be planted with 1,400 Goodding willow (*Salix gooddingii*) saplings, 100 Frémont cottonwoods (*Populus fremontii*), 500 buttonwillow shrubs (*Cephalanthus occidentalis*), 450 velvet ash trees (*Fraxinus velutina*), 400 netleaf hackberries (*Celtis laevifolia*), and 150 Arizona black walnuts (*Juglans major*). Kim says that willow is the main woody species of the deciduous forest in the ciénega because it is typically the most abundant species at the margin of low-elevation ciénega and can tolerate the shallow groundwater depths more than the cottonwoods, ashes, and walnuts.

The 16-acre mesquite bosque area, which already has some natural mesquite recruitment, will receive 900 *Prosopis velutina* saplings. In a fairly bold move, the plan calls for using cattle to further propagate mesquite in the target area, since mesquite seeds need to be scarified by flood scour or run through animals' digestive systems before they can germinate. A temporary electric fence will corral a high number of cattle, which will be fed mesquite beans. The combination of grazing on exotic weeds, deposition (with manure as fertilizer) of processed mesquite seeds, and soil disturbance, a sort of nonmechanical tilling, should be a recipe for successful establishment of a mesquite bosque. Preserve staff will hand-thin the new growth.

Walking across the first of the planted sacaton fields, Kim explains that labor for the plantings comes from volunteers, many of them schoolchildren from St. David, Benson, San Manuel, Oracle, and Mammoth, as well as the Kellys and their family. Kim tells me of one young girl who is in a special needs program and helped plant this field, which began choked with weeds. She was able to return after the first planting and see the plants, now ten times bigger, and got really excited about making a difference.

Money for the project comes from numerous grants, including the Arizona Water Protection Fund, the Partnership Program with U.S. Fish and Wildlife, Arizona Game and Fish, and the Wallace Genetic Fund, as well as TNC and community volunteers.

The field we're in is studded with about 20,000 new sacaton plants, which were planted in August as tiny seedlings in 2-inch mulch containers. After a wet summer and nice warm fall, the plants are now 12 to 18 inches tall, and well over half are blooming. Kim is ecstatic with the survivorship, which is about 97 percent. Weed control is painstaking, though. The new grass is planted in rows so that a mower can take down weeds in between, and staff spot-spray with Roundup and hand pull what can't be mowed. Kim is also experimenting with permaculture techniques for weed control, including using cardboard and mulch. In one corner of the field she laid down several layers of cardboard, and mulch on top of that, before planting the sacaton. Although labor intensive, the technique is worth it, Kim feels, because the sacaton grass in this section is the most robust.

"I'm trying to use low-disturbance methods," she explains. "The more you disturb the land the more weeds are a problem. The land is trying to heal itself. To go back to ground zero [using herbicides and plowing]—that's going back to where we don't want to be."

Still, another of the sacaton fields will be planted using just such "ground-zero" methods, so that each method might be evaluated for success. Whichever works best will be used in the future, Kim says.

Once the sacaton grassland is established, fire will be used as a management tool, Kim says. Sacaton thrives on fire, which adds important nutrients to the soil and takes out the accumulation of thatch from older plants, invigorating growth.

As we walk back to the trucks at the end of our tour, Kim muses about the project: "I think [the restoration] will have a big effect on the community. We're not just planting sacaton, but the concept of land conservation and stewardship. It's got other community members thinking about planting sacaton as erosion control.

"I think it's very powerful."

A HUNDRED FIFTY miles northwest of the lower San Pedro River live over 2 million people. Many have lush green lawns, swimming pools, and decorative fountains at their homes, and many regularly play golf at one of dozens of courses on miles of greens around the Valley of the Sun, also known as Phoenix, Glendale, Tempe, and Scottsdale. They live in the desert but act like it's as wet as the Pacific coast. To help preserve this illusion, besides the lawns and water features they run air conditioners in summer, electricity courtesy of hydroelectric plants at reservoirs around the state.

To help meet these needs, in the early 1990s the Bureau of Reclamation decided it needed to raise the height of Roosevelt Dam, on the Gila River, by 70 feet, thus equally raising the level of Roosevelt Lake. One major problem reared its ugly head: the higher water level would obliterate a large swath of Goodding willow habitat and with it the nesting sites for numerous federally endangered southwestern willow flycatchers.

But rather than derail the project, U.S. Fish and Wildlife struck a curious deal with Bureau of Reclamation: the bureau could destroy the Roosevelt habitat if it bought and preserved an equal amount of identical habitat elsewhere. So in 1994 the bureau, with the help of the Nature Conservancy (TNC), identified acreage along the lower San Pedro River, near its confluence with the Gila River, as an ideal mitigation site, complete with willows and willow flycatchers. The Nature Conservancy helped negotiate the purchase of the property, but the bureau did not want to manage the land, so the purchase money as well as an endowment to cover management costs was granted to TNC by the bureau, and a twenty-year management plan hammered out, with TNC working on habitat restoration and U.S. Fish and Wildlife overseeing the willow flycatchers.

On my only visit to Dudleyville, I was lucky enough to spy this little willow flycatcher for just a few seconds before he flitted off upriver

A light rain is leaving muddy prints on my dusty windshield as I near San Manuel on the river road that runs from Cascabel to Highway 77. The weather is schizophrenic today; half the sky is sunny and the other half, over me, gunmetal gray and weepy, a stiff wind blowing clouds and rain and ravens across the sky. To my right the land drops away a half mile to the San Pedro, which winds resolutely north ever nearer its confluence with the Gila River. A huge mesquite bosque stretches for several miles on the east side of the river between San Manuel and Mammoth.

At San Manuel I pass the large copper complex, which processes ore from the nearby strip mines. Over a square mile of tailings ponds sit poised, oily green and glistening, a mile or so from the river. Today the smelter is not running, so the telltale black plume does not rise from the stacks.

I am already half an hour late for a meeting with Steve Huckett, manager of the Nature Conservancy's Lower San Pedro River Preserve at Dudleyville. I pass an empty ore truck and risk a speeding ticket as I zip through the notorious speed trap of Mammoth, over the dry bed of the San Pedro, then the trickling waters of Aravaipa Creek, and on to Dudleyville where a dirt side road drops into the floodplain. The closer the road gets to the river, the more densely packed are the young willows and cottonwoods; as my truck splashes across the now-flowing San Pedro— thanks to the additional water of Aravaipa Creek, which accounts for 70 to 80 percent of the surface flow to the confluence—I can see but a few feet into the dark green thickets, which are growing back after a very large flood in 1993.

I arrive at the preserve an hour late, cross a large abandoned farm field that slopes gently down to a pecan orchard, a large pond, and the river, and find Steve waiting for me in one of several old farm buildings that serve as offices, staff quarters, and workshops. Steve is easy-going and friendly, and he immediately puts me at ease about being late. After a few minutes of chatting we agree to head over to the mining town of Kearney for chile burgers and fries at the old cafe.

Waiting for our cholesterol bombs, sipping iced tea, Steve tells me the story of the mitigation purchase, which was finalized in 1997. He says that the mitigation property includes 660 acres around the headquarters and another 180 acres four miles farther north at the confluence. The parcels are separated by private, state, and Asarco-owned land. I ask about the intermittent riparian habitat that stretches between Benson and the confluence. He says that vegetation intervals closely correlate to surface flow, with the exception of areas that burned such as the site about four miles south of Dudleyville where about half the old cottonwoods in a large grove are dead. The Nature Conservancy owns the water rights on their acreage; upstream of TNC 's property Asarco owns water rights to the PZ Ranch, where wells pump water to 4-foot-diameter supply pipes every day of the year, 24 hours a day.

Like most of the large landowners along the lower San Pedro, the former owners of the preserve ran cattle as well as farmed the land. When the economy toughened, they tried many different schemes, from pecan orchards to aquaculture. At one time there were 11 ponds stocked with bass, sunfish, and channel cats, which were sold as stockers or fished on site by fishermen who paid for the privilege. The big flood in 1993 wiped out all but one pond, and after that the family abandoned farming and took up trucking.

Restoration plans for the property will keep Steve, who has been site manager for the preserve since its acquisition, busy for many years. Steve will oversee grading the old ponds back to their natural topography and drainage patterns; taking out the pecan orchard; fencing 4½ miles of the property boundary along the river to keep out cattle and all-terrain vehicles; establishing monitoring programs for water and wildlife; and developing an experimental agricultural field where TNC and other researchers can test methods for growing out native plants such as sacaton for revegetation programs.

After lunch we head back to the preserve and lounge around a big porch overlooking the remaining pond. A belted kingfisher hovers like a hummingbird over the water, taking aim on a hapless fish before plunging into the water. He comes out empty-beaked and perches on a nearby wire, preening. A vermilion flycatcher calls nearby, and overhead a kestrel passes. The orchard removal project, Steve explains, will be a joint project with Kearney's Ray High School science club. The kids will cut and sell the wood, and the proceeds will be used for science field trips and classroom supplies. Steve, whose teenage son attends Ray High School, is a volunteer advisor with the club. When he first got involved there were 35 kids in the club; the following year there were 110 kids, most of whom will get a chance to work on the preserve and learn conservation biology and restoration first-hand. Science teacher Jim Nyhoff claims that Steve, with his easy manner and apparently boundless energy, is the catalyst for the renewed interest in the club.

As we wind up our meeting, Steve points out Bassett Peak across the valley, location of the Muleshoe Preserve, a joint-management area for TNC, BLM, and Coronado National Forest in the Galiuro Mountains. Hot Springs Wash, the main drainage of the Muleshoe Preserve, joins the San Pedro near Cascabel. The Nature Conservancy also manages a preserve at lower Aravaipa Creek, the most important tributary on the lower San

Pedro. In 1998 the owners of Buehman Canyon, a large drainage feeding the San Pedro on the northeast slope of the Catalina Mountains, donated the canyon to TNC. And best news of all: it was just announced the week I meet Steve that TNC is involved in acquiring the Bellota Ranch in Redington Pass, an irreplaceable 25,000-acre open space, wildlife corridor, and watershed linking the Catalina Mountains, the Rincon Mountains, Saguaro National Park, the lower San Pedro, and the Galiuro Mountains.

It's all about connections—corridors, Steve says. The Nature Conservancy began as an organization that bought and sealed off discrete chunks of endangered habitat, but over the last decade it has committed to preserving the bigger picture so that its preserves don't become just living relics, mere islands of dying species.

We sit in silence for a few minutes. I shade my eyes and look from the Galiuros to the Catalinas, imagining the far shoulder of the Rincons, and the connections between them all to the place we sit and beyond: the Whetstones, Huachucas, Sierra Madres, the Sea of Cortés. Migratory birds and giant cottonwoods, bears and lions, fish and beavers, drinking water and clean air.

I say goodbye to Steve, having taken up too much of his busy day. I drive over to Kearney to look for the General Kearney Inn, where Steve says there are photos of the river from around 1904, but I can't find it. Instead I pass Ray High School, and it dawns on me that the links in the ecological chain of the San Pedro are growing each year—that the links, those myriad stories that make up a river, are not just animals and habitat. They are human as well. The 110 kids of the Ray High School Science Club, the kids in the schools at Oracle and Benson and Mammoth who work at Bingham ciénega, and the Sierra Vista volunteers who lead nature walks on the upper San Pedro all represent stories that are part of the river and also are key to its future. So are the ecologists and birders and ranchers and farmers and Sierra Vistans and Phoenicians. Only time will tell if the connections these stories represent are strong enough to save this last, great free-flowing river in the Southwest.

❧ Exploration Guide ❧

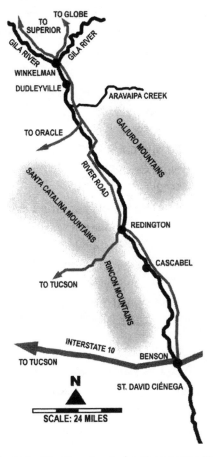

St. David to Gila River San Pedro River Access Map

HIGHLIGHTS

Several scenic drives, suitable for trucks and sport utilities, crisscross the area, and there is good camping in nearby Coronado National Forest. There is an ecotourism-friendly bed and breakfast/guest ranch in Oracle.

ACCESS

From Benson to the Gila River, the land along the San Pedro River is nearly all privately owned and not open to public access.

RECREATION

Cascabel and River Roads extend from Benson to San Manuel but are very rough and suitable mostly for trucks and sport utilities. Fall and spring are the best seasons for this drive, but they are also dusty seasons. Redington Road, which begins in east Tucson at the end of Tanque Verde Road and winds over Redington Pass to the San Pedro at River Road, is also very rough but does cross public land. There are many opportunities for hiking, camping, backpacking, mountain biking, and hunting in the Redington Pass area. Coronado National Forest is the primary land owner; 300 W. Congress, Tucson AZ 85701; 520-670-4552.

The Redington Land and Cattle Company offers horseback rides and jeep tours in the Aravaipa, Cascabel, and Galiuro Mountains areas; HC-1, Box 730, Benson, AZ 85602; 520-212-5555.

Each fall, the artists of Cascabel host an art fair for early Christmas shoppers. Contact the Benson Chamber of Commerce for dates and information (see "Other Attractions Nearby," below).

The Arizona Nature Conservancy operates preserves at Bingham ciénega, Aravaipa Creek, and Dudleyville. None are open to the public, but visits for groups may be scheduled. Contact TNC at 300 E. University Blvd., Suite 230, Tucson AZ 85705; 520-622-3861.

ACCOMMODATIONS

Cherry Valley Ranch in Oracle is a small bed-and-breakfast operation with a special interest in natural history and recreation. The ranch can help arrange visits to the Nature Conservancy sites and also schedule horseback riding trips on the river. For information call 520-896-9639.

See below for information on Benson, which is about 20 miles south of Cascabel on I-10.

OTHER ATTRACTIONS NEARBY

Benson is a good hub for exploring the lower San Pedro River. There are several motels and chain hotels either in Benson or just west of town at Highway 90, where all the service businesses are located for Kartchner Caverns State Park. This new state park, just a few miles south of Benson on Highway 90, is a spectacular look at one of the best-preserved limestone caves in North America; for information call 520-586-2283.

Don't miss the Horseshoe Cafe in "downtown" Benson (just east of Safeway, which is at Ocotillo Road), which cooks up killer green chile cheeseburgers (not to be confused with chili burgers) and home fries. And a hidden jewel, just 2½ miles north of Benson on Ocotillo Road (I-10 exit 304), is Winifred Bundy's magical Singing Wind Bookshop (520-586-2425), tucked into the front rooms of her working ranchhouse on the banks of the San Pedro River. Winifred often staffs the small but excellent shop, which offers the best selection of Western and Southwestern literature and nonfiction in the country.

For more information on lodging and recreation in the Benson area, contact the Benson Chamber of Commerce at 520-586-2842.

SPECIES LISTS

❧ HABITATS AND COMMON PLANTS OF THE SAN PEDRO RIVER

In a Southwestern riparian area the distribution of plants, and therefore the animals to some degree, is controlled by the ebb and flow of the river itself. This appendix, based on David E. Brown's *Biotic Communities, Southwestern United States and Northwestern Mexico* and information from the Bureau of Land Management, describes the basic plant habitats as they are arranged along a river, particularly the San Pedro River in the conservation area, referred to as SPRNCA (San Pedro Riparian National Conservation Area) or RNCA. The mosaic of these communities is what constitutes the greater riparian ecosystem. Each community description begins with a list, including

Mature woody plants—common species of mature shrubs or trees found in this habitat.

Herbaceous plants—common species of annuals, perennials, grasses, and other "forbs" found in this habitat.

Indicator wildlife—common or significant species of wildlife that depend exclusively or to a large degree on this habitat for breeding, food, or shelter.

Example in the SPRNCA—names a place where there is a good example of the habitat type (of course, these habitats occur throughout the RNCA).

These are not complete lists of flora and fauna of these communities; rather, they are the species that best typify the community for identification. The first time a plant is listed, its scientific name is also listed; scientific names of birds, mammals, arthropods, reptiles, and amphibians are not listed.

Use these descriptions as your beginning "dictionary" for getting to know the language of the plants and animals of the San Pedro Riparian National Conservation Area. Following this section are more complete lists of birds, mammals, and reptiles and amphibians. See the "Suggested Reading" section at the end of the book for suggestions of specific field guides and books about riparian ecology.

Riparian—Within or along the Banks of the River Corridor

Although "riparian area" usually is used to describe the whole ecosystem—all the habitats combined—of a watercourse or lake, for the purposes of this chapter and this section, the riparian habitat zone encompasses those areas within or along the banks of the river. It can be split into aquatic, semiaquatic, broad-leaved deciduous forest, scrublands, and mesquite bosque communities. Some of these communities can be further defined by subcommunities, such as the submerged aquatic community or the strand community, below.

Aquatic and Semiaquatic

River, Marshland, and Pond Submergent—Plants Living Entirely (or Nearly So) Submerged Underwater.
Aquatic habitats along a Southwestern river include the river itself; adjacent ponds formed by old oxbow bends in the river that become cut off from the main river flow but maintain aboveground water; and ciénegas, or natural springs, near the river. These latter are often just referred to as marshlands. All of these habitats are dependent on the same water table for their existences. Submergent communities are those that occur in or directly on the surface of ponds, ciénegas (marshlands), and rivers.

The water in the main river channels of Southwestern rivers is often intermittent, retreating belowground for a few hundred yards or a mile or more before resurfacing. It is usually shallow and therefore, except where it is shaded all day by overhanging branches, quite warm. The plants and animals that live in the river must be pretty hardy—able to withstand warm and often turbid water, periodic floods, or no water at all. Native fishes such as the longfin dace and desert sucker are adapted to withstand several hours of total stranding when riverflow stops during midday heat in summer; they hide out under damp mats of algae or other plants. Floods and muddy water are no problem for them. Other native river fauna survive by retreating to the shrinking pools and ponds. The common aquatic plants are just as hardy.

The most common aquatic plants in the river and ponds are called thallophytes, a group that includes algae, bacteria, and fungi. Many of these lower plants are single celled and microscopic. The bacteria are important reducers—they feed on dead plants and animals, and return vital nitrogen, sulphur, and phosphorus to the nutrient cycle. Algae is nonvascular, contains chlorophyll, reproduces cell by cell, and is very important as one of the primary base foods for the entire food pyramid, providing grazing fodder for the countless little animals that are eaten by larger animals, which are eaten by larger animals, and so on. Also, filaments of algae joined together in long, waving "beards" are often seen in the river; these are like miniature kelp forests—an important habitat for aquatic animals of all sizes. Thallophytes also contribute vital oxygen to the river water, which aquatic animals depend on. From tadpoles to grown frogs and toads, from insect larvae to flies and beetles, and from snakes and turtles to mammals and birds, thousands of species depend on the microscopic but complex aquatic forests of pond and river water.

Larger vascular plants we might see underwater or on the surface of the water, in ponds and ciénegas, include water ferns, poolmat, pepperworts, pondweeds, and duckweeds. Duckweeds are so named because waterfowl feed on the lush, floating carpet of small leaves. Duckweeds are among the smallest known flowering plants, but their tiny flowers are rarely borne; instead, they usually reproduce vegetatively. Insects and their larvae, and small vertebrates such as tadpoles, take cover and feed on and around the submerged stems, leaves, and roots of aquatic vascular plants.

HERBACEOUS PLANTS: algae, duckweed (*Lemna gibba*), Mexican water fern (*Azolla mexicana*), hairy pepperwort (*Marsilea vestita*), pondweeds (*Potamogeton* spp.), common poolmat (*Zannichellia palustris*)

INDICATOR WILDLIFE: breeding and feeding—Sonoran mud turtle, Texas spiny softshell turtle, bullfrog, Woodhouse's toad, nymphs of dragonflies and other flying insects, water boatmen, giant water bugs, predaceous diving beetles, crayfish (introduced); **fishes in river and permanent large ponds**—longfin dace, desert sucker, channel catfish (introduced), bluegill (introduced), mosquitofish (introduced)

EXAMPLE IN THE SPRNCA: Kingfisher Pond, near the San Pedro House, and St. David ciénega

Marshland and Pond Emergent—Plants Rooted in Water or in Very Damp Soil at Water's Edge, with Most Parts above Water.

The moist, nutrient-rich shallows and water's-edge habitats of ponds and ciénegas are vital nurseries for young riparian woody plants, as well as feeding and breeding grounds for hundreds of species of large and small vertebrates.

Most notable among the plants are the aquatic emergents—those that grow with their roots in water, or in saturated soil, but most of their stems and leaves above the water. The larger, more conspicuous of these are the rushes, cattails, bulrushes, and sedges. In fact, when we think of marshland habitats, we usually picture a calm pond that is clear of emergent vegetation in the center, with dense, tall cattails and rushes lining the shores, sometimes even completely surrounding the pond and making human or other predator access difficult. That's precisely why so many birds, especially blackbirds, use these emergent plants for cover while feeding and build their nests in them.

The protected and nutrient-rich habitat of an emergent marshland is vital for nurturing young seedlings of key riparian species such as Goodding willow. Birds such as willow flycatchers and black phoebes hunt from and breed in the young woody vegetation, and bird-eating snakes such as whipsnakes hunt there as well.

In the Southwest, riverine marshland eventually fills in with accumulated detritus, which forms soil, and in place of a marshland grows a mature riparian forest, which will be replaced by mesquite bosque, and eventually scrubland. If the water table rises again, a marshland will begin anew.

WOODY SEEDLINGS: seep willow (*Baccharis salicifolia*), Goodding willow (*Salix gooddingii*)

HERBACEOUS PLANTS: Torrey's rush (*Juncus torreyi*), wire rush (*Juncus balticus*), spike rush (*Eleocharis macrostachya*), bulrush (*Scirpus acutus*), giant bulrush (*Scirpus californicus*), cattail (*Typha domingensis*), sedge (*Carex chihuahensis*), aster (*Aster subulatus*), knotgrass (*Paspalum distichum*), willow smartweed (introduced) (*Polygonum lapathifolium*), pinkweed (*Polygonum pensylvanicum*), water smartweed (*Polygonum punctatum*), and water speedwell (*Veronica anagallis-aquatica*)

INDICATOR WILDLIFE: **breeding**—red-winged blackbird, common yellowthroat; **feeding**—black-bellied whistling duck, marsh wren, great blue heron, green kingfisher, black phoebe; beaver

EXAMPLE IN THE SPRNCA: St. David ciénega, and Kingfisher Pond, near the San Pedro House

Strands—Alternately Dry/Deluged Sand or Gravel Bars within the River Channel.

It's hard to think of the sand and gravel bars of a river as a habitat. But many plants and animals have adapted to use these seemingly sterile and definitely transient life zones in a variety of ways.

Plants we think of as weeds thrive in strands: seep willow, burrobush, amaranths, ground cherries, and cockleburs. These are hardy plants that grow fast and hang on tight in floods. Seep willows are so pliable they can endure floods of surprising magnitude; after the water recedes, they pop right back up and keep growing or, if their branches are buried, sprout again from the buried limbs. These strand-adapted plants are vital to slowing the flow of water, mitigating the rapid changes of the riverbed topography, and adding to the riverwater decaying organic matter, which is one of the building blocks of aquatic life. Hundreds of species of beetles and bugs that feed on—or reduce—both living and dead plant matter, especially flood debris, are also vital to the strand system.

The strand is a popular foraging and resting zone for many riparian animals. Spadefoot toads hunt for terrestrial and aquatic insects while black-necked garter snakes hunt for toads. Spiny softshell turtles not only bask in the sun on the moist strand edges, they lay their eggs in the soft, wet sand. Throughout the day killdeer dart across the gravelly stretches looking for insects, while at night migrating waterfowl may hunker down to roost among the vegetation. But by far the most remarkable strand-adapted animal is the longfin dace, a native to the San Pedro River watershed. This little inch-long fish, when faced with the daily drying of its stream during the hot, dry summer months, will slip under the drying but still-moist mats of thick algae and survive for hours in the barest amount of moisture. So desert-stream-adapted is the species that only one female need survive a drought cycle—she can lay enough eggs after the river fills up again to reestablish a small population.

WOODY SEEDLINGS AND PLANTS: seep willow, burrobush (*Hymenoclea monogyra*), rabbitbrush (*Chrysothamnus* spp.)

HERBACEOUS PLANTS: amaranths (*Amaranthus* spp.), ground cherries (*Solanum* spp.), sunflowers (*Helianthus* spp.), sacred datura (*Datura meteloides*), rumex (*Rumex* spp.), rabbitsfoot grass (*Polypogon monspeliensis*), cocklebur (*Xanthium strumarium*), cowpen daisy (*Verbesina enceloides*)

INDICATOR WILDLIFE: **breeding**—northern rough-winged swallow (cutbanks), spiny softshell turtle (egg deposition); **feeding**—killdeer, fungus beetles and plant bugs, raccoon, black-necked garter snake, spadefoot toad; **roosting**—great blue heron; **refuge**—longfin dace (can survive short dry periods under damp algae); **basking**—spiny softshell turtle

EXAMPLE IN THE SPRNCA: throughout the riverbed

Riparian Understory

Scrubland.
Scrubland is a bit of a catchphrase to indicate the dense thickets of small to medium-large shrubs and young trees that make up the understory of a riparian forest. Although some plant community classification systems include 10 or more scrubland types for Southwestern riparian systems, defined by specific plant associations such as burroweed-rabbitbrush-

mesquite or sapling-willow-cottonwood, we have elected to stick to one major type—the thicketlike scrubland itself (sometimes referred to as thornscrub, or shrubland).

If you picture a cottonwood-willow forest or mesquite bosque as a kind of natural highrise apartment complex, the scrubland understory creates the second to middle "floors" of the vertically stacked foraging and nesting habitats, after the leaf-litter ground floor. The density and diversity of the understory—with dozens of closely growing woody and herbaceous plant species—are among the more important features of a riparian forest, providing protective cover for animals while they feed and raise their young, as well as plenty of plant and animal food.

When scrubland understories are permanently removed in a riparian community, such as by grazing cattle, a big chunk of the food chain disappears with them—the insects, birds, reptiles, and mammals that depended on the scrublands and each other. The ground no longer benefits from all the leaf litter and animal detritus, and it becomes bare, hard-packed, and sterile. No seedlings can sprout, and water runs off and away instead of soaking into the local water table. The cycle of drying that begins is sometimes nonending if the cattle are not removed.

Many animals are scrubland specialists. Towhees are excellent bird examples. The spotted, green-tailed, and canyon towhees are most often seen flitting around low in the understories or scratching around in the leaf litter—they are first- and second-floor dwellers of the forest apartment complex. Above them, in the middle floors, are where birds such as Lucy's warblers and blue grosbeaks feed and breed. Snakes such as Sonoran whipsnakes specialize in hunting for birds and their eggs in low thickets in the first through middle stories. And many butterflies and moths lay their eggs, and their larvae develop, in the foliage of scrublands. Gray hawks specialize in hunting the reptiles and small mammals of the scrublands and bosques. When the BLM acquired the San Pedro RNCA in 1986, there were just nine pairs of breeding gray hawks along the river—the last of these magnificent birds known in our region. Cattle grazing along the river corridor was still common, and the understory virtually nonexistent in most places. By 1993 the breeding pairs had doubled to 18, and by 1996 there were 25 pairs. Today these hawks are more common along the San Pedro than anywhere else in the Southwest.

Historically, large and secretive vertebrates such as jaguars and ocelots most likely depended on the thick cover afforded by scrublands for moving around their ranges, which probably once included southern Arizona.

SEEDLING AND MATURE WOODY PLANTS: Frémont cottonwood, Goodding willow, seep willow, desert broom (*Baccharis sarothroides*), burrobush, rabbitbrush, velvet mesquite, desert hackberry (*Celtis pallida*), catclaw acacia (*Acacia greggii*), wolfberries (*Lycium* spp.), buttonwillow (*Cephalanthus occidentalis*), desert willow (*Chilopsis linearis*), tamarisk (introduced)

HERBACEOUS PLANTS: spiny aster (*Aster spinosus*), cup grass (*Eriochloa* spp.), ragweeds (*Ambrosia* spp.), sunflowers, sand dropseed (*Sporobolus cryptandrus*), spiny aster, Canada wild rye (*Elymus canadensis*), horsetail (*Equisetum laevigatum*), cocklebur, cowpen daisy

INDICATOR WILDLIFE: breeding—Crissal thrasher, yellow-breasted chat, Abert's towhee, yellow-billed cuckoo, willow flycatcher, blue grosbeak; feeding—Lucy's warbler, Madrean alligator lizard, side-blotched lizard, Sonoran whipsnake, beaver, jaguar (potentially historically)

EXAMPLE IN THE SPRNCA: between Kingfisher Pond and the river, near the San Pedro House

Riparian Canopy

Mature Cottonwood-Willow Forest.
The upper canopies of the mature cottonwood-willow forest represent the top floors and "penthouse" suites of the forest apartment complex. Just as there are species that specialize in understory habitat, there are those that make their livings almost exclusively in the canopy, as well as those that depend on the canopy for just breeding or roosting. There is an old joke about the malady "Warbler Neck" among serious birders; it is a crick-in-the-neck pain that comes from spending too much time trying to see migrating or breeding warblers as they forage in their favorite habitat: the tops of very tall, broad-leafed deciduous trees.

Along the San Pedro's cottonwood gallery, common warblers include the yellow and, in winter, the yellow-rumped; more than 35 species of migrating or breeding warblers have been seen along the San Pedro. Other birds that breed or feed there are Bullock's and hooded orioles, summer tanagers, vermilion flycatchers, Cassin's kingbirds, brown-crested flycatchers, and lesser goldfinches. Gray hawks build their well-hidden nests in the forked branches of the biggest cottonwoods. Great-horned owls breed and roost in the cottonwoods, joining silver-haired, big brown, and red bats. Cavity-nesting owls such as the Western screech owl nest in the hollowed-out limbs of dead or dying cottonwoods.

MATURE WOODY PLANTS: Frémont cottonwood, Goodding willow, Arizona walnut (*Juglans major*), velvet ash (*Fraxinus velutina*)

INDICATOR WILDLIFE: **breeding**—gray hawk, Cooper's hawk, yellow warbler, Cassin's kingbird, vermilion flycatcher, summer tanager, Bullock's oriole, blue grosbeak; **roosting**—great-horned owl, silver-haired, big brown, and red bat; **feeding**—yellow warbler, yellow-billed cuckoo, lesser goldfinch

EXAMPLE IN THE SPRNCA: throughout the RNCA, but a nice mature stand occurs just north and south of the river bridge at Highway 90

Mesquite Bosque.

Along Southwestern rivers you will find a unique forest called a mesquite bosque, believed by some to be the second most faunally rich habitat in the Southwest, after the cottonwood-willow forest. Because of the richness of insects in a bosque (representing a low trophic level), densities of birds (at a high trophic level) are correspondingly extremely high.

From about the turn of the century until about 50 years ago, mesquite bosques along southern Arizona's waterways were up to six miles wide and many miles long, with huge trees over 55 feet tall and 4 feet in diameter. Today, because of woodcutting and clearing, a mature bosque is increasingly rare and usually only a few hundred feet wide and infrequently more than a mile long. Though not giants, the trees are big, up to 40 feet tall and a few feet in girth.

Dominated by tall, thick-trunked old mesquites with very wide umbrellalike canopies, the understory of a mesquite bosque can be surprisingly dark and cool. Mesquite is a highly adaptable plant, and in a bosque it appears in its most robust form; for this reason it is called a facultative riparian plant, since it occurs in other habitats but occurs most robustly in riparian zones.

The ground of a mesquite bosque is covered with inches of nutrient-rich decaying duff from mesquite beans and leaves. The woody shrubs and herbaceous plants that grow there sometimes form dense thickets, but more often than not they cluster around areas where light penetrates the canopy, leaving other areas open. Vines—gourds, morningglories, wild beans—are common in late summer, ascending the rough-barked mesquites toward the promise of sun.

The plants of mesquite bosques were very important to early Southwestern people. In fact, mesquite might have been one of the single most important plants. Its wood, bark, and beans were gathered for food, medicine, lumber, fiber, dye, weapons, and games. Like supermarkets, bosques also offered wild beans, gourds, lysine-rich grains and greens from amaranths, and fruits from hackberries, elderberries, mulberries, and wolfberries, not to mention good hunting grounds for small mammals such as rabbits.

A number of Sonoran and Chihuahuan Desert birds rely heavily on mesquite bosques for breeding and feeding. The diminutive elf owls and cactus ferruginous pygmy owls both are found in bosques; both are cavity nesters, co-opting old woodpecker nests. Another bird closely tied to bosques is the Lucy's warbler, one of two cavity-nesting warblers in North America. Phainopeplas feed on the berries of the desert mistletoe, which is common in mesquites. These silky black birds also build their nests in mistletoe clumps—kind of like having your own fast-food joint in your living room.

Usually, a mesquite bosque grows adjacent to the river or in the first or second terrace above the rivercourse, in deep alluvial soil, and often at the confluence of a river's tributary. Along the upper San Pedro River, there is a nice bosque at the Babocomari River, and along the lower San Pedro, at Hooker Wash near Cascabel.

MATURE AND SEEDLING WOODY PLANTS: velvet mesquite (*Prosopis velutina*), graythorn, catclaw acacia, desert hackberry, netleaf hackberry (*Celtis laevigata*), Texas mulberry (*Morus microphylla*), Mexican elder (*Sambucus mexicana*), four-wing saltbush (*Atriplex canescens*)

HERBACEOUS PLANTS: Palmer's amaranth (*Amaranthus palmeri*), vine mesquite grass (*Panicum obtusum*), buffalo gourd (*Cucurbita foetidissima*), goldeneye (*Viguiera dentata*), morningglories (*Ipomoea* spp. and *Evolvulus* spp.), desert mistletoe (*Phoradendron californicum*)

INDICATOR WILDLIFE: **breeding**—elf owl, Bell's vireo, Lucy's warbler, phainopepla, varied bunting; **roosting**—white-winged dove; **feeding**—vermilion flycatcher, Abert's towhee, varied bunting, Clark's spiny lizard, desert pocket mouse

EXAMPLE IN THE SPRNCA: at the confluence of the San Pedro and Babocomari Rivers

Floodplain: First Terrace above River Level

Sacaton-Mesquite Grassland.

The mature mesquite-sacaton grassland might be the second-most endangered riparian community after Fremont cottonwood–Goodding willow forests. Growing in the first terrace above the river, usually where the water table is from 6 to 15 feet below the surface, but also in a less robust form where the water table is up to 24 feet below the surface, the sacaton grassland is dominated along the San Pedro by big sacaton, a perennial bunch-forming grass. In moist alluvial floodplains, sacaton can form nearly monotypic (one species), 3- to 6-foot-high grasslands. More typically, it is robust, not quite as tall, and interspersed with mesquite, catclaw, and graythorn shrubs.

Sacaton-mesquite grasslands are crucial to the health of many riparian areas: by their dense, bunch-forming nature they bind the silty alluvial soil, slow down flood flows, and spread out the flows over greater areas, which increases groundwater recharge. Many birds use the dense cover for feeding and nesting; the Botteri's sparrow is a sacaton "old growth" specialist. After the San Pedro's years of entrenchment and industrial development, sacaton grasslands nearly disappeared, as did Botteri's sparrows. As the native habitats of the San Pedro RNCA return to health, wildlife such as Botteri's sparrows are returning for the first time in decades. Another sacaton user, the common yellowthroat, forages and builds nests in the dense clumps.

HERBACEOUS PLANTS: sacaton (*Sporobolus wrightii*), green sprangletop (*Leptochloa dubia*), tobosa grass (*Hilaria mutica*), vine mesquite grass

MATURE WOODY PLANTS: velvet mesquite, graythorn (*Zizyphus obtusifolia*), catclaw acacia, whitethorn acacia (*Acacia constricta*), wolfberries (*Lycium* spp.)

INDICATOR WILDLIFE: Botteri's sparrow, Cassin's sparrow, Western kingbird, Eastern meadowlark, burrowing owl (extirpated from San Pedro valley), Sonoran Desert toad, Mexican hognosed snake, Mojave rattlesnake, Botta's pocket gopher, kangaroo rats

EXAMPLE IN THE SPRNCA: just east of the parking lot at Hereford Road bridge, on the east side of the river

Uplands: Second and Third Terraces above River Level

Chihuahuan Desertscrub.

In the uplands above the river, along the uppermost and oldest of the terraces, begin the true desert habitats. The desertscrub is a thornbush- and cactus-dominated landscape in rocky, poor soil. The plants and animals that live there are hardy—very heat and drought tolerant, and since this is the Chihuahuan Desert, cold tolerant as well.

Historically, before wide-scale industrial ranching began in the late 1800s and early 1900s, the desertscrub and desert grassland habitats of the San Pedro River valley were much more distinct than they are today. Years of overgrazing coupled with drought altered both the plant associations and the soil compositions (because of erosion) so that today it is harder to tell where desertscrub stops and desert grassland begins. Usually, the habitats are subtly intergraded, with many desertscrub species, such as mesquites and rabbitbrush, now invading the grasslands.

Chihuahuan desertscrub is dominated by low-growing shrubs such as creosote bush, blackbrush, crucifixion thorn, condalia, wolfberries, and Mormon tea. Interspersed throughout are succulents such as Palmer's agave and larger woody species such as ocotillo. Desert-specialist wildlife that seldom show up in the riparian habitats include black-chinned sparrows, round-tailed ground squirrels, Mojave rattlesnakes, Texas horned lizards, and black-tailed jackrabbits.

MATURE WOODY PLANTS AND SUCCULENTS: Palmer's agave (*Agave palmeri*), ocotillo (*Fouquieria splendens*), creosote bush (*Larrea tridentata*), crucifixion thorn (*Koeberlinia spinosa*), blackbrush (*Coleogyne ramosissima*), desert sumac (*Rhus microphylla*), condalia (*Condalia warnockii*), wolfberries, desert honeysuckle (*Anisacanthus thurberi*), Mormon tea (*Ephedra trifurca*), tarbush (*Flourensia cernua*), whitethorn acacia, catclaw acacia, wait-a-minute bush (*Mimosa biuncifera*), burrobush, rabbitbrush, snakeweed (*Gutierrezia sarothrae*)

HERBACEOUS PLANTS: desert zinnia (*Zinnia acerosa*), butterweed (*Senecio longilobus*), stinkgrass (*Eragrostis megastachya*), bush muhly (*Muhlenbergia porteri*), silver morningglory (*Ipomoea hirsuta*)

INDICATOR WILDLIFE: **breeding and feeding**—black-chinned sparrow, black-tailed gnatcatcher, scaled quail, roadrunner, mule deer, round-tailed ground squirrel, Mojave rattlesnake, banded gecko, Texas horned lizard, Arizona desert whiptail, spiny lizard, lyre snake

EXAMPLE IN THE SPRNCA: surrounding the archaeological sites at Murray Springs and the Presidio San Juan de Terrenate

Chihuahuan Desert Grassland.

The once-widespread desert grasslands of the San Pedro River valley are all but gone today, invaded and sometimes replaced by desertscrub habitat. Chihuahuan desert grassland usually occurs at slightly higher elevations than desertscrub and is marked by mixed-grass cover of various gramas—sideoats, Rothrock, and blue—as well as cane beardgrass, plains bristlegrass, spidergrass and bush muhly, among others. Standing sentinel-like at regular intervals across the grassy hills are soaptree yuccas, tall woody succulents in the lily family, and stately ocotillos. Whitethorn acacia and spicebush are common shrubs.

The desert grasslands have a unique fauna—such as the prairie dogs that were once common throughout the Southwest but were nearly extirpated early this century. It is thought that a few black-tailed prairie dogs are recolonizing the grasslands of the upper San Pedro valley, in Mexico.

These ubiquitous diggers, in their huge numbers, once amounted to the most important herbivores in a grassland, controlling the spread of mesquite and other woody shrubs by consuming their seeds and seedlings, while providing important soil disturbances—adding air, moisture, and organic matter throughout the soil layers and mixing nutrients in different soil layers with their extensive digging. Today, kangaroo rats fill a similar role, or niche, and you can see their giant multiholed mounds throughout the desert grasslands. Their mounds also house burrowing owls, skinks, many different snakes, and countless small arthropods.

Desert grasslands are also important feeding and breeding habitats for seed-eating birds, such as the many sparrows in our region—Botteri's, vesper, Cassin's, and lark, to name a few—and Eastern and Western meadowlarks. In some years it is thought that seed consumption by birds exceeds that of even all the rodents and harvester ants combined. (In a desert grassland, up to 95 percent of each year's seed crop may be consumed by rodents, arthropods, and birds.)

MATURE WOODY PLANTS: soaptree yucca (*Yucca elata*), ocotillo, whitethorn acacia, spicebush (*Aloysia wrightii*)

HERBACEOUS PLANTS: cane beardgrass (*Bothriochloa bardinodis*), sideoats grama (*Bouteloua curtipendula*), Rothrock grama (*Bouteloua rothrockii*), blue grama (*Bouteloua gracilis*), plains bristlegrass (*Setaria macrostachya*), spidergrass (*Aristida ternipes*), bush muhly, desert zinnia

INDICATOR WILDLIFE: Cassin's sparrow, burrowing owl (extirpated in the San Pedro valley), lark sparrow, Swainson's hawk, American kestrel, loggerhead shrike, Eastern meadowlark, Southern grasshopper mouse, desert box turtle, large-spotted leopard lizard, Big Bend patch-nosed snake

EXAMPLE IN THE SPRNCA: Chihuahuan Desert grassland is a recovering habitat in the RNCA; healthy examples still exist just outside the RNCA just off Middlemarch Road, entering Cochise Stronghold West.

〰 BIRDS OF THE SAN PEDRO RIVER

The San Pedro Riparian National Conservation Area harbors over 100 species of breeding birds and provides invaluable habitat for another 250 species of migrant and wintering birds. Located between the Huachuca and Mule Mountains, and adjacent to Mexico, the RNCA attracts a myriad of bird species from a wide variety of habitats.

Concerns have increased over population declines of migrant bird species that breed in North America, from northern Mexico up to the Arctic, and winter south of the United States (Neotropical Migratory Birds), from southern Mexico to the tip of South America. The Bureau of Land Management follows careful management plans to monitor and enhance populations of bird species that utilize BLM lands throughout North America.

This bird checklist, which documents over 370 bird species, was compiled by BLM biologist Dave Krueper from historical avian records within the upper San Pedro River Valley and from biological inventories within the RNCA. Please report any new species to the Bureau of Land Manage-ment, San Pedro RNCA, 1763 Paseo San Luis, Sierra Vista, AZ 85635; 520-458-3559.

Bird names in this checklist follow the American Ornithological Union's policy of full capitalization. With apologies to ornithologists worldwide, I opted not to use capitalization in the main text.

Abbreviations Used in Checklist

Abundance

C - **Common** = Present in proper habitat and during the proper season in moderate to large numbers annually.

U - **Uncommon** = Present in proper habitat in small to moderate numbers annually, or locally in specific habitats.

R - **Rare** = Present in proper habitat singly or in very small numbers annually or semiannually. This designation also applies to species that breed extremely locally or in very small numbers.

Ca - **Casual** = Greater than five records, but not occurring annually. Records in the area are very few, but a general vagrancy pattern may be evident based on records from surrounding areas in Southeast Arizona in the proper season.

I - **Irregular** = Irruptive or an invasion species.

Residency

P - Permanent

S - Summer resident

W - Winter resident

T - Transient or migrant

* Indicates accidental or historical record and not expected again

# Indicates Neotropical Migratory Bird species

Federal Conservation Status

Th - Threatened

En - Endangered

SoC - Species of concern

Checklist

Loons (Family Gaviidae)
- Pacific Loon T *
- Common Loon Ca T

Grebes (Family Podicipedidae)
- Least Grebe T *
- Pied-billed Grebe U W T #
- Eared Grebe U W #
- Western Grebe R T #
- Clark's Grebe R T #

Cormorants & Allies (Families Phalacrocoracidae, Pelecanidae, & Fregatidae)
- American White Pelican Ca T #
- Brown Pelican Ca T
- Neotropic Cormorant R T
- Magnificent Frigatebird T *
- Double-crested Cormorant R T #

Swans, Geese, & Ducks (Family Anatidae)

- Black-bellied Whistling Duck U S #
- Tundra Swan Ca T
- Greater White-fronted Goose R W
- Snow Goose R W
- Ross' Goose R W
- Canada Goose R W
- Wood Duck R W
- Green-winged Teal U W #
- Mallard C P #
- Northern Pintail U W #
- Blue-winged Teal U T R W #
- Garganey T *
- Cinnamon Teal U W T #
- Northern Shoveler C W
- Gadwall U W #
- American Wigeon U W #
- Canvasback U W #
- Redhead R W #
- Ring-necked Duck C W #
- Greater Scaup Ca T
- Lesser Scaup U W
- Surf Scoter Ca T
- Common Goldeneye Ca W
- Bufflehead U W #
- Hooded Merganser Ca T
- Common Merganser R W U T
- Red-breasted Merganser Ca T
- Ruddy Duck U W #

Raptors (Families Cathartidae, Accipitridae, & Falconidae)

- Turkey Vulture C S #
- Osprey R T #
- White-tailed Kite R T
- Mississippi Kite R T #
- Bald Eagle R W Th
- Northern Harrier C W #
- Sharp-shinned Hawk U W #
- Cooper's Hawk C P #
- Northern Goshawk Ca T
- Common Black Hawk R T #
- Great Black Hawk T *
- Harris' Hawk R P
- Gray Hawk C S SoC #
- Broad-winged Hawk Ca T #
- Swainson's Hawk U S #
- Zone-tailed Hawk R T #
- Red-tailed Hawk C P
- Ferruginous Hawk R W
- Rough-legged Hawk R W
- Golden Eagle R T
- Crested Caracara Ca T
- American Kestrel C P #
- Merlin R W #
- Peregrine Falcon R W #
- Aplomado Falcon T En *
- Prairie Falcon R W

Quail & Allies (Family Phasianidae)

- Wild Turkey R T
- Montezuma Quail Ca T
- Scaled Quail C P
- Gambel's Quail C P

Rails & Allies (Families Rallidae & Gruidae)

- Black Rail T *
- Virginia Rail U W #
- Sora U W #
- Purple Gallinule Ca T #
- Common Moorhen U P
- American Coot U P
- Sandhill Crane Ca T

Shorebirds (Families Charadriidae, Haematopodidae, Recurvirostridae, & Scolopacidae)

- Black-bellied Plover Ca T #
- Snowy Plover Ca T #
- Semipalmated Plover R T #
- Killdeer U P
- Black-necked Stilt U T #
- American Avocet U T #
- Greater Yellowlegs U T #
- Lesser Yellowlegs U T #
- Solitary Sandpiper R T #
- Willet R T #
- Spotted Sandpiper U T #
- Whimbrel Ca T #
- Long-billed Curlew R T #
- Marbled Godwit R T #
- Ruddy Turnstone Ca T #
- Sanderling R T #
- Semipalmated Sandpiper R T #
- Western Sandpiper U T #
- Least Sandpiper C T U W #
- Baird's Sandpiper U T #
- Pectoral Sandpiper R T #
- Dunlin Ca T #
- Stilt Sandpiper R T #
- Short-billed Dowitcher Ca T #
- Long-billed Dowitcher U T #
- Common Snipe C W #
- Wilson's Phalarope C T #
- Red-necked Phalarope R T #
- Red Phalarope Ca T #

Gulls & Terns (Family Laridae)

- Long-tailed Jaeger T *
- Franklin's Gull R T #
- Bonaparte's Gull R T #
- Heermann's Gull Ca T
- Ring-billed Gull U T #
- California Gull R T
- Herring Gull Ca T #
- Black-legged Kittiwake Ca T
- Sabine's Gull Ca T
- Common Tern Ca T #
- Forster's Tern R T #
- Least Tern T *
- Black Tern U T #

Pigeons & Doves (Family Columbidae)

- Rock Dove C P
- Band-tailed Pigeon Ca T
- White-winged Dove C S R W #
- Mourning Dove C P #
- Inca Dove U P
- Common Ground-Dove U P
- Ruddy Ground-Dove Ca T

Cuckoos & Allies (Family Cuculidae)

- Yellow-billed Cuckoo U S SoC #
- Greater Roadrunner C P
- Groove-billed Ani Ca T

Owls (Families Tytonidae & Strigidae)

- Common Barn Owl U P
- Flammulated Owl T * #
- Western Screech-Owl U P
- Great Horned Owl C P
- Elf Owl U S #
- Burrowing Owl Ca P #
- Long-eared Owl U T U W
- Short-eared Owl Ca T #
- Northern Saw-whet Owl T *

Nightjars (Family Caprimulgidae)

- Lesser Nighthawk C S #
- Common Nighthawk U S #
- Common Poorwill C S #
- Whip-poor-will Ca T #

Swifts (Family Apodidae)

- Black Swift T * #
- Chimney Swift T * #
- Vaux's Swift U T #
- White-throated Swift U P #

Hummingbirds (Family Trochilidae)

- Broad-billed Hummingbird
  R T #
- Violet-crowned Hummingbird
  R T #
- Blue-throated Hummingbird
  Ca T #
- Magnificent Hummingbird
  Ca T #
- Plain-capped Starthroat T *
- Lucifer Hummingbird Ca T #
- Black-chinned Hummingbird
  C S #
- Anna's Hummingbird U P
- Costa's Hummingbird R T #
- Calliope Hummingbird R T #
- Broad-tailed Hummingbird
  U T #
- Rufous Hummingbird U T #
- Allen's Hummingbird Ca T #

Trogons & Kingfishers (Families Trogonidae & Alcedinidae)
- Elegant Trogon T * #
- Belted Kingfisher U W #
- Green Kingfisher U P

Woodpeckers (Family Picidae)
- Lewis' Woodpecker I W
- Acorn Woodpecker R T
- Gila Woodpecker C P
- Yellow-bellied Sapsucker Ca T #
- Red-naped Sapsucker U W #
- Red-breasted Sapsucker Ca T
- Williamson's Sapsucker Ca W #
- Ladder-backed Woodpecker C P
- Hairy Woodpecker Ca T
- Strickland's Woodpecker Ca T
- Northern Flicker C P
- Gilded Flicker U P

Flycatchers & Allies (Family Tyrannidae)
- Northern Beardless-Tyrannulet U S #
- Olive-sided Flycatcher R T #
- Greater Pewee R T #
- Western Wood-Pewee C S #
- Willow Flycatcher, Southwest R T En #
- Least Flycatcher Ca T #
- Hammond's Flycatcher U W #
- Dusky Flycatcher U W #
- Gray Flycatcher U W #
- Pacific-slope Flycatcher C T #
- Buff-breasted Flycatcher T * #
- Black Phoebe C P
- Eastern Phoebe R T W #
- Say's Phoebe C P #
- Vermilion Flycatcher C S R W #
- Dusky-capped Flycatcher U S #
- Ash-throated Flycatcher C S #
- Brown-crested Flycatcher C S #
- Sulphur-bellied Flycatcher Ca T #
- Tropical Kingbird Ca T #
- Cassin's Kingbird C S #
- Thick-billed Kingbird Ca T #
- Western Kingbird C S #
- Eastern Kingbird Ca T #
- Scissor-tailed Flycatcher Ca T #
- Rose-throated Becard Ca T #

Larks & Swallows (Families Alaudidae & Hirundinidae)
- Horned Lark C P #
- Purple Martin U T #
- Tree Swallow C T #
- Violet-green Swallow C T #
- Northern Rough-winged Swallow C S #
- Bank Swallow U T #
- Cliff Swallow C S #
- Barn Swallow C S #

Jays, Crows, & Ravens (Family Corvidae)

- Steller's Jay I W
- Blue Jay T *
- Scrub Jay I W
- Gray-breasted Jay Ca T
- Pinyon Jay I W
- Clark's Nutcracker I W
- American Crow R T
- Chihuahuan Raven C P
- Common Raven C P

Titmice, Bushtits, & Wrens (Families Paridae, Remizidae, Sittidae, Certhiidae, & Troglodytidae)

- Bridled Titmouse U W
- Verdin C P
- Bushtit C P
- Red-breasted Nuthatch Ca T
- White-breasted Nuthatch C P
- Pygmy Nuthatch T *
- Brown Creeper U W #
- Cactus Wren C P
- Rock Wren C P
- Canyon Wren U P
- Bewick's Wren C P
- House Wren U W #
- Winter Wren R W
- Marsh Wren U W #

Gnatcatchers, Kinglets, & Thrushes (Family Muscicapidae)

- Golden-crowned Kinglet Ca W
- Ruby-crowned Kinglet C W #
- Blue-gray Gnatcatcher U T #
- Black-tailed Gnatcatcher U T
- Eastern Bluebird I W
- Western Bluebird U W #
- Mountain Bluebird U W #
- Townsend's Solitaire Ca W #
- Veery T * #
- Swainson's Thrush R T #
- Hermit Thrush U W #
- Rufous-backed Robin Ca T
- American Robin I W
- Varied Thrush Ca T

Mockingbirds & Thrashers (Family Mimidae)

- Gray Catbird Ca T #
- Northern Mockingbird C P
- Sage Thrasher R W #
- Brown Thrasher Ca T #
- Bendire's Thrasher R P #
- Curve-billed Thrasher C P
- Crissal Thrasher C P

Pipits & Waxwings (Families Motacillidae & Bombycillidae)

- American Pipit U W #
- Sprague's Pipit Ca W #
- Bohemian Waxwing T *
- Cedar Waxwing U W T #

Silky Flycatchers & Shrikes (Families Ptiligonatidae & Laniidae)

- Phainopepla U P #
- Northern Shrike T *
- Loggerhead Shrike C P #

Starlings (Family Sturnidae)

- European Starling C P

Vireos (Family Vireonidae)

- White-eyed Vireo T * #
- Bell's Vireo C S #
- Gray Vireo R T #
- Solitary Vireo C T #
- Yellow-throated Vireo T * #
- Hutton's Vireo U T #
- Warbling Vireo C T #
- Philadelphia Vireo T * #
- Red-eyed Vireo T * #
- Yellow-green Vireo T *

Wood Warblers (Family Emberizidae, Subfamily Parulinae)

- Golden-winged Warbler Ca T * #
- Tennessee Warbler Ca T #
- Orange-crowned Warbler C T #
- Nashville Warbler U T #
- Virginia's Warbler R T #
- Lucy's Warbler C S #
- Northern Parula Ca T #
- Yellow Warbler C S #
- Chestnut-sided Warbler Ca T #
- Magnolia Warbler T * #
- Cape May Warbler T * #
- Black-throated Blue Warbler Ca T #
- Yellow-rumped Warbler C W #
- Black-throated Gray Warbler U T #
- Townsend's Warbler U T #
- Hermit Warbler R T #
- Black-throated Green Warbler Ca T #
- Blackburnian Warbler T * #
- Yellow-throated Warbler T * #
- Grace's Warbler Ca T #
- Pine Warbler T * #
- Palm Warbler Ca T * #
- Black-and-white Warbler R T #
- American Redstart R T #
- Prothonotary Warbler Ca T #
- Worm-eating Warbler T * #
- Ovenbird Ca T #
- Northern Waterthrush R T #
- Kentucky Warbler T * #
- Mourning Warbler T * #
- MacGillivray's Warbler U T #
- Common Yellowthroat C S R W #
- Hooded Warbler Ca T #
- Wilson's Warbler C T #
- Red-faced Warbler T * #
- Painted Redstart R T #
- Yellow-breasted Chat C S #

Tanagers (Family Emberizidae, Subfamily Thraupinae)

- Hepatic Tanager Ca T #
- Summer Tanager C S #
- Scarlet Tanager T * #
- Western Tanager C T #

Grosbeaks & Allies (Family Emberizidae, Subfamilies Cardinalinae & Emberizinae)

- Northern Cardinal U P
- Pyrrhuloxia C P
- Yellow Grosbeak T * #
- Rose-breasted Grosbeak Ca T #
- Black-headed Grosbeak C T #
- Blue Grosbeak C S #
- Lazuli Bunting C T R S #
- Indigo Bunting R S #
- Varied Bunting R S #
- Painted Bunting R T #
- Dickcissel Ca T #
- Green-tailed Towhee C W #
- Rufous-sided Towhee I W
- Canyon Towhee C P
- Abert's Towhee C P
- Botteri's Sparrow C S #
- Cassin's Sparrow C S #
- Rufous-winged Sparrow Ca T
- Rufous-crowned Sparrow U P
- Chipping Sparrow C W #
- Clay-colored Sparrow Ca T #
- Brewer's Sparrow C W #
- Black-chinned Sparrow R T #
- Vesper Sparrow C W #
- Lark Sparrow U W #
- Black-throated Sparrow C P
- Sage Sparrow R W #
- Lark Bunting U W #
- Savannah Sparrow U W #
- Baird's Sparrow R W #
- Grasshopper Sparrow R W #
- Fox Sparrow Ca W
- Song Sparrow C P
- Lincoln's Sparrow C W #
- Swamp Sparrow R W
- White-throated Sparrow R W
- Golden-crowned Sparrow Ca W
- White-crowned Sparrow C W #
- Harris' Sparrow Ca W
- Dark-eyed Junco I W
- Yellow-eyed Junco T *
- McCown's Longspur Ca T
- Chestnut-collared Longspur R W #

Blackbirds & Allies (Family Icterinae)

- Bobolink Ca T #
- Red-winged Blackbird C P#
- Eastern Meadowlark C P
- Western Meadowlark C W
- Yellow-headed Blackbird C W #
- Rusty Blackbird Ca T #
- Brewer's Blackbird C W #
- Great-tailed Grackle C P
- Common Grackle T *
- Bronzed Cowbird R P #
- Brown-headed Cowbird C P #
- Orchard Oriole Ca T #
- Hooded Oriole U S #
- Bullock's Oriole C S #
- Scott's Oriole U S #

Finches & Allies (Family Fringillidae)

- Purple Finch Ca W
- Cassin's Finch Ca W #
- House Finch C P
- Red Crossbill Ca T
- Pine Siskin U W #
- Lesser Goldfinch C P
- Lawrence's Goldfinch I W
- American Goldfinch R W
- House Sparrow C P

✎ MAMMALS OF THE SAN PEDRO RIVER

Marsupials (Order Marsupialia)
OPOSSUMS (FAMILY DIDELPHIDAE)

- Virginia opossum (*Didelphis virginiana*)
- Mexican opossum (*Didelphis virginiana californicus*)

Insectivores (Order Insectivora)
SHREWS (FAMILY SORICIDAE)

- Desert shrew (*Notiosorex crawfordi*)

Bats (Order Chiroptera)
AMERICAN LEAF-NOSED BATS (FAMILY PHYLLOSTOMIDAE)

- California leaf-nosed bat (*Macrotis californicus*)
- Long-tongued bat (*Choeronycteris mexicana*)
- Lesser long-nosed bat (*Leptonycteris curasoae*) [endangered]

VESPERTILIONID BATS (FAMILY VESPERTILIONIDAE)

- California myotis (*Myotis californicus*)
- Yuma myotis (*Myotis yumanensis*)
- Cave myotis (*Myotis velifer*)
- Southwestern myotis (*Myotis auriculus*)
- Fringed myotis (*Myotis thysanodes*)
- Long-legged myotis (*Myotis volans*)
- Small-footed myotis (*Myotis leibii*)
- Silver-haired bat (*Lasionycteris noctivagans*)
- Western pipistrelle (*Pipistrellus hesperus*)
- Big brown bat (*Eptesicus fuscus*)
- Red bat (*Lasiurus borealis*)
- Hoary bat (*Lasiurus cinereus*)

- Southern yellow bat (*Lasiurus xanthinus*)
- Spotted bat (*Euderma maculatum*)
- Townsend's big-eared bat (*Plecotus townsendii*)
- Allen's lappet-browed bat (*Idionycteris phyllotis*)
- Pallid bat (*Antrozous pallidus*)

FREE-TAILED BATS (FAMILY MOLOSSIDAE)
- American free-tailed bat (*Tadarida brasiliensis*)
- Pocketed free-tailed bat (*Tadarida femorosacca*)
- Big free-tailed bat (*Tadarida macrotis*)
- Western mastiff bat (*Eumops perotis*)

Hares, Rabbits, & Pikas (Order Lagomorpha)
HARES & RABBITS (FAMILY LEPORIDAE)
- Desert cottontail (*Sylvilagus audubonii*)
- Black-tailed jackrabbit (*Lepus californicus*)

Rodents (Order Rodentia)
SQUIRRELS & ALLIES (FAMILY SCIURIDAE)
- Harris' antelope squirrel (*Ammospermophilus harrisii*)
- Rock squirrel (*Spermophilus variegatus*)
- Spotted ground squirrel (*Spermophilus spilosoma*)
- Round-tailed ground squirrel (*Spermophilus tereticaudus*)
- Black-tailed prairie dog (*Cynomys ludovicianus*)

POCKET GOPHERS (FAMILY GEOMYIDAE)
- Botta's pocket gopher (*Thomomys bottae*)

KANGAROO RATS, POCKET MICE, & ALLIES (FAMILY HETEROMYIDAE)
- Silky pocket mouse (*Perognathus flavus*)
- Rock pocket mouse (*Perognathus intermedius*)
- Desert pocket mouse (*Perognathus penicillatus*)
- Bailey's pocket mouse (*Perognathus baileyi*)
- Hispid pocket mouse (*Perognathus hispidus*)
- Merriam's kangaroo rat (*Dipodomys merriami*)
- Ord's kangaroo rat (*Dipodomys ordii*)
- Banner-tailed kangaroo rat (*Dipodomys spectabilis*)

BEAVERS (FAMILY CASTORIDAE)
- Beaver (*Castor canadensis*)

NEW WORLD MICE & RATS
(FAMILY MURIDAE, SUBFAMILY CRICETINAE)
- Western harvest mouse (*Reithrodontomys megalotis*)
- Plains harvest mouse (*Reithrodontomys montanus*)
- Fulvous harvest mouse (*Reithrodontomys fulvescens*)
- Deer mouse (*Peromyscus maniculatus*)
- Cactus mouse (*Peromyscus eremicus*)
- White-footed mouse (*Peromyscus leucopus*)
- Brush mouse (*Peromyscus boylii*)
- Northern pygmy mouse (*Baiomys taylori*)
- Southern grasshopper mouse (*Onychomys torridus*)
- Northern grasshopper mouse (*Onychomys leucogaster*)
- Arizona cotton rat (*Sigmodon arizonae*)
- Fulvous cotton rat (*Sigmodon fulviventer*)
- Yellow-nosed cotton rat (*Sigmodon ochrognathus*)
- White-throated woodrat (*Neotoma albigula*)

OLD WORLD RATS & MICE
(FAMILY MURIDAE, SUBFAMILY MURINAE)
- House mouse (*Mus musculus*)

NEW WORLD PORCUPINES (FAMILY ERETHIZONTIDAE)
- Porcupine (*Erethizon dorsatum*)

Carnivores (Order Carnivora)
DOGLIKE MAMMALS (FAMILY CANIDAE)
- Coyote (*Canis latrans*)
- Kit fox (*Vulpes macrotis*)
- Gray fox (*Urocyon cinereoargenteus*)
- Bears (Family Ursidae)
- Black bear (*Ursus americanus*) [transient]

RACCOONS & ALLIES (FAMILY PROCYONIDAE)
- Ringtail (*Bassariscus astutus*)
- Raccoon (*Procyon lotor*)
- Coatimundi (*Nasua nasua*) [transient]

WEASELS, SKUNKS, & ALLIES (FAMILY MUSTELIDAE)
- Badger (*Taxidea taxus*)
- Spotted skunk (*Spilogale gracilis*)
- Striped skunk (*Mephitis mephitis*)
- Hooded skunk (*Mephitis macroura*)
- Hog-nosed skunk (*Conepatus mesoleucus*)

CATS (FAMILY FELIDAE)
- Mountain lion (*Felis concolor*) [transient]
- Bobcat (*Felis rufus*)

Hooved Animals (Order Artiodactyla)
PECCARIES & PIGS (FAMILY TAYASSUIDAE)
- Javelina (*Tayassu tajacu*)

DEER, ELK, & ALLIES (FAMILY CERVIDAE)
- Mule deer (*Odocoileus hemionus*)
- White-tailed deer (*Odocoileus virginianus*)

Sources: Table 13, carnivore occurrence records, San Pedro Riparian National Conservation Area, Cochise County, Arizona, 1987–1988; table 7, shrew and rodent occurrence records, San Pedro Riparian National Conservation Area, Cochise County, Arizona, 1986–1988; table 6, bat occurrence records and bats observed and collected, San Pedro Riparian National Conservation Area, Cochise County, Arizona, 1987–1988.

✏ REPTILES AND AMPHIBIANS OF THE SAN PEDRO RIVER

Frogs & Toads (Order Anura)
SPADEFOOT TOADS (FAMILY PELOBATIDAE)
- Couch's spadefoot toad (*Scaphiopus couchii*)
- Southern spadefoot toad (*Scaphiopus multiplicatus*)

TRUE TOADS (FAMILY BUFONIDAE)
- Sonoran desert toad (*Bufo alvarius*)
- Southwestern Woodhouse's toad (*Bufo woodhouseii australis*)
- Great Plains toad (*Bufo cognatus*)
- Red-spotted toad (*Bufo punctatus*)

TRUE FROGS (FAMILY RANIDAE)
- Bullfrog (*Rana catesbeiana*) [introduced]

Turtles (Order Testudines)
MUSK & MUD TURTLES (FAMILY KINOSTERNIDAE)
- Sonoran mud turtle (*Kinosternon sonoriense*)

LAND TORTOISES (FAMILY TESTUDINIDAE)
- Desert tortoise (*Gopherus agassizii*)

BOX & WATER TURTLES (FAMILY EMYDIDAE)
- Western box turtle (*Terrapene ornata ornata*)
- Slider (*Trachemys scripta*)

SOFTSHELL TURTLES (FAMILY TRIONYCHIDAE)
- Texas spiny softshell (*Trionyx spiniferus emoryi*)

Lizards (Order Squamata, Suborder Sauria)
COLLARED AND LEOPARD LIZARDS (FAMILY CROTAPHYTIDAE)
- Longnose leopard lizard (*Gambelia wislizenii wislizenii*)

IGUANID LIZARDS (FAMILY IGUANIDAE)
- Southwestern earless lizard (*Cophosaurus texanus scitulus*)
- Zebra-tailed lizard (*Callisaurus draconoides draconoides*)
- Twin-spotted spiny lizard (*Sceloporus magister bimaculosus*)
- Clark's spiny lizard (*Sceloporus clarkii*)
- Southern prairie lizard (*Sceloporus undulatus consobrinus*)
- Tree lizard (*Urosaurus ornatus*)
- Regal horned lizard (*Phrynosoma solare*)
- Texas horned lizard (*Phrynosoma cornutum*)

GECKOS (FAMILY GEKKONIDAE)
- Tucson banded gecko (*Coleonyx variegatus bogerti*)

WHIPTAIL LIZARDS (FAMILY TEIIDAE)
- Arizona desert whiptail (*Cnemidophorus tigris gracilis*)
- Sonoran spotted whiptail (*Cnemidophorus sonorae*)
- Desert grassland whiptail (*Cnemidophorus uniparens*)
- Giant spotted whiptail (*Cnemidophorus burti stictogrammus*)

ALLIGATOR LIZARDS & ALLIES (FAMILY ANGUIDAE)
- Madrean alligator lizard (*Gerrhonotus kingii*)

VENOMOUS LIZARDS (FAMILY HELODERMATIDAE)
- Gila monster (*Heloderma suspectum*)

Snakes (Order Squamata, Suborder Serpentes)
BLIND SNAKES (FAMILY LEPTOTYPHLOPIDAE)
- Texas blind snake (*Leptotyphlops dulcis*)

COLUBRID SNAKES (FAMILY COLUBRIDAE)
- Regal ringneck snake (*Diadophis punctatus*)
- Mexican hognose snake (*Heterodon nasicus kennerlyi*)
- Coachwhip snake (*Masticophis flagellum*)
- Sonoran whipsnake (coachwhip) (*Masticophis bilineatus*)
- Big Bend patch-nosed snake (*Salvadora hexalepis deserticola*)
- Sonoran gopher (bull) snake (*Pituophis melanoleucus affinis*)
- Desert kingsnake (*Lampropeltis getulus splendida*)
- Western long-nosed snake (*Rhinocheilus lecontei lecontei*)
- Checkered garter snake (*Thamnophis marcianus*)
- Northern Mexican garter snake (*Thamnophis eques megalops*) [species of concern]
- Plains black-headed snake (*Tantilla hobartsmithi*)
- (Spotted) Night snake (*Hypsiglena torquata*)
- Sonoran lyre snake (*Trimorphodon biscutatus lambda*)

CORAL SNAKES, COBRAS & ALLIES (FAMILY ELAPIDAE)

- Arizona coral snake (*Micruroides euryxanthus euryxanthus*)

RATTLESNAKES, MOCCASINS & OLD WORLD VIPERS (FAMILY VIPERIDAE)

- Western diamondback rattlesnake (*Crotalus atrox*)
- Mojave rattlesnake (*Crotalus scutulatus*)

Source: Corman, Troy E. 1988. Abundance, Distribution, and Habitat Management of the Reptiles and Amphibians of the San Pedro RNCA. U.S. Department of the Interior, BLM, San Pedro Project Office.

RESOURCES

Conservation Groups

Arizona Nature Conservancy, 1510 E. Fort Lowell, Tucson, AZ 85719; 520-622-3861; <www.tnc.org>.

Arizona Riparian Council, Arizona State University, Center for Environmental Studies, Tempe, AZ 85287-1201; <www.asu.edu/ces/ARC/arc.htm>.

Arizona State Parks, Streams and Wetlands Heritage Program, 800 W. Washington, Phoenix, AZ 85007.

Center for Biological Diversity, P.O. Box 710, Tucson, AZ 85702-0710; 520-623-5252; <www.biologicaldiversity.org>.

Friends of the San Pedro River, Inc., c/o Bureau of Land Management, 1763 Paseo San Luis, Sierra Vista, AZ 85635; 520-459-2555.

Huachuca Audubon Society, Huachuca Audubon Society, P.O. Box 63, Sierra Vista, AZ 85636.

Sky Island Alliance, P.O. Box 41165, Tucson, AZ 85717; 520-624-7080; <www.skyislandalliance.org>.

Southeastern Arizona Bird Observatory, P.O. Box 5521, Bisbee, AZ 85603; 520-432-1388; <www.sabo.org>; sabo@SABO.org.

Tucson Audubon Society, 300 E. University Blvd., Suite 120, Tucson, AZ 85705; 520-629-0510; <www.audubon.org/chapter/az/tucson>.

Recreation in the San Pedro River Area

Friends of the San Pedro River (FSPR) sponsors guided activities along the river, including general hiking, archaeology, birdwatching, horseback riding, and children's activities. Call 520-439-6400, the BLM office in Sierra

Vista, or stop by the San Pedro House on Highway 90 at the river for information.

ARCHAEOLOGY: Center for Desert Archaeology, 3975 N. Tucson Blvd., Tucson, AZ 85716; 520-881-2244; <www.cdarc.com>; center@desert. com.

BIRDING: See Huachuca and Tucson Audubon Societies, in the "Conservation Groups" section, above. See also nature guides in the "Suggested Reading" section at the end of the book.

BUTTERFLIES: Southeastern Arizona Butterfly Association, P.O. Box 1012, Hereford, AZ 85615; <www.naba.org/chapters/nabasa/home.html>.

HIKING: Huachuca Hiking Club, P.O. Box 3555, Sierra Vista, AZ 85636; <www.primenet.com/~tomheld/hhc.html>.

HORSEBACK RIDING: Call 520-458-3559, the BLM office, for current contact information for the trail rides coordinator as well as for information on Sierra Vista–area horseback riding associations.

MOUNTAIN BIKING: Dawn to Dust Mountain Biking Club, Dawn to Dust Mountain Bike Club, 164 W. Fry Blvd., Sierra Vista, AZ 85635; <www.primenet.com/~tomheld/dd.html>.

NATURE GUIDES: High Lonesome Ecotours, Inc., 570 S. Little Bear Trail, Sierra Vista, AZ 85635, (800) 743-2668, <www.hilonesom.com>; Stuart Healy, 220 Stardust Street, Sierra Vista, AZ 85635, 520-458-7603, <www.aztrogon.com>; Melody Kehl, Outdoor Adventures, 9402 E. El Cajon Dr., Tucson, AZ 85710, 520-296-9437, outdoor@azstarnet.com; Southeastern Arizona Bird Observatory, see "Conservation Groups" section, above.

Finding Out More

For more information about the San Pedro River, contact the Bureau of Land Management's San Pedro field office at 1763 Paseo San Luis, Sierra Vista, AZ 85635; 520-439-6400. The Tucson-area office of the BLM is at 12661 E. Broadway, Tucson, AZ 86748; 520-722-4289; <tucson.az. blm. gov/tfo.html>. The state office is at 3707 N. 7th St., Phoenix, AZ 85014; <tucson.az.blm.gov>.

The Friends of the San Pedro River, Inc., was incorporated in 1987 as a non-profit membership organization supporting the Bureau of Land Management's San Pedro Riparian National Conservation Area. The goals of the FSPR include "providing environmental education to further the conservation, protection, and enhancement of the NCA; designing and/or implementing projects that utilize contributed labor and/or funding to enhance the NCA; operating and managing FSP resources; and becoming proactive in community affairs, specifically as they impact the San Pedro ecosystem."

FSPR volunteers operate a bookstore at the San Pedro House on Highway 90 at the river. It is also an unofficial BLM visitor center, providing information to over 50,000 visitors annually. A BLM visitor and environmental education center is planned near the San Pedro House, but construction is still a long way off.

FSPR volunteers also provide education experiences for children and adults. San Pedro River docents, who receive eight weeks of training, lead nature walks and give programs in the Sierra Vista community. The Junior Naturalist program is for children ages 7–13 and includes two summer camp programs.

To join FSPR, contact them through the Bureau of Land Managment at the address and phone number, above, or visit the San Pedro House on Highway 90, at the river.

Visitor Use Information and Regulations, SPRNCA

• Public recreation is limited to daylight hours only, except for backcountry camping purposes or special group events.

• Backcountry camping requires a permit ($2 per person), and you must camp at least one mile from any parking areas.

• Campfires are allowed only in designated areas.

• Vehicles are allowed only in designated parking areas and on designated roads. The road east of the river near Palominas off Highway 92 is open to vehicles.

• Bicycles are permitted only on the designated road listed above, and on designated trails. (See the "Discovery Guide" texts for each chapter for details.)

- Horses are permitted throughout the RNCA. Call the BLM for current access information and tips on riding hazards.

- Pets must be leashed at all developed facilities. Unleashed hunting dogs may be used during the recognized hunting period and only in the areas open to firearm discharge.

- Firearm discharge is permitted only for the purpose of regulated hunting and only in the area north of Charleston Road and the area south of Highway 92 from September 1 through March 31, except within ¼-mile of developed facilities and residences.

- Bowhunting is permitted anywhere in the RNCA during established hunting periods except within ¼-mile of developed facilities and residences.

- Activities prohibited within the RNCA are off-road vehicle use, metal detecting and artifact collection (bottles, cans, arrowheads, potsherds, etc.), cutting or gathering of wood, prospecting including gold panning, mining, and trapping.

Other Southern Arizona Riparian Areas

Arivaca Ciénega and Brown Canyon, Baboquivari Mountains. U.S. Fish and Wildlife Service, Buenos Aires National Wildlife Refuge, P.O. Box 109, Sasabe, AZ 85633; 520-823-4251.

Gila Box National Riparian Conservation Area. Bureau of Land Management, 425 E. 4th St., Safford, AZ 85546; 520-428-4040.

Ciénega Creek. Pima County Parks and Recreation, 1204 W. Silverlake Road, Tucson, AZ 85713; 520-740-2690.

Hassayampa River Preserve. Arizona Nature Conservancy, P.O. Box 3290, Wickenburg, AZ 85385; 520-684-2772.

Patagonia–Sonoita Creek Nature Conservancy Preserve. Arizona Nature Conservancy, P.O. Box 815, Patagonia, AZ 85624; 520-394-2400.

Sabino Canyon National Recreation Area. U.S. Forest Service, Federal Building, 300 W. Congress, Tucson, AZ 85701; 520-670-4552.

Santa Cruz River. Santa Cruz River Alliance, 350 S. Grande Ave., Tucson, AZ 85745.

CHAPTER NOTES AND CITATIONS

Exploration Guides

All information in the chapter-end "Exploration Guides" is from personal experience of the author and from printed sources from and direct communication with staff at the San Pedro office of the Bureau of Land Management, 1763 Paseo San Luis, Sierra Vista, AZ 85635; 520-458-3559. Birding information was graciously supplied by Dave Krueper and horseback riding information by Sierra Vistan Katie Salwei.

Chapter 1, Border to Palominas

Monsoons: Whenever I use this word in print, I always get in trouble regarding its usage and origin. For a good overview of the usage of *monsoon* as a meteorological term, see "The North American Monsoon" in the October 1997 issue of the *Bulletin of the American Meteorological Society*.

Early hydrology: Nils Roar Sælthun, "So what is hydrology?" (internet: Norwegian Institute for Water Research, 1997): <http://www.uio.no/~nilsroar/nrsinde.html>.

Watershed and physical statistics of the San Pedro: Barbara Tellman, R. Yarde, and M. G. Wallace, *Arizona's Changing Rivers: How People Have Affected the Rivers* (Tucson: Water Resources Research Center, University of Arizona, College of Agriculture, 1997), p. 29; Laurel J. Lacher, *Hydrologic and Legal Issues of the Upper San Pedro River Basin, Arizona* (Tucson: University of Arizona, Department of Hydrology and Water Resources, 1997).

Rainfall for San Pedro valley: Gary Paul Nabhan, "Alternative Land Uses and Food Resources for a Semi-arid Rangeland Watershed" (unpublished manuscript, 1975). The extremes listed are for Fairbank, with a low annual rainfall of 4.8 inches and Fort Huachuca, with the high of 25 inches.

Colorado River impoundment facts: Joe Gelt, "Managing the Flow to Better Use, Preserve Arizona's Rivers," *Arroyo* 4 (University of Arizona Water Resources Research Center, 1997):5.

Cuckoo natural histories, general: Kenn Kaufman, *Lives of North American Birds* (New York: Houghton Mifflin, 1996); Paul R. Ehrlich, D. S. Dobkin, and D. Wheye, *The Birder's Handbook* (New York: Simon and Schuster, 1988).

Important facts about riparian habitats: "Fact Sheet #1" (Arizona Riparian Council, n.d.); Sandy Anderson, ed., *Friends of the San Pedro River Docent Notebook* (Sierra Vista: Friends of the San Pedro River, 1997) (hereafter cited as FSPR *Docent Notebook*).

Proportion of biological interest and importance of Southwestern riparian areas: David E. Brown, *Biotic Communities, Southwestern United States and Northwestern Mexico* (Salt Lake City: University of Utah Press, 1994), p. 224.

Ecology of cottonwood-willow forests: Brown 1994, pp. 250–251.

Amphibians: Description and ecology are from Robert C. Stebbins, *A Field Guide to Western Reptiles and Amphibians,* Peterson Field Guides (Boston: Houghton Mifflin, 1985); and W. G. Degenhardt, C. W. Painter, and A. H. Price, *Amphibians and Reptiles of New Mexico* (Albuquerque: University of New Mexico Press, 1996). Food consumption and emergence are from M. A. Dimmitt and R. Ruibal, "Environmental Correlates of Emergence in Spadefoot Toads," *Journal of Herpetology* 14, no. 1 (1980):21–29.

Historical overview: Greg M. Yuncevich, "The San Pedro Riparian NCA" (Tucson: Bureau of Land Management, 1984); Tellman, Yarde, and Wallace 1997, pp. 28–38. On abandoned cattle: Conrad Joseph Bahre, *A Legacy of Change: Historic Human Impact on Vegetation of the Arizona Borderlands* (Tucson: University of Arizona Press, 1991), p. 115. San Pedro archaeology chronology: Amy Campbell, "Archaeological Facts: The San Pedro Valley," FSPR *Docent Notebook*.

Chapter 2, Palominas to Hereford

Lehner and Murray Springs site excavation details: Emil W. Haury, E. B. Sayles, W. W. Wasley, E. Antevs, and J. F. Lance, "The Lehner Mammoth Site," *American Antiquity* 25, no. 1 (1959):1—42; C. Vance Haynes, Jr., "Murray Springs and Lehner Clovis Sites; Miscellaneous data for field trip for the visit of Soviet archaeologists to the University of Arizona" (1991); Haynes, "Mammoth-Bone Shaft Wrench from Murray Springs, Arizona," *Science* 159, no. 3811 (1968):186–187; Haynes, "Curry Draw, Cochise County, Arizona: A Late Quaternary Stratigraphic Record of Pleistocene Extinction and Paleo-Indian Activities," *Geological Society of America Centennial Field Guide—Cordilleran Section* (Geological Society of America, 1987), pp. 23–28.

Climate and vegetation of southeastern Arizona during the Pleistocene: Andrew William Amann, Jr., J. V. Bezy, R. Ratkevich, and W. M. Witkind, *Ice Age Mammals of the San Pedro River Valley, Southeastern Arizona* (Tucson: Arizona Geological Survey, 1998), pp. 1–3.

Current theories of first man in the Americas: Charles W. Petit, "Rediscovering America: The New World May Be 20,000 Years Older Than Experts Thought," *U.S. News & World Report* 125, no. 14 (1998):57–64.

Paleo-humans of the San Pedro and the Pleistocene extinctions: Amann, Bezy, Ratkevich, and Witkind 1998, pp. 15–17. An excellent and concise discussion of man's expansion into North America, and the subsequent megafauna extinctions, may be found in chapter 1 of Jared Diamond's *Guns, Germs, and Steel* (New York: Random House, 1997), pp. 41–52.

Mammoth and other Pleistocene mammal natural history: Amann, Bezy, Ratkevich, and Witkind 1998, pp. 5–14; Ulf Carlberg, "Mammoth Saga" (internet: Swedish Museum of Natural History, Department of Information Technology, website transcript of exhibit, January 1995): <http://www.nrm.se/>.

Plant community descriptions and ecology: Brown 1994. Seep willow resprouting after floods: Dave Gori, "Riparian Vegetation Dynamics, San Pedro River: Hydrology-Vegetation Relationships" (Tucson: Arizona Nature Conservancy, 1996); FSPR *Docent Notebook*. Plant natural histories: FSPR

Docent Notebook; Anne Orth Epple, *Plants of Arizona* (Mesa: LewAnn Publishing, 1996); Janice Emily Bowers, *Shrubs and Trees of the Southwest Deserts* (Tucson: Southwest Parks and Monuments Association, 1993); Francis H. Elmore, *Shrubs and Trees of the Southwest Uplands* (Tucson: Southwest Parks and Monuments Association, 1976); and Thomas H. Kearney and Robert H. Peebles, et al., *Arizona Flora* (Berkeley: University of California Press, 1960).

Chapter 3, Hereford Road to Highway 90

Sacaton grasses: Mitchell P. MacClaran and T. R. Van Devender, *The Desert Grassland* (Tucson: University of Arizona Press, 1995). Quote of early explorers: P. Davis Goode, Jr., *Man and Wildlife in Arizona—The American Exploration Period 1824–1865* (Phoenix: Arizona Game and Fish Department, 1986).

Riparian plants, flood relationships, and succession: Gori 1996; Brown 1994, pp. 224–286.

Desert sucker and longfin dace ecology: "Fish Fauna of the San Pedro," FSPR *Docent Notebook*. Colorado squawfish description and occurrence: Charles H. Lowe, ed., *The Vertebrates of Arizona* (Tucson: University of Arizona Press, 1964), p. 140.

Aquatic ecology: George K. Reid, *Pond Life: A Guide to Common Plants and Animals of North American Ponds and Lakes* (New York: Golden Press, 1967).

Plant natural histories: FSPR *Docent Notebook*; Epple 1996; Bowers 1993; Elmore 1976; and Kearney and Peebles 1960.

Green kingfisher repopulation and natural history: FSPR *Docent Notebook*; Kaufman 1996; and Ehrlich, Dobkin, and Wheye 1988.

Arizona's largest cottonwood: American Forests keeps a National Register of Big Trees, which is run by volunteers in each state. At press, Arizona's "keeper of big trees" was Bob Zahner of Tucson; American Forests, National Register of Big Trees, P.O. Box 2000, Washington, D.C. 20013. Cottonwood natural history: Epple 1996; Bowers 1993; Elmore 1976; and Kearney and Peebles 1960.

The Southeastern Arizona Bird Observatory (SABO), located in Bisbee, is run by Tom Wood and Sheri Williamson, numerous volunteers, grants, memberships, and donations. For more information, contact SABO at P.O. Box 5521, Bisbee, AZ 85603.

Chapter 4, Highway 90 to Charleston

Bird migration: Ehrlich, Dobkin, and Wheye 1988.

Birdwatching statistics: "Fact Sheet—Birding as an Economic Asset" (American Birding Association, 1997).

Plant transpiration and atmospheric oxygen: Robert A. Wallace, J. L. King, and G. P. Sanders, *Biology: The Science of Life* (Santa Monica: Goodyear Publishing Company, 1981).

Desert riparian ecosystem living matter production: "Arizona Riparian Council, Fact Sheet #1" (Tempe: Arizona State University, Center for Environmental Studies, n.d.).

Reptile and amphibian natural history: Carl H. Ernst, *Venomous Reptiles of North America* (Washington, D.C.: Smithsonian Institution Press, 1992); Degenhardt, Painter, and Price 1996; Stebbins, 1985. Hoofed browser–rattle evolution theory: Desert grassland interpretation material, Arizona–Sonora Desert Museum, 1995. For a list of herpetofauna of the San Pedro RNCA, see the appendix.

Fire in southwestern riparian plant communities: David E. Busch and S. D. Smith, "Effects of Fire on Water and Salinity Relations of Riparian Woody Taxa," *Oecologia* 94 (1993):186–194. Busch and Smith also cite anthropologist Henry F. Dobyns (*From Fire to Flood: Historic Human Destruction of Sonoran Desert Riverine Oases,* Ballena Press, 1981), historian Conrad Bahre (A *Legacy of Change,* University of Arizona Press, 1991), and ecologist Thomas Swetnam in their assertion that fire in riparian areas was infrequent prior to the advent of Europeans in the Southwest.

Historical vegetation changes in the Southwest: J. R. Hastings and R. M. Turner, *The Changing Mile: An Ecological Study of Vegetation Change with Time in the Lower Mile of an Arid and Semiarid Region* (Tucson: University of Arizona Press, 1965); Richard Hereford, *Entrenchment and Widening of the Upper San Pedro River, Arizona,* Special Paper 282 (Boulder: Geological Society of America, 1993). Richard

Hereford also supports the finding that extensive gallery forests of cottonwoods and willows are new (since the turn of the century) to the banks of the San Pedro River.

Sacaton natural history: see citations at beginning of chapter 3 notes.

Chapter 5, Charleston to Fairbank

Woodcutting: Tellman, Yarde, and Wallace 1997.

Population numbers and description of Charleston: ibid.

Early accounts and arroyo downcutting: Gori 1996.

Soil building and erosion: Robert E. Ricklefs, *The Economy of Nature* (Concord, Mass.: Chiron Press, 1976).

Entrenchment, stabilization, and revegetation facts: Hereford 1993. Cienéga disappearance: D. A. Hendrickson and W. L. Minckley, "Cienegas—Vanishing Climax Communities of the American Southwest," *Desert Plants* 6 (1984).

Groundwater depletion: *Arizona Water Resource* 3, no. 4 (Aug.–Sept. 1994):3.

Jaguars in the Southwest: Donald F. Hoffmeister, *The Mammals of Arizona* (Tucson: University of Arizona Press, 1986), pp. 519–520.

Bat natural history and San Pedro bat facts: Ronnie Sidner, personal communication and presentation, "Bats of Southern Arizona," Tucson Audubon Society, September 13, 1994; William H. Burt, *A Field Guide to the Mammals of America North of Mexico*, Peterson Field Guides (Boston: Houghton-Mifflin Company, 1976), pp. 24–25.

San Pedro geology: Peggy Wenrick, "Geology 2, San Pedro National Conservation Area," FSPR *Docent Notebook*; Halka Chronic, *Arizona Roadside Geology* (Missoula, Mont.: Mountain Press, 1983).

Monarch butterflies: Robert Michael Pyle, *Handbook for Butterfly Watchers* (Boston: Houghton-Mifflin, 1992), p. 84.

San Pedro Valley railroads: James Herrewig, "An Overview of the San Pedro Riparian Management Area" (Sierra Vista: Friends of the San Pedro River, 1988).

Chapter 6, Fairbank to St. David Ciénega

Presidio Santa Cruz de Terrenate information: Bureau of Land Management, *Presidio Santa Cruz de Terrenate,* Publication No. BLM-AZ-G1-92-019-4333 (Bureau of Land Management, 1992).

Early people of the San Pedro: Overview taken from Jane Kolber, "The Rock Art of the San Pedro River, Cochise County, Arizona," *American Indian Rock Art* 17 (American Rock Art Research Association, 1997):1–7. Estimates of Sobaipuri population during the 16th century are from Tellman, Yarde, and Wallace 1997, p. 29.

Beavers, trapping statistics: Tellman, Yarde, and Wallace 1997, p. 30. Ecology: William H. Burt, *A Field Guide to the Mammals of America North of Mexico,* Peterson Field Guides (Boston: Houghton-Mifflin Company, 1976), pp.151–152.

Biodiversity article: Reported by Douglas Kreutz, October 1, 1994, *Arizona Daily Star.*

Appendix 1, Species Lists

Sources for species lists are included with each list.

Profiles of plant communities: Gori 1996; Brown 1994, pp. 224–286.

Suggested Reading

Arthropods

Bailowitz, Richard A., and James P. Brock. *Butterflies of Southeastern Arizona*. Tucson: Sonoran Arthropod Studies, 1991.

———. *70 Common Butterflies of the Southwest*. Tucson: Southwest Parks and Monuments Association, 1998.

Pyle, Robert Michael. *National Audubon Society Field Guide to North American Butterflies*. New York: Alfred A. Knopf, 1994.

Werner, Floyd, and Carl Olson. *Learning about and Living with Insects of the Southwest*. Tucson: Fisher Books, 1994.

Birds

Ehrlich, Paul R., David S. Dobkin, and Darryl Wheye. *The Birder's Handbook*. New York: Simon and Schuster, 1988.

Kaufman, Kenn. *Lives of North American Birds*. New York: Houghton-Mifflin, 1996.

National Geographic Society. *Field Guide to the Birds of North America*. Rev. ed. Washington, D.C.: National Geographic Society, 1999.

Taylor, Richard Cachor. *A Birder's Guide to Southeastern Arizona*. Rev. ed. Colorado Springs: American Birding Association, 1999.

Tucson Audubon Society. *Finding Birds in Southeast Arizona*. Rev. ed. Tucson: Tucson Audubon Society, 1999.

Mammals

Burt, William H. *A Field Guide to the Mammals of America North of Mexico*. Peterson Field Guide Series. Boston: Houghton Mifflin Company, 1976.

Cockrum, E. Lendell, and Yar Petryszyn. *Mammals of the Southwestern United States and Northwestern Mexico*. Tucson: Treasure Chest Books, 1992.

Halfpenny, James. *A Field Guide to Mammal Tracking in North America*. 2nd ed. Boulder: Johnson Books, 1986.

Hanson, Roseann Beggy, and Jonathan Hanson. *Animal Tracks*. Old Saybrook, Conn.: Globe Pequot Books, 2001.

Plants

Arnberger, Leslie P. *Flowers of the Southwest Mountains*. Tucson: Southwest Parks and Monuments Association, 1982.

Bowers, Janice Emily. *100 Desert Wildflowers of the Southwest*. Tucson: Southwest Parks and Monuments Association, 1989.

——. *100 Roadside Wildflowers of Southwest Woodlands*. Tucson: Southwest Parks and Monuments Association, 1987.

——. *Shrubs and Trees of the Southwest Deserts*. Tucson: Southwest Parks and Monuments Association, 1993.

Dodge, Natt N. *Flowers of the Southwest Deserts*. Tucson: Southwest Parks and Monuments Association, 1985.

Elmore, Francis H. *Shrubs and Trees of the Southwest Uplands*. Tucson: Southwest Parks and Monuments Association, 1976.

Epple, Anne Orth. *Plants of Arizona*. Mesa, Ariz.: LewAnn Publishing, 1996.

Niehaus, Theodore F. *Southwestern and Texas Wildflowers*. Peterson Field Guide Series. Boston: Houghton Mifflin Company, 1984.

Petrides, George A., and Olivia Petrides. *Western Trees*. Peterson Field Guide Series. Boston: Houghton Mifflin Company, 1992.

Reptiles and Amphibians

Hanson, Jonathan, and Roseann Beggy Hanson. *50 Common Reptiles and Amphibians of the Southwest*. Tucson: Southwest Parks and Monuments Association, 1996.

Lowe, Charles H., Cecil R. Schwalbe, and Terry B. Johnson. *Venomous Reptiles of Arizona*. Phoenix: Arizona Game and Fish Department, 1986.

Stebbins, Robert C. *Western Reptiles and Amphibians.* 2nd ed. Boston: Houghton Mifflin Company, 1985.

Rivers and Water

Dennis, Jerry. *The Bird in the Waterfall: A Natural History of Oceans, Rivers, and Lakes.* New York: HarperCollins, 1996.

Rea, Amadeo. *Once a River: Bird Life and Habitat Changes along the Middle Gila.* Tucson: University of Arizona Press, 1983.

Reid, George K. *Pond Life: A Guide to Common Plants and Animals of North American Ponds and Lakes.* New York: Golden Press, 1967.

Tellman, Barbara, R. Yarde, and M. G. Wallace. *Arizona's Changing Rivers: How People Have Affected the Rivers.* Tucson: Water Resources Research Center, University of Arizona, College of Agriculture, 1997.

Natural History

Hanson, Jonathan, and Roseann Beggy Hanson. *Southern Arizona Nature Almanac.* Boulder: Pruett Publishing, 1996.

Pyle, Robert Michael. *Chasing Monarchs.* Boston: Houghton-Mifflin, 1999.

INDEX

W

wash, as riparian habitat type, 13
water: cycle, description of, 9–10, 76;
    table, lowering of, 97–99; use, 10,
    17, 77, 99, 106, 128, 146–147
watershed: map of, 2; of the
    Colorado River (including the
    San Pedro River), 8–9; mountains
    in the San Pedro, 9
whiptail lizards, natural history of,
    80

White Tanks Associates, 19
wildlife, microscopic, 56
willow, Goodding, natural history
    of, 39–40. *See also* habitats
willow, seep. *See* seep willow
wolf (*Canis* spp.): dire, 35; gray, 35
woodcutting, volume of, 95

Y

yellow-billed cuckoo: locations of,
    67; natural history of, 11

About the Author

Roseann Beggy Hanson, a native Tucson naturalist and author, has coauthored a dozen natural history and outdoor books with her husband, Jonathan, including the *Southern Arizona Nature Almanac* and the award-winning *50 Common Reptiles and Amphibians*. She studied writing and ecology and evolutionary biology at the University of Arizona and has been exploring the San Pedro since she was a little girl. The Hansons live in Tucson, where Roseann is executive director of the Sky Island Alliance.